DIRECTED BY WILLIAM BEAUDINE: AN OVERVIEW

BY JAMES L. NEIBAUR

Directed by William Beaudine: An Overview
By James L. Neibaur
Copyright © 2020 James L. Neibaur
No part of this book may be reproduced in any form or by any means, electronic, mechanical, digital, photocopying, or recording, except for inclusion of a review, without permission in writing from the publisher or Author.

Published in the USA by:
BearManor Media
4700 Millenia Blvd.
Suite 175 PMB 90497
Orlando, FL 32839
www.bearmanormedia.com

Paperback ISBN 978-1-62933-558-2
Hardcover ISBN 978-1-62933-559-9
BearManor Media, Orlando, Florida
Printed in the United States of America
Book design by Robbie Adkins, www.adkinsconsult.com

Table of Contents

ACKNOWLEDGEMENTS v
INTRODUCTION vii
THE EARLY YEARS 1
THE SILENT COMEDY SHORT FILMS 7
THE SILENT FEATURES 20
THE EARLY SOUND FEATURES 43
THE FILMS IN ENGLAND 58
RETURNING TO AMERICA 65
DIXIE NATIONAL PRODUCTIONS 72
PRODUCERS RELEASING CORPORATION 81
MONOGRAM STUDIOS AND AN INCREASE IN PRODUCTIVITY 93
POST WAR FREELANCING AT MONOGRAM, PRC, AND ELSEWHERE 107
THE BOWERY BOYS 120
BELA LUGOSI MEETS A BROOKLYN GORILLA 132
RELIGIOUS AND EXPLOITATION FILMS 140
INVESTIGATING 1950s TELEVISION 146
BEAUDINE AND DISNEY 152
BILLY THE KID VERSUS DRACULA & JESSE JAMES MEETS FRANKENSTEIN'S DAUGHTER 160
LASSIE AND THE FINAL YEARS 167
REDISCOVERY OF "THE CANDADIAN" AND BEAUDINE'S FINAL YEAR 171
APPENDIX A: FILMOGRAPHY 175
BIBLIOGRAPHY 224
INDEX 226

ACKNOWLEDGEMENTS

Special thanks, as always, to Katie Carter, who continues to live each book with me and offer insights and suggestions that always make a positive difference. Amazing to think she wasn't even born when I wrote my first two books. Katie may never forgive me for having her sit through *Bela Lugosi Meets a Brooklyn Gorilla*.

Special thanks also to Oscar winning film historian and archivist Kevin Brownlow, who kindly shared a great deal of material on William Beaudine's work in silent films, including photos and printed information.

And special thanks to Wendy Marshall for penning a biography of her grandfather, William Beaudine, which was a very helpful research tool for this book that focuses on his work.

I also extend my deep appreciation to:

Thomas Reeder for sharing his research on William Beaudine as well as his subsequent story in Filmfax.

Dave Lord Heath and his Another Fine Mess website for the information on William Beaudine's work with Hal Roach.

Charles Tranberg for giving permission to use quotes from interviews he conducted with actors who worked with Beaudine.

Further thanks to the following:

Terri Lynch, Ted Okuda, Phil Hall, Steve Massa, Brent Walker, Paul Gierucki, Gary Schneeberger, Peter Jackel, Lea Stans, Allie Schulz, Richard Finegan, Jon Provost, Dale Wamboldt, Kelly Parmelee and the late Jerry Lewis, Bill Cappello, Emil Sitka, Gabe Dell, Sammy Petrillo, and my dear late son Max Neibaur.

DEDICATION

This book is dedicated, with great respect, to Oscar winning film historian and archivist Kevin Brownlow.

Thank you for teaching us.

INTRODUCTION

William Beaudine may very well be the most poorly represented director in motion picture history. Because so much of his career was spent working in B product at the low budget studios, latter day snark has claimed he was a hack whose talents were limited to that which was cheap and exploitative. Even worse, he is frequently called "One-Shot," claiming he rarely, if ever, shot a second take.

There is also a story where director William Beaudine is on the set of a low budget movie he's directing and is told to hurry it along. Beaudine allegedly responded, "You mean somebody is actually waiting for this picture?" The incongruity of the efficient Beaudine being told to hurry up makes this anecdote highly suspect. This was probably a myth that was created to help support the contention that Beaudine was a "one-shot" director who cared so little about his low budget projects, he simply zipped through them without much attention, and that their eventual cult status was because they were campy bad movies.

In fact, the very moniker "One-Shot" was not something Beaudine was ever called in his entire career.

This misrepresentation all began during the nostalgia boom in the 1970s when older films became hipster subjects on college campuses. Along with the acknowledged cult worship for The Marx Brothers and Humphrey Bogart, there were groups that took perverse delight in watching B movies and pointing out their limitations rather than appreciating what a filmmaker was able to do within those restrictive parameters. Popular books were released offering snarky comments on "bad movies" according to this perspective, and in one of these, William Beaudine was hailed as cinema's worst director. They were wrong. But, sadly, their misrepresentative moniker "one-shot" has stuck with him.

William Beaudine had a long and varied career that lasted from the silent era into the television age. The idea that he carelessly limited himself to one take is a wild misrepresentation of the fact that Beaudine was able to do a lot within the confines of a low budget and limited shooting schedule. He originally became known for creative efficiency back when he was helming one and two reel comedy subjects during the silent era. When he much later was directing films for the poverty row studios, he was able to offer solidly entertaining vehicles despite threadbare budgets and brief shooting schedules. He directed comedies, westerns, musicals, horror movies, adventure sagas, adaptions from great literature, and exploitation films. And in a career that spanned nearly 60 years and hundreds of movies, William Beaudine made a discernible impact that has for too long been unfairly dismissed and misrepresented.

There was a time when William Beaudine was considered one of the best and most reliable directors in the movie industry, with consistent success in silent films that continued into the pre-code sound era. Just as his momentum was steadily rising, Beaudine went to England for a few years and directed some of their top comedy stars. When he returned, he discovered that the American film industry had moved on and forgotten him. During the year 1931, a few years before traveling to England, Beaudine directed nine films. In 1938, upon returning to the United States, he could only secure work in one; an entry in the Warner Brothers "Torchy" series. In 1939, he directed one more Torchy film, and no others. It was not until 1940, when old friends who'd known his work from the silent era, and had some clout at the low budget studios like PRC and Monogram, that Beaudine once again found steady work.

Despite being paid less than he had prior to working in England, Beaudine accepted the jobs mostly out of necessity and partially because he loved to be active. He didn't refuse projects, and brought his approach to a variety of offbeat and exploitative films that were a part of his filmography, but do not define it.

This text is an overview of William Beaudine's career as a director, beginning in the silent era and extending into the TV age. In each chapter, we will point out specific films and discuss their significance to Beaudine's filmography as well as cinema history overall. While most of the chapters will concentrate on a specific period in the director's career, The Bowery Boys will get their own chapter, because Beaudine directed so many of the features in that series, and helped to guide its concept. There will also be a singular chapter on the cult film *Bela Lugosi Meets a Brooklyn Gorilla* because of its lasting status among bad movie aficionados, and its connection to Dean Martin and Jerry Lewis. Quotes from Jerry Lewis, told to the author and exclusive to this book, will be included.

Finally, the two films Beaudine directed at the end of his career - *Billy The Kid Versus Dracula* and *Jesse James Meets Frankenstein's Daughter* - will also be given a chapter of their own because they are the last theatrical movies Beaudine directed and have also generated a cult following.

It is because of films like the aforementioned that William Beaudine is looked upon as a hack director who made throwaway low budget fodder that is only interesting as a result of its campiness. Too often Beaudine's entire long career is defined by movies like *Bela Lugosi Meets a Brooklyn Gorilla* which is tantamount to Buster Keaton's career being defined by *How to Stuff a Wild Bikini*. Buster Keaton is one of the most creative filmmakers in movie history, but after his silent screen career, he struggled in sound films, not because of his ability but because of the circumstances of his career and the limited opportunities afforded him. Still, Keaton did not suddenly stop making great movies after the silent era. There are many highlights among his sound shorts at Educational Studios and Columbia Pictures, and, years later, his cameos in the popular Beach movies included some fun comedy bits that were among those films' highlights. And he kept working until the very end.[1]

Beaudine, like Keaton, took the jobs that were available to him at any point in his career, be it a major production for a top level studio, or a B movie made for a specialized audience.

William Beaudine directed films with Mary Pickford, Tom Mix, Jean Harlow, W.C. Fields, Bela Lugosi, and The Bowery Boys; he

---

1 For more on this, see my book on Buster Keaton's sound films, *The Fall of Buster Keaton*, for Scarecrow Press.

worked for Fox, Warner Brothers, MGM, Paramount, Universal, and Walt Disney, as well as Monogram, Republic, and Producers Releasing Corporation. He directed TV episodes of *Lassie, The Green Hornet, Wild Bill Hickok,* and *Naked City.* Beaudine helmed everything from one-reel silent slapstick comedies to the literary screen adaption of Robert Louis Stevenson's *Kidnapped*.

This book is not a biography, but will also provide some biographical information as it pertains to the filmography. It is an overview of the director's work in an effort to better understand and appreciate the length, and depth, of his motion picture career. William Beaudine's more significant films will be singled out and discussed as to their merit and lasting impact. The text will also include memories from actors and directors, photo illustrations and ad graphics. But, most of all, the intention is to point out that William Beaudine was a talented and versatile filmmaker whose work in a wide range of genres and sub-genres resulted in some of the most beloved, timeless movies.

And that he was not a "One-Shot" director.

THE EARLY YEARS

William Washington Beaudine was born January 15, 1892 in New York City. Not long after he graduated from high school in 1910, Beaudine was hired to work odd jobs at the old Biograph studios. At the time, David Wark (D.W.) Griffith was at Biograph making landmark films that would be considered the syntax of cinematic language. During 1909, Griffith had explored the possibilities of the moving picture's vast capabilities at telling stories and conveying emotions. Films like *A Corner in Wheat*, *The Violin Maker of Cremona*, and *What Drink Did* are good examples of D.W. Griffith exploring cinema's possibilities. Griffith created nearly 150 short films that year alone.

While focusing on drama and melodrama, Griffith was less comfortable with comedy. As a result, Griffith enlisted the help of Biograph actor Mack Sennett, who had a wealth of comic ideas that he was eager to connect to the cinematic process. While credited to Griffith, comedies like *Those Awful Hats* and *The Curtain Pole* were far more Mack Sennett's vision. Both of these men would figure prominently in William Beaudine's life and career during his own Biograph employment, as their directorial ideas progressed.

Because there were already too many Bills and Williams at Biograph, D.W. Griffith affectionately nicknamed the hard working Beaudine kid "Beau." According to author Wendy L. Marshall:[2]

> Six days a week, Beau mopped floors, carried towels, and film cans, and got lunches. He fetched props, and hauled the heavy iron tripod from one setup to the next. He swept up the constant river of celluloid silvers spewing from the massive Biograph camera as it perforated the edges of film. He took bit parts and tried his hand at writing scenarios.

---

[2] Marshall, Wendy L. *William Beaudine: From Silents to Television*. Lanham, MD. Scarecrow Press. 2002

Beaudine made $8 per week which was quite a comfortable sum for a high school graduate in 1910. He worked hard, gained the respect of his peers and employers, and during this period, Beaudine learned a great deal about the rudiments of motion picture production. He was able to watch cinema grow during its infancy, learning from Griffith the way Griffith had learned from Edwin S. Porter.

Cinema's most basic ideas were being formed and utilized as the concept of the narrative film evolved from a storefront attraction to a veritable art form. While D.W. Griffith had bigger ideas, soon to create such groundbreaking epics as *The Birth of a Nation* (1915) and *Intolerance* (1916), at the time Beaudine was working for him, he was still experimenting with his more basic concepts in shorter films. Griffith explored how a close-up of a movie bad guy caused him to become more menacing. He understood, from Porter's work, how editing was responsible for the rhythm of a film. Establishing shots, camera angles, the movement and the expression of the actors, all were fundamentals that were being discovered and investigated in these early movies.

According to Wendy L. Marshall, Beaudine worked closely with Griffith's cameraman Billy Bitzer:

> It was Beau's job to help Bitzer with the camera and film every morning after breakfast. With Griffith, every frame of film had to contribute, compressing the tightest possible essence of story values into each scene. Bitzer knew exactly how much film he would need for the day.

While learning such foundational elements from Griffith was certainly important to Beaudine's own eventual vision as a filmmaker, he capitalized further when working with Mack Sennett, who was, by now, forming his own comedy unit under the Biograph umbrella. Griffith had a lot of respect for Sennett's thorough understanding of comedy, realizing that was not a genre in which he excelled. Beaudine contributed in various capacities, including prop man, assistant cameraman, and, eventually, assistant director. Beaudine connected the fundamentals he'd learned from Griffith and responded even better to Mack Sennett's approach. The basics had laid the foundation. Sennett's concepts added more to the process of comedy, something that attracted Beaudine more so than drama.

Sennett also was careful not to waste a frame of film, but his approach to the cinematic process was quicker and more frenetic. Garish makeup, bulging eyes, flailing arms, wild pratfalls, and breathless chases were natural ingredients. Sennett would map out the construction of each scene with chalk marks on the floor, and his method as a director was to keep all of the action within the frame, each character stationed carefully to present the most effective mise-en-scène.

The Manicure Lady, for example, features Sennett as a barber with some interest in one of the girls doing manicures at his shop (Vivian Prescott). She flirts with male customers, who become so distracted by her, they will often get out of the barber chair and decide upon a manicure over a haircut. Sometimes, the men's wives will take them out by the ear, abruptly ending the flirtation. The manicurist is really only having a bit of innocent fun while drawing decent tips from her smitten customers, until a rich cad comes in and convinces her to go to lunch. She has a nice time, so he comes to pick her up again after work. The barber is upset by this rival, and hops on the back of the rich man's chauffeur driven car. When he sees the man try to make a move on the manicurist, the barber climbs into the back window, beats the man up, throws him out the same back window, and slips a ring on the manicurist's finger.

The simple comedy was conveyed through complex filmmaking, especially for so early in the process. Sennett has the manicurist seated at the left, while the barber works at his chair on the right. On one side we see the manicure and flirtation, on the other we see a haircut and a shave. His girl giving attention to her customers distracts the barber. Sennett frames the shot with each person on either side of the frame. The casual flirtation at left is a distraction that is hampering the barber's effectiveness on the right side of the screen. There is movement on both sides, and it conflicts within the frame, displaying the tension from the barber on the right and the carefree manicurist on the left.

Beaudine also noticed the effectiveness of Sennett's use of movement. He has the barber stand rigid, stiff with anger and jealousy, as his girl gleefully waves to the rich cad outside and prepares to leave with him. The fluttery movement of the happy manicurist offsets the seething tension of the barber.

The comparison-contrast aspect of the film is most effective during the lunch sequence. The barber and manicurist prepare to leave together, but the rich customer, who has a chauffeur driven limo that plans to take her to a fancy restaurant, sidetracks the woman. She goes, quite willingly, while the dejected barber is forced to eat alone. Sennett cross-cuts between the manicurist and the rich customer dining el fresco in a ritzy place surrounded by attentive waiters, and the barber eating alone in a seedy diner with a grouchy waitress. The observant Beaudine would watch the creation of a short like this and understand the most effective method of presenting visual comedy in a slapstick short film.

In *A Dash Through The Clouds* there is a long shot of an airplane coming in for a landing, flying toward the screen. The pilot, Phil Parmalee, and actress Mabel Normand leave the plane and walk into the foreground toward the camera. It is all done in a single shot, with no edits. The positioning of the camera, and the movement of the actors, not only make this a really impressive visual for a 1912 movie, but it shows that Mabel was indeed on that plane for the scene. Aviation was less than ten years old by this time, and the plane in the movie looks more like a kite. The Wright Brothers themselves had trained Parmalee, an actual pilot.

When Beaudine would observe these methods of filming, how Sennett explored the possibilities of filmmaking, he learned not only the fundamentals, but some of the artful approaches to the visual image. It was magnificent training. But Beaudine benefited even more greatly from the way the characters performed and how Sennett presented his outrageous comedy through these players. In *A Dash Through the Clouds,* Fred Mace does a beautiful comic turn as the chubby schnook with the rumpled suit and crooked tie. His misgivings about air travel are understandable in that aviation was so much in its infancy, and quite dangerous (pilot Phil Parmalee was actually killed in a plane crash shortly after appearing in this movie). But Mace's reaction has all the comic gusto of a Mack Sennett comedian. He holds up his hands, shakes his head, puts his hand on his heart, and offers other, similar responses to the trepidation he has over going up in the air. Beaudine's observation of Mace's definition of his character, and Mack Sennett's presentation of the slapstick, would be of tremendous help in a couple of years.

Not long after filming *A Dash Through The Clouds*, Mack Sennett left Biograph and formed his own Keystone studios. Beaudine remained active with Biograph for another two years, working closely with director Dell Henderson, and continuing to learn more about comedy filmmaking. In 1914, the studio needed to cut costs and Beaudine's job was terminated. Having just gotten married, Beaudine was in need of finding work quickly. After several failed attempts to secure employment in New York, Beaudine heard from his friend Marshall Neilan, with whom he'd worked at Biograph. Neilan was currently directing films at the Kalem company, and beckoned William Beaudine to this west coast studio. Beaudine and his new bride borrowed money from her mother and headed to California, where he went to work for Kalem.

William Beaudine

THE SILENT COMEDY SHORT FILMS

William Beaudine walked onto the Kalem lot off Sunset Boulevard in Los Angeles on October 20, 1914 and began working for the studio. It was a comfortable experience right away. Along with Marshall Neilan, who had summoned him there, Beaudine's friend D.W. Griffith was currently shooting his magnificent epic *Intolerance* on an adjoining lot to where Beaudine would be working on the simple Ham and Bud slapstick comedies.

Lloyd Hamilton and Bud Duncan were a very early comedy team that relied mostly on violent slapstick and frenetic action. There was never any real finesse to their one-reel shorts, but they were fast and funny and audiences enjoyed them. For decades, it was believed by exhibitors that a drama or melodrama should be coupled with a comedy short subject in order to have a more balanced program. At theaters, the Ham and Bud films were a cheerful accompaniment to a heavily dramatic feature film.

Ham and Bud were a study in contrasts, with Hamilton standing over six feet tall and Bud under five feet. Shabbily dressed and engaging in the sort of rough and tumble comedy that was a bluntly visceral experience for the viewer, the Ham and Bud one-reelers were usually shot in three days and heavily distributed to theaters. Anthony Balducci stated, in his biography of Lloyd Hamilton:[3]

> Ham and Bud occupy a remote recess of movie history. Being a century removed from the team, a contemporary audience might perceive them as curious creatures. They could react to ancient footage of the duo much differently than they would to a magical video tape of an actual brontosaurus or triceratops. Ham and Bud were obvious reprobates. Their appearance was not as shabby as their behavior. The pair, lustful and aggressive, was the embodiment of

---
3 Balducci, Anthony. *Lloyd Hamilton: Poor Boy Comedian of Silent Cinema*. Jefferson, NC: McFarland, 2009

the rampaging id. They were indifferent to everything except their most immediate needs and interests. Being amoral, they broke the rules of convention. They were frightfully ill-mannered, recklessly violent, grossly self-centered, unduly envious, and completely untrustworthy. They would readily cheat or rob in order to get what they wanted. By radiating a childish innocence and charm, this iconoclastic pair were seen by their fans as lovable bad boys.

Marshall Neilan had been directing the Ham and Bud films, but when he left Kalem, his assistant, Chance Ward, moved into the director's chair. But Ward didn't want to direct, and preferred to act as assistant to the director. He had good ideas, but not a fully formed vision of how a complete film should be structured, even something like the wild, uninhibited slapstick of the Ham and Bud series. He offered the directorial job to William Beaudine, and while Beaudine wanted the job, he realized his own limited experience and suggested that they collaborate.

After Ward left the studio, Beaudine felt he was ready to start directing the films himself, with Rube Miller as his assistant. One of William Beaudine's directorial efforts during this period was *Ham the Diver*, featuring Lloyd Hamilton diving underwater while Bud pumps air to him. The comedy happens when Bud is distracted by a pretty woman, leaving Ham to suffer without oxygen. The comedy is very broad, but quite funny in a most visceral sense, and it shows Beaudine's efficiency in that these comedies were shot in three days.

Rube Miller had been a stunt man, so he would often double for the actors and do the more dangerous stunts. Despite this, Lloyd Hamilton still managed to suffer a broken leg while doing a gag for one of the films, and was sidelined for several weeks. In order to provide sufficient product for movie distributors, who were requesting more Ham and Bud films to balance their programs with dramatic features, Bud Duncan continued working without his partner. In an attempt to recreate the comedy team dynamic, Rube Miller stepped in Hamilton's place, and the pair called themselves Bud and Dud. When that didn't seem to click, William Beaudine acted opposite Duncan, but the Bill and Bud comedies weren't well received either. This makes sense, for when the two actors eventually went off on their own, Lloyd Hamilton became a top comedy star, while Bud Duncan was relegated to supporting and bit roles. So it is Ham whose presence was most needed in these comedies.

Many years later, William Beaudine would recall for Phillip Scheuer how improvisational these comedies were:[4]

> The script was just a bare outline and most of the gags were invented on the set. In fact, it's true the scrip was often written off the cuff, and if your wife sent the shirt to the laundry.... Everything had to be sent to New York just like we shot it; there is was developed, printed, and cut. If any of it was fogged or out of focus, they'd wire us back for retakes. I never saw any of the damn things till they opened at theaters downtown.

By the time Lloyd Hamilton recovered and returned to the series, William Beaudine was no longer employed at Kalem. After working there six months and directing 24 films, Beaudine was fired in another cost-cutting move. Not long afterward Kalem shut down operations.

While William Beaudine's training with Biograph was cinematic research, his initial efforts as a director with Kalem were his initial active experience. He felt prepared to manage a comedy unit of his own, and sought that opportunity at other studios that featured short subjects in production.

Beaudine eventually connected with Universal studios' vice president H.O. Davis and his assistant Cy Burr, finding work at one of the several comedy companies active throughout that studio. Beaudine had been making $75 at Kalem, but told Davis and Burr that his weekly salary was $150. They said they could only afford to give him $100, so Beaudine got a $25 per week raise from employers who thought they were getting him for $50 per week less than he'd been getting at Kalem.

William Beaudine was put in charge of the Joker Comedies unit, featuring such comic performers as Billy Franey, Gale Henry

---

4 "60 Years in Films." *Action* July-August, 1969

Milburn Morante, Heinie Conklin, and Lillian Peacock among the regulars. Beaudine's approach to the Joker shorts was quite effective, in that he had some background in working on comedy shorts including directing them and even some acting. After a few productions, H.O. Davis told Cy Burr that the Joker shorts Beaudine directed were the best the unit had ever offered and increased the popularity of the unit. Because of moviegoers' reactions, theater owners asked for more product. William Beaudine was given a raise in salary and continued to achieve success with his own comedy unit.

While Beaudine's tenure at Joker was very successful, and an overall positive experience, it was not without tragedy. Pretty comic actress Lillian Peacock and lanky comedienne Gale Henry were injured while filming a stunt for the Beaudine-directed comedy *Bombs and Business* on March 12, 1916. Peacock suffered a fractured wrist and internal injuries, while Henry badly injured her knee during a scene in which the two of them leaped out of a car as it tumbled over a cliff. In these primitive days of movie production, especially the lower budget short comedies, doubles and stunt people were a luxury that just weren't considered. Injuries were frequent.

Although she sustained some pretty serious injuries on the stunt with Gale Henry, follow-up articles on Lillian Peacock indicated that she was recovering well and would be back to work in movies by May 1st. However, despite returning to work, Peacock never fully recovered from internal injuries sustained in the stunt. After a painful two years, Lillian died on August 18, 1918 at the home of her parents. She was only 28 years old.

One of Beaudine's most successful Joker comedies was his 1917 takeoff on Jules Verne's *20,000 Leagues Under the Sea*, entitled *The Cross-Eyed Submarine (or 20,000 Peeks Under the Sea)*." It starred Billy Franey as Prince Ducker/Captain Nebo, Gale Henry as Ducker's wife, Lillian Peacock as their daughter, and Milburn Morante as Charlie Denvere. According to the October 27, 1917 issue of *The Moving Picture Weekly*:

> *The Cross-Eyed Submarine,* Universal's satire on *20,000 Leagues Under the Sea,* had a week's run at the Casino

Theater in Chicago, and Manager Schaffer reports that it kept the audience roaring from start to finish.

Running an uncharacteristically lengthy three reels, *The Cross-Eyed Submarine* became one of the most popular comedies from the Joker unit.

At the end of 1917, H.O. Davis was hired by the Triangle Film Corporation and Beaudine followed him there, *The Cross-Eyed Submarine* being his last Joker release. A week later, Beaudine's first comedy for Triangle was already in theaters.

Beaudine worked in several units at Triangle, including for his old friend and mentor Mack Sennett. One of Beaudine's first directorial efforts for Triangle was the ambitious comedy *Won by a Fowl* (1917). Screening this three-reel silent today, it comes off as a pretty standard slapstick effort, but with the added layer of Beaudine's own vision. The film features a restaurant, a theater, and a park setting. There are mix-ups, mistaken identities, flirting, and jealousy. The film concludes with a slapstick chase and there is knockabout humor strewn throughout the otherwise situational approach.

However, amidst all of this typical Keystone structure, is Beaudine's concept of presenting the characters as more than face-value caricatures. He establishes each one separately, presents the relationships each has, and manages to meld the diverse personalities into a conflicted ensemble. Paddy McGuire is cast as a down-and-out sort, and rises to the level of a restaurant's head cook within the course of the narrative. Fritz Schade goes from being an open, awkwardly flirtatious middle ager into one who realizes the importance of his marriage. While it does not feature any of the more noteworthy top talent at Keystone during this period, *Won by a Fowl* is a significant representative of William Beaudine's early career.

H.O. Davis's contract with Triangle was for one year, and when that year was up, it was not renewed. Gone also were the directors that Davis brought on board, so William Beaudine was once again out of a job as of June, 1918. However, he was, by now, generating some notoriety in the industry as a result of his good work. Not long after his dismissal from Triangle, William Beaudine was hired by Henry Lehrman to direct for his Sunshine Comedies, but that gig only lasted about a month. Beaudine recalled for Phillip Scheuer:[5]

> Whenever Lehrman was off the lot we'd post a lookout for him; everybody was either shooting crap or playing poker. When he drove in, the dice and cards would disappear.

He then found work with Al Christie's productions. This job lasted five years and resulted in Beaudine directing over 50 comedies.

Al Christie had taken over the Nestor studios in 1911 and was in charge of production while his brother Charles handled the business. The studio was very successful, growing over the next several years while distributing through Universal. By the time William Beaudine joined the studios, the Christie brothers had broken with Universal and had gone into independent production. Eventually they acquired their own studio property due to the independent success of their comedies.

Beaudine joined Christie at about the same time comedy actor Bobby Vernon did. Bobby had been working at Mack Sennett's Keystone studios, starring opposite Gloria Swanson in the Keystone classic *Teddy at the Throttle* (1917). Vernon would recall for *Motion Picture Classic* magazine:[6]

> When Gloria Swanson and I were working for Sennett, it would take sometimes two or three months to make a two-reeler. We'd rehearse for a week or so before we'd crank a camera. But the weather had something to do with it, too. You see, photography in those days wasn't what it is now and most of our scenes were exteriors. Cheaper, you know. Didn't have to build sets. If we had a call for the next day and we woke up to find it cloudy or raining, we'd just go back to bed again. And it sure can rain out here during the wet season.

Vernon joined Christie in December of 1917 and Beaudine directed most of his comedies. Leaving the frenetic Keystones

---

5 "60 Years in Films." *Action* July-August, 1969
6 Lubou, Dorothy. "Grinding Out Grins". *Motion Picture Classic*. May 1929

for the more subdued, situational Christie productions was a big change for Vernon, but, being a very good actor and comedian, he was able to adapt nicely. However, the pace of making the comedies was still tight, and Bobby recalled this in another interview:[7]

> Short comedies are nerve-wracking, in addition to the chances we constantly take of receiving dangerous injuries. In the shorts there are no long shots, and the result is that we do not employ doubles. We must work fast, for our action is speeded in order to tell the story in two reels. Comedy that drags along is not real comedy. The shooting schedules on our pictures never run more than a week. It is nothing to work from eight o'clock in the morning until midnight. When I get through, comfortable slippers, a dressing gown and a newspaper look better to me than all the restaurants and theaters in the world

Vernon worked hard, and the pratfalls took their toll on his body. He underwent a spine operation in 1929 as a result of those falls, and eventually left performing and turned to writing. He only lived to be 42 years old, dying in 1939.

William Beaudine responded well to Vernon's boyish charm, and his striking leading lady Vera Steadman, as well as frequent co-star Jimmy Harrison. One of his better films, *Why Wild Men Go Wild* (1920), features Harrison as college boy Jimmy, who is known for his wild antics. His roommate, Bobby (Vernon) is even wilder. When Jimmy goes home to visit family, he has to play down his antics and seem much more sober and subdued. He is accompanied by Bobby, who changes his appearance to appear like a prudish minister's son in order to gain the approval of Jimmy's father, so he is not cut off financially. The problem is, Bobby is smitten with Jimmy's sister (Vera), who likes wild guys (which Bobby actually is) and finds her brother's roommate boring in his prudishness.

In just one reel, Beaudine uses this set-up to maintain a narrative where the characters are well-drawn and the antics are fast paced and funny. Hearing about an escaped wild man, Bobby con-

---

7 Moak, Bob "Hollywood Draws the Line". *Picture-Play Magazine*. September 1929

vinces Jimmy to pose as such in front of his sister, so Bobby can run in and beat him up to attract her. Of course, the actual wild man comes along to spoil things. Mistaken identities and slapstick gags are strewn about the narrative that manages to complete its trajectory within a twelve-minute running time.

William Beaudine continued to enjoy success with Christie, directing most of the Bobby Vernon films, as well as comedies with Neal Burns, Dorothy Devore, and Earle Rodney, among others.

Along with his Christie comedies, Beaudine would also branch out and do the occasional film for Hal Roach (*Punch the Clock* with Snub Pollard) and Sennett (*Step Forward* with Ben Turpin). Interestingly, William Beaudine's brother, Harold Beaudine, also secured work directing comedies for Christie, and was quite successful in his own right.

Punch the Clock is one of the better Snub Pollard shorts for Roach, and Beaudine responds well to the fusion of slapstick gags and situational comedy. The film opens with Snub is sleeping in the doorway of his employment. A police officer confronts him and Snub produces a letter indicating he will lose his job if he is ever late again, so he must "punch the clock" on time hereafter or be fired. Thus, he sleeps overnight in the doorway of his work to make sure.

This bit of absurdity is an amusing opener to the subsequent situations that involved mistaken identities. Beaudine shifts to a domestic setting where young wife is planning to step out on her husband and rendezvous with a man wearing a carnation. Her husband overhears and follows her. The admirer sees him, and Snub ends up with the carnation, which he unwittingly affixes to his coat. Of course the husband believes he is the admirer and comically accosts him.

The next several sequences show Snub inadvertently getting between the husband and the woman, whom he does not even know. Another comic layer is added when every time the husband gets ready to hit Snub, a policeman walks by so the husband stops and pretends to be friendly with his victim. There are variations on slapstick gags throughout. Snub and the woman end up rolling down the on a crate that has been propelled by a clumsy worker, landing at the husband's feet. Snub hides in a laundry basket that ends up being delievered to their home. Snub is knocked off a bridge into a coal truck that delivers him back into their house once again. After all this, Snub finally gets back to his place of employment, happy to realize he still made it on time, only to discover it is Sunday and the place is closed anyway.

Punch the Clock was filmed in early 1922, and is remarkable in that it contains all of these situations and slapstick sequences in the course of only one reel. It shows that Beaudine had now perfected his ability to helm a well-structured short comedy, and because he continued to allow the comedian a lot of creative freedom, Snub Pollard enjoyed adding a lot of comic nuance to his reactions.

Now that William Beaudine had very firmly established himself in short comedies, it was time he graduated to feature length movies. He was called upon to direct his first feature by Samuel Goldwyn, who signed him to a two picture deal. While he would continue churning out shorts for Christie, William Beaudine was about to direct his first feature film.

Ethel Teare, Lloyd Hamilton, and Bud Duncan in Ham Takes a Chance.

Trade ad for The Cross-Eyed Submarine.

Lillian Peacock.

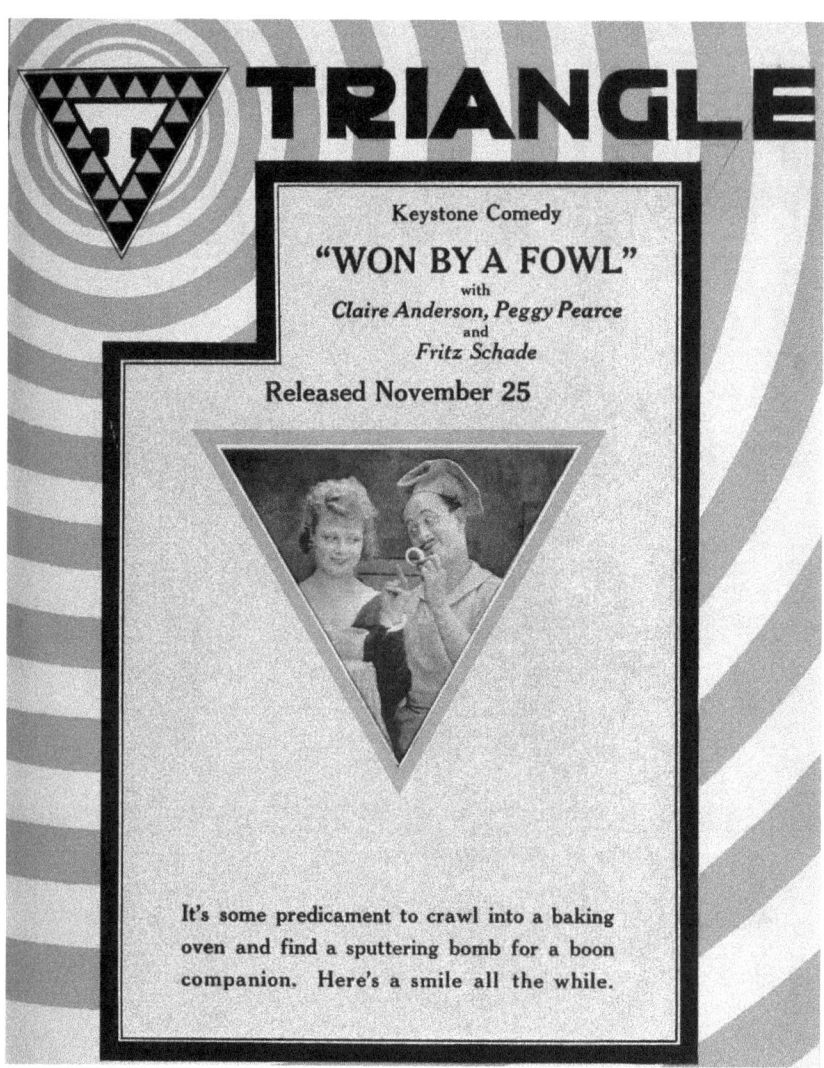

Trade ad for Won By a Fowl.

Bobby Vernon.

THE SILENT FEATURES

Upon signing with Samuel Goldwyn to direct two features for $2500 per film, William Beaudine wrapped work on the Christie short he had in production and began making preparations for *The City Feller*, based on a story and screenplay by Julien Josephson. Cullen Landis, an actor who began his career as a director, was cast as the lead, with Patsy Ruth Miller as his female co-star. The cast was rounded out by capable character actors like Bert Woodruff, Henry Rattenbury, and Cordelia Callahan. By the time it was released, the film's title was changed to *Watch Your Step*.

The story deals with Landis as Elmer Slocum, a typical 20s-era go-getter who has a penchant for speeding in his beloved roadster. After being jailed for constant speeding violations, Elmer, upon his release, races at a harrowing 85 miles per hour to bring a doctor to an emergency call. The car is wrecked and when Elmer knocks down the pursuing policeman, he believes he has killed him so he quickly leaves town. His clothes are stolen by some tramps, so a disheveled Elmer wanders shabbily into a midwestern town. While there, he falls for the daughter of the town's richest man, but is soon discovered by a detective. It turns out the policeman was not killed, and, in fact, was back to work the next day.

While no screening print is available for *Watch Your Step*, period reviews indicate that it was extremely well received by audiences. Beaudine drew from his influences by everyone from D.W. Griffith, to Marshall Neilan, to Mack Sennett, to Dell Henderson, as well as his own experiences, and came up with a thoroughly entertaining feature. And it was pure entertainment, with no pretentions beyond that. Critics believed it to be Cullen Landis' best role yet, with *Motion Picture News* stating: "William Beaudine directed *Watch Your Step* and has brought out excellently the author's truthful record of small town characters and happenings."[8]

---

8 "Cullen Landis Featured in 'Watch Your Step'" *Motion Picture News* January 24, 1922

To give us an idea of at least one of this elusive film's scenes, *Variety* stated in their May 19, 1922 review:[9]

> One incident of the story may indicate the spirit of the comedy. Russ (the general store owner) is out on some business when a telephone message comes that Ky Wilson wants him in a hurry. The store clerk sends his assistant to find Russ, adding "I don't know what it's about, but you better take Russ' plumbing tools along. Russ takes the message and starts on the mysterious mission, observing casually, "I guess that leaky bathtub of Ky's is in trouble again. When he gets to Ky's cottage, ky meets him at the dooer grinning broadly and informs him, "Never Mind, I got Doc Harrison instead. It's a boy!" For a surprise laugh, it was a whale, and the picture is full of the same sort of fresh and amusing touches.

Other reviews refer to action sequences including the car crash and a fistfight. Beaudine is praised for his ability to depict small town life earnestly and not as parody. *Watch Your Step* was the 14th most profitable film of 1922, besting the box office of *Blood and Sand* with Rudolph Valentino and *Just Tony* with Tom Mix.

Filming was not without incident, however. William Beaudine told *Film Daily* in their June 11, 1922 issue:[10]

> It was necessary to show a very convincing scene of a wrecked racing car. The transportation department hired a big Dusenberg special that was guaranteed to do 110 miles per hour. The technical department drew extensive plans for turning the car over without damaging it. Cullen Landis wanted to drive the car to the location. While trying to find out how fast it would go, he narrowly missed a car that came out of a side road and had landed at the bottom of an eight foot ravine, right side up, without a scratch to either passenger. The car, however, was most artistically wrecked. So we moved back and shot the rea wreck.

---

9 "Watch Your Step" *Variety* May 19, 1922
10 "In Which An Auto Figured" *Film Daily* June 11, 1922

However, despite the film's success at the box office, Samuel Goldwyn was disappointed. *Watch Your Step* was biggest in rural areas and small towns, which was not the demographic that Goldwyn desired. Beaudine was quite unhappy when Goldwyn paid him off and cancelled the proposed second planned feature. Beaudine returned to short films at Christie.

In June of 1922, William Beaudine was beckoned by producer Harry Rapf to direct a feature for Warner Brothers. *Heroes of the Street* was planned as a vehicle for child star Wesley Barry. Beaudine had directed Barry at Kalem back in 1916 when the nine year old played Bud Duncan as a child in a Ham and Bud comedy. Barry was now crowding adolescence. Many child actors usually lose their careers during this awkward stage, but Rapf (and Warners) believed Barry had enough talent to overcome any growing pains.

Heroes of the Street is the sort of melodrama that already seemed old fashioned in 1922, but Beaudine's approach, and the strength of the performances, made it a popular box office hit. The story deals with officer Mike Callahan, who is killed on duty, forcing his son Mickey to become the man of the house. Beaudine's establishing scenes show the peaceful tranquility of the happy family, while Wesley Barry's performance as Mickey responds to his father being killed, is first rate acting. Mickey sets out to avenge his father's death, resulting in a lot of action and suspense.

Marie Prevost is one of Barry's co-stars in the film, *Heroes of the Street* being one of six films she made in 1922. A popular and sought-after performer throughout the silent era, Prevost's career began to slip once talkies arrived. She had a good voice and handled dialog well, but was putting on weight. Her attempts to lose weight resulted in starving herself coupled with alcoholism. She died alone in January of 1936. Beaudine never forgot actors with whom he worked successfully, and would later cast Marie in the Jean Harlow vehicle *Three Wise Girls* in 1931, which turned out to be one of her best performances in talkies.

Warner Brothers realized with *Heroes of the Street* that they had a potential hit on their hands, and also knew that families and children would be their chief audience. Some of their promotional gimmicks included the distribution of Wesley Barry writing tablets to school children. Other theatres had newfangled motorcycles on display as they were presented as law enforcement transport in the movie.

Unlike Samuel Goldwyn, who dismissed the success of *Watch Your Step* because he was dissatisfied as to where the box office was coming from, Warners were elated with the success of *Heroes of the Street*. William Beaudine was given a contract and signed to directed the next few Wesley Barry vehicles, including *Printer's Devil* and *The Country Kid*. Beaudine would remain with Warner Brothers for the next four years.

The Country Kid features Wesley Barry as Ben Applegate, who is orphaned at 14 and works on his late parents' farm to take care of his two little brothers. Ben's uncle arranges to have Ben work for him, while the younger boys are sent to an orphanage. Ben must help his brothers escape from the orphanage and prove to a judge that their uncle is an unfit guardian. The review in *Bioscope* for *The Country Kid* stated:[11]

> This is a pleasing picture of the humor and pathos of child life whic will appeal to any class of audience. The story is slight but sufficient as a thread on which to hang some very effective scenes, which are rendered delightful by the charm and talent of some attractive children and a dog of super intelligence. Their youthful ailments brought on by ill-assorted foodstuffs and the drastic remedies, their reversals of fortune, and eventual attainment of perfect childish happiness are set forth in a series of scenes in which humor is skillfully mingled with simple sentiment.

Based on the success of his films with Wesley Barry, William Beaudine had proven himself to have a knack for working with youngsters. Thus, producer J.K. McDonald hired Beaudine to direct a film version of Booth Tarkington's *Penrod and Sam* for First National Pictures. Tarkington's book was a sequel to his previous *Penrod*, and a film version of that book had been made the previous year. That film, made by Marshall Neilan for his

---

[11] "The Country Kid" *Bioscope* January 10, 1924

own company, had starred Wesley Barry as Penrod and Gordon Griffith as Sam. Thus, Beaudine wanted Barry for his film, but he was working with Mal St. Clair on a screen version of George M. Cohan's play *George Washington, Jr.* Plus, Warners was allowing the 16 year old Barry to age out of juvenile parts and start playing teenagers. Ben Alexander was cast as Penrod, Joe Butterworth was hired to play Sam, and the cast was rounded out with child actors Gertrude Messinger, her brother Buddy Messinger, Newton Hall, Joe McGray, and Eugene Jackson. The adult actors included Rockliffe Fellowes, Gladys Brockwell, Mary Philbin, and William Mong.

William Beaudine attempted something different for this film. Wanting a more natural look from his youthful actors, Beaudine chose to film them without makeup. While makeup in comedies during the teens was often quite garish, as the cinematic process developed during the twenties, everything was more tempered, from the outrageous makeup to the bulging eyes and florid gestures. Stage trained actors began to understand the intimacy of the movie camera that could register the mere lift of an eyebrow, making it unnecessary to perform so broadly with the sweeping gestures that often unfairly define silent movie acting. Beaudine believed that with camera work and lighting, he could present his young actors more naturally.

Much of the film deals with Penrod and Sam initiating prissy Georgie Bassett into their exclusive club. They don't like Georgie, because they believe him to be a sissy, but Penrod's dad recommends they allow the effete youngster into the club because he comes from a prominent wealthy family. The initiation that the boys concoct for poor Georgie include dumping him in a tub of paint, smearing his hair with glue, and sticking him in a furnace and threatening to start a fire. These scenes fit well into William Beaudine's wheelhouse. Not only was he adept at working with youngsters, he had a great deal of experience with physical gags and slapstick comedy. These scenes of Georgie's initiation resulted in gales of laughter from moviegoers. *Penrod and Sam* was a huge hit for Warner Brothers, drawing in children and parents alike. The books were themselves quite popular, so the film had a ready-made audience of readers wanting to see the literature as a movie.

William Beaudine's knack for directing children had a lot to do with patience and understanding, but also his allowing a break during each day of filming for a pickup baseball game in which the director himself woult participate with the kids. This generated a real loyalty from his young actors, who never received this sort of attention and understanding from other directors.

J.K. McDonald next asked William Beaudine to direct Ben Alexander in *Boy of Mine*, a melodrama based on another Booth Tarkington story. Ben plays a young boy whose father is a strict disciplinarian who shows no warmth for his son. His mother leaves, taking the youngster with her, and leaving the father with an ultimatum. Beaudine was comfortably surrounded by actors with whom he was already familiar; not only Alexander, but Rockliffe Fellows, who had been in *Penrod and Sam*, plays a doctor in this movie. Henry B. Walthall, who had acted for D.W. Griffith when Beaudine was working at Biograph, played the father. The mother was Irene Rich, whose career lasted from the teens until the end of the 1940s (she lived almost to the end of the 1980s). Jack Jungmeyer in a syndicated article published in newspapers on June 14, 1924, stated:[12]

> Every American boy has a friend at the court of parental autocracy in the person of William Beaudine, motion picture director. *Boy of Mine*, made from Booth Tarkington's story, gives him that status. As a screen play it has exceptional merit. But it is even more laudable as a sensitive treatment of childhood's crucial hours, especially in defense of the juvenile's sharp sense of justice so flagrantly violated by elders in the name of discipline. Beaudine, himself a family man and one of those rare adults who take time to fathom childish motives, understands the dramatic vigor of domestic commonplace. His ingredients are very simple but profoundly effective. The picture unfolds the misunderstanding between a father and son,

---

12 Jungmeyer, Jack. "Beaudine Friend of Boyhood." *The Reading Times*. June 14, 1924

amusingly, pathetically, trenchantly. The father is a man of intense family pride. The boy's energies, often devastating. Ben Alexander gives such a convincing, poignant portrayal that every family will recognize in him the counterpart of an ebullient son. Fathers may be loath to identify themselves with Henry Walthall, the sire who inflicts discipline without examining motive or permitting the child a hearing, but it is these precisely who should see the film. Walthall contributes his fine talents with discernment and a pathetic bewilderment. Irene Rich, always distinguished, will be applauded by every sensitive parent and by picture critics for her splendid handling of the maternal role. The doctor friend of the family, whose good offices averts disaster, is played by Rockcllffe Fellowes, and boasts no finer player in a characterization of this type.

William Beaudine's status in the movie industry continued to grow with these First National releases, and his status as a director for Warner Brothers continued to flourish.

Beaudine was pleased to be reunited with Lloyd Hamilton for his next J.K. McDonald production, *A Self-Made Failure* which was filmed not long after *Boy of Mine*. Beaudine liked to work with actors he'd directed before, and he had good history with Hamilton. Beaudine rounded out the cast with other actors he'd worked with previously, including Patsy Ruth Miller, who had co-starred in his first feature length directorial effort *Watch Your Step,* and, once again, Ben Alexander.

Lloyd Hamilton had become quite a popular solo star in short comedies since breaking with Bud Duncan, and First National believed he could advance to feature films like Charlie Chaplin, Buster Keaton, and Harold Lloyd had. Hamilton's bumbling screen character had a certain style of his own, and it was believed that adding more layers to his performance would still keep the heart of the characterization and allow for feature-length productions. Chaplin, Keaton, and Lloyd had expanded past gags with their feature-length films. It was believed that Lloyd Hamilton could do so as well.

Before embarking on what would become *A Self-Made Failure*, Hamilton starred in the five-reel *His Darker Self*. Initial screenings flopped, and the film was edited down to a two-reeler. Disappointed by the failure of *His Darker Self*, but still undaunted, Hamilton embarked on his next feature with the same zest and concentration that marked his best short films. Producer J.K. McDonald believed in Hamilton, and felt that having the seasoned William Beaudine direct the film would result in a box office hit. Hamilton recalled the respect he had enjoyed from Beaudine's direction of the Ham and Bud shorts, and appreciated having the room to be creative. *A Self-Made Failure* looked like a winning project.

Producer McDonald came up with a story that would allow Hamilton to not only be funny, but to use his established screen persona for pathos. It was important that the audience cared about the central character in a feature film. Hamilton was a good actor who was able to rise to the occasion. McDonald's story was adapted by Tamar Lane, and a screenplay was written with contributions from Violet Clark, John Grey, and Lex Neal. Neal had adapted Beaudine's feature *Boy of Mine* and would later contribute to scripts of Buster Keaton, Harold Lloyd, and W.C. Fields films. Grey had written for Ben Turpin and Mabel Normand.

Cameo the dog had been in *Penrod and Sam* and was already something of a screen veteran. A female, Cameo might best be remembered for appearing with Billy Bevan in the Sennett comedy *Nip and Tuck* (1923). In a 1924 article for *Exhibitor's Herald*, trainer Hap Ward talked about Cameo's film career, indicating *Penrod and Sam* had been her favorite movie experience:[13]

> Cameo just loves kiddies. And she played all day with Penrod and his gang. She liked *A Self-Made Failure* too. Cameo has worked in four different pictures with William Beaudine. He takes great delight in rehearsing all the people and then saying 'Come on, let's go.' Then I ask him what the dog does and he tells me and Cameo goes through the scene without a rehearsal. I'll tell her to do

---

13 Nichols, Harry E. "Are Animals Abused in Films?" *Exhibitors Herald*. November 29, 1924

something and Mr. Beaudine changes his mind and tells her to do something else and she does it. Then he will tell me, 'You might as well go home, the dog knows more than you do.' Mr. Beaudine is a regular fellow. Everybody who works for him says so.

First National worked publicity and special events for *A Self-Made Failure* including a special screening for disabled children at the Crystal Theater in Brown's Lake, Wisconsin.

Sadly, *A Self-Made Failure* is a lost film so we cannot judge for ourselves as to the feature's merit. Some critics liked it, others did not. Some exhibitors reported that their patrons enjoyed the film, others complained of walk-outs.

There are a lot of factors that might have caused *A Self-Made Failure* to perform disappointingly, and we can only address these through research, with no film to screen. First, it was very long for a comedy of its time – eight reels. There were scenes with Ben Alexander and Cameo the Dog in which Hamilton didn't appear, distracting from his status as the central figure of the narrative. And while Hamilton appears to have been adept at getting audience sympathy while also being funny, the film was overlong and disjointed enough to make his acclaimed performance skills less impressive in this context. Finally, a lot of the ideas were recognized as having been inspired by the films of others, such as the relationship between a hobo (Hamilton) and a child (Ben Alexander) and its resemblance to Chaplin's *The Kid* (1921).

Still, it would be quite interesting to screen *A Self-Made Failure* today. The idea of expanding on the sympathetic aspect of Lloyd Hamilton's comical screen persona, and deriving from it the sort of pathos that Chaplin was able to successfully exhibit, might hold up a bit better this many years later. Often when a film is looked at from the perspective of the 21st century, and examined as a historical piece, it can be more aesthetically impressive as to its era and its method. But, in 1924, *A Self-Made Failure* was a disappointment. No further Lloyd Hamilton features were considered, and he returned to short subjects. And while Hamilton would thereafter make some of his best two-reelers (*Jonah*

Jones, Move Along, etc), he would remain disappointed that his feature film attempts had not worked out.

Despite the disappointing returns for A Self-Made Failure, William Beaudine continued to be a top director for Warner Brothers studio, now commanding a salary of $1,750 per week. Beaudine was presented on the cover of the February, 1925 issue of Director magazine. The story therein gave an overview of Beaudine's career up to that time:[14]

> In the lowly position of assistant property boy, Bill Beaudine had plenty of opportunity for using his eyes and the events of the past few years afford ample indication that he did so. Events moved rapidly in those old days and the opportunities for advancement were much more frequent than they are today. He had not been on the coast for very long before an opportunity came for him to wield the director's megaphone on the Triangle lot. That was some nine years ago, and Bill Beaudine confined his directorial activities to mirth-makers, winding up his comedy direction at the Christie studios. Forsaking straight comedy for drama....two years ago he was signed on a long term contract by Warner Brothers. When Mary Pickford decided to make Little Annie Rooney, she picked out Bill Beaudine as the logical man to direct.

Mary Pickford, one of the biggest stars and most powerful people in Hollywood, had been away from movies for a year and was ready to make a comeback film that would restore her status as a major Hollywood star.

Mary Pickford was one of the first, and greatest, stars of silent movies. The 4 foot 11 inch actress played youngsters well into her 20s for a captivated moviegoing public that dubbed her "America's Sweetheart." In 1922, Pickford had just completed one of the finest films of her career, Tess of the Storm Country, and decided that, at age 30, she should start playing characters closer to her own age. However, her next two films: Rosita (1923) and Dorothy Vernon of Haddon Hall (1924), in which she

---

14 "The Man on the Cover" Director February, 1925

played adult characters, were flops. Pickford recalled in her biography *Sunshine and Shadow*:[15]

> It would worry me that I was becoming a personality instead of an actress. I would suddenly resent the fact that I had allowed myself to be hypnotized by the public into remaining a little girl. It was sometime in 1922 that rebellion led me to a somewhat disastrous reaction. So much for *Rosita*, my first punishment for wanting to grow up on screen. I now decided to do *Dorothy Vernon of Haddon Hall*. That picture cost me $1,000,000 to make. The public just refused to accept me in any role older than the gawky, fighting age of adolescent girlhood.

Mary Pickford wrote a story called *Little Annie Rooney*, and because it required a cast that included children in principal roles, Pickford wanted William Beaudine to direct. Pickford and Beaudine had become friendly at the Biograph studios, when he was merely a helper and she was making some of her first films for D.W. Griffith.

William Beaudine was interested in directing *Little Annie Rooney*, but also under contract to Warner Brothers, who were not at all interested in lending one of their top directors to another studio. Pickford, of course, was, by now, part owner of United Artists, a studio she founded along with husband Douglas Fairbanks, Charlie Chaplin, and, for a time Griffith. She was one of the most powerful people in films, had the resources behind her, and was able to meet any price that Warner Brothers commanded for the use of their director.

An actual poll was taken, and the moviegoing public indicated that they wanted Mary Pickford to continue being "America's Sweetheart," despite her age. Pickford recalled:[16]

> After *Rosita* and *Dorothy Vernon* I was quite ready to surrender to public demand and become a child again. My two adventures in adulthood had been costly and embarrassing, but instructive too.

---

15 Pickford, Mary *Sunshine and Shadow* NY: Doubleday, 1955
16 Pickford, Mary *Sunshine and Shadow* NY: Doubleday, 1955

Pickford indicated that if *Little Annie Rooney* flopped, she was done with movies. William Beaudine was taking a real chance with this assignment. If the movie did flop, he would be blamed, not her. It would be considered his fault if she left movies. Fortunately, *Little Annie Rooney* was not only a success, it was one of the biggest hits in Mary Pickford's entire career.

Beaudine's approach to filming this feature seemed to be a bit more engaged, especially since the star of the movie was also the owner of the studio. His vision was supported, with beautiful establishing shots, camera placement, and his adeptness at working with younger actors. Pickford had an entire tenement set build on her studio's backlot, to represent the Bowery. A myriad of different nationalities and ethnic groups were represented. And Beaudine's long held method of allowing the actors to creatively add to their roles was also in evidence. Actor Eugene Jackson recalled for the writer in a 1985 interview:[17]

> I had worked with Mr. Beaudine in some other pictures, and he remembered me. I was working in the Our Gangs and he brought me over to this big production. I used to do a little shimmy, a little dance, in vaudeville back in those days, and I showed Ms. Pickford on the set. He and Ms. Pickford came up with a scene where I could do it in the picture. Little things like that would get an actor like me noticed and would get me more work.

Beaudine also arranged to use Joe Butterworth who had played Sam in *Penrod and Sam*, as well as his beloved Cameo the dog. Both were met with approval by Mary Pickford.

One casting decision failed, however. A young unknown named Alan Hughes was picked by Mary as the leading man, given the name Hugh Allan as an actor. He initially showed promise. A story in the Oakland Tribune reported:[18]

> A short time ago it was noted here that an Oakland lad is to play leading man in Mary Pickford's new film *Little Annie Rooney*. Alan Hughes was graduated from the Fremont

---

17 Interview with the author for a 1985 article
18 "High School to Hollywood" *Oakland Tribune* May 17, 1925

High School over in Oakland but two years ago. After working here' for a time in the office of a steamship company he went to Hollywood to be a secretary for a film company. Then he became an assistant camera man and a film cutter and from that an actor of small parts. All of this in two years he had no dream of a sudden rise to a chance for fame and was as surprised as anyone else when he received the word that Miss Pickford wished him to sign his name on the dotted line. Explanation is in the fact that Miss Pickford studies every role in. her productions and make her selections from screen tests. This is the story of how Alan Hughes of East Oakland became Hugh Allan motion picture star. He reversed his name because another actor, Lloyd Hughes is under contract with the same company.

This, however, did not work out. Hugh Allan was too inexperienced to play such a significant role in such an important feature. Mary liked him and was sad that she had to fire him from the movie. To save face, her studio's publicity department put out a story that he was injured.[19]

> Repairing his aerial one day, Hugh fell from the roof of his home, and when he picked himself up, one wrist was broken. Mary regretted the blow she had to offer, but she could not wait for the wrist to heal. However, disappointed and heartsick as he was, Hugh smiled, an honest boyish smile. And because he smiled, this eighteen year old boy has a long contract with First National, and he's to have another chance as soon as the wrist is free of its sling

Hugh Allan remained active in movies for the rest of the 1920s, and lived until 1997 when, at the age of 94, he committed suicide.

Filming was quite an experience for all involved. Mary kept an open set, so there were visitors quite regularly, from tourists to major stars like Pickford's husband Douglas Fairbanks, studio co-owner Charlie Chaplin, even a visit one day from Rudolph Valentino.

---

19 "Boyish Smile, In Spite of Sickness, Gives Hugh Allen a Chance with Mary Pickford". *Lincoln Star* June 14, 1925

Little Annie Rooney enjoyed much publicity while it was in production. Even the fact that William Beaudine wore a visor to shade his eyes from the sun, instead of the traditional cap, made the syndicated newspaper columns. And when the movie came out and broke box office records at some theaters, exhibitors wrote that their audiences both laughed at the slapstick battles between the rival teenage gangs, and cried as Little Annie volunteered to give a young man she loved a blood transfusion, her child's mind believing that it would be fatal to her. The makeshift will she scribbles out, where she wrote that there were no hard feelings between Annie and her main neighborhood rival, brought tears to moviegoers throughout the nation.

Newspapers announced that Warner Brothers had planned for William Beaudine to next direct *Bunker Bean*, based on the story by Harry Leon Wilson. He was to go right into production on that movie as soon as he wrapped *Little Annie Rooney*. However, buoyed by the success of *Little Annie Rooney*, Pickford announced that she was to make three more features in rapid succession. She wanted to continue with the momentum of her success. And she wanted William Beaudine to direct her next planned film, which would turn out to be *Sparrows*.

While it was a massive success and continues to be considered perhaps the best film in Mary Pickford's career, *Sparrows*, was an especially difficult project for William Beaudine. He clashed so frequently with Pickford that he experienced facial paralysis. When he left toward the end of the project, allowing his assistant director, Tom McNamara, to finish the film, the facial paralysis went away.

Although she was pleased with Beaudine's direction of *Little Annie Rooney*, Mary Pickford asserted her considerable authority on the set of *Sparrows*. In later interviews, she claimed Beaudine put her, and a baby she was holding, in danger by having them venture across water that was filled with alligators, but cinematographer Hal Mohr refuted this and stated that the actors got nowhere near the alligators, and the scenes were all done in process. Beaudine did not refute Pickford, hoping she would eventually tell the truth. She did not, and in her autobiography, *Sunshine and Shadow*, she doesn't even mention Beaudine's name, referring to him only as "the director" of the film.

One thing worth mentioning in regard to *Little Annie Rooney* and *Sparrows* is how they further point out the fact that Beaudine is certainly not a hurried "one-shot" director as claimed by those not knowledgeable about his work. In both of these films, he lingers for a long time on the actors, especially Pickford. There are several more emotional scenes in which the camera stays on a close-up of her for a while, allowing her to exhibit the extent of her formidable acting skills. Both of these movies have a lot of action, a lot of comedy, and, particularly with *Sparrows*, deeper, even religious themes. Beaudine proves himself adept at handling all these different genres as he does a great job framing these shots as well, and getting the most out of his actors. All of these elements would effectively serve to inform Beaudine's direction when he later explored different genres more completely.

The success, both critical and financial, of *Sparrows* caused William Beaudine to become and even more highly respected director. He continued to be employed with Warner Brothers, but was also loaned to other studios who requested his services. And while he never made another silent feature quite at the level of *Sparrows*, Beaudine's subsequent films through the end of the 1920s were popular and successful. *The Canadian* (1926) was a strong adaption of the W. Somerset Maugham play. It was made for Famous Players-Lasky and released by Paramount. This silent feature would figure prominently at the end of William Beaudine's life and is discussed at greater length in the final chapter of this book.

When William Beaudine appeared as the cover story of the February, 1925 issue of the trade magazine *Director*, the article stated:

> Bill Beaudine's rise to the top of the ladder has been steady and sure. Today he is sitting on top of the world, ranking among the foremost motion picture directors in the business, president of The Motion Picture Director's Association, and recognized as one of the dominant figures of the industry.

He was also the first director to appear on the cover of this magazine, something the article similarly touted.

Two of William Beaudine's more interesting productions during this period were the features he directed for comedian Douglas MacLean. MacLean was a stage performer who entered movies in the teens and had been acting in films for about a dozen years when Beaudine began directing him. Since MacLean was his own producer, having just signed a new contract with Paramount, he wanted to meet with Beaudine before hiring him to direct. MacLean was familiar with Beaudine's background in directing comedies, all the way back to the Ham and Bud one-reelers, and thought he'd be a good fit for his method.

During their meeting Beaudine was honest about not having particularly liked MacLean's latest feature, *Seven Keys to Baldpate* (1925). MacLean appreciated Beaudine's honesty and candor, and as the two continued to talk, they discovered they had similar attitudes about comedy, and similar approaches. MacLean asked Beaudine to direct his first film on his new Paramount contract, *That's My Baby* (1926). Of course Beaudine was still under contract with Warner Brothers, but that studio profited by loaning him out.

That's My Baby had Douglas MacLean engaged to be married to a woman he was madly in love with. However, she dumps him and goes off with another, so he swears off women forever. Then he sees a girl who has twisted her ankle, so he goes to the rescue and the two fall in love. But her father turns out to be his business rival, and her mother has her beau all picked out. A scheme is set up to accuse Doug of bigamy, hiring a midget to claim to be his long lost son.

Under William Beaudine's direction, *That's My Baby* was hailed as one of Douglas MacLean's biggest hits. It started out slowly as the conflict was presented, but then it picked up as a fast and exciting comedy, perfectly in line with MacLean's past successes. So pleased was he with Beaudine's direction, MacLean hired him to helm his next movie while this film was still in production.

Beaudine's next movie with Douglas MacLean was *Hold That Lion*, a wild farce where Doug is invited by a girl he's in love with to hunt for "cats." He is then surprised to discover that the "cats" are lions and the hunt will take place in the jungles of Africa. This was another hit. But one of the amusing connections to *Hold That Lion* involved an off-screen contest between the skinny Beaudine and the rotund comedy actor Walter Hiers. The two made a bet where every time Beaudine lost a pound he'd lose a dollar, and every time Hiers gained a pound, he lose a dollar. The two men weighed themselves every morning, and money changed hands a reported 70 times!

As the 1920s continued, Beaudine's other silent features included *The Life of Riley* (1927), which was a fun comedy with Charley Murray and George Sidney. *Home James* (1928), is another one of the better features during this period; a very funny comedy featuring Laura LaPlante. This was a time when the silent film could be determined as perfected. After decades of experimenting, silent movies were now an art form unto themselves, and even the cheerful comedies Beaudine had been directing with the likes of Murray, Sidney, and La Plante have an essence that defined them for the era. But as the 1920s concluded and the bigger studios began experimenting with sound on film, William Beaudine was assigned to work on his first movies with sound.

Fugitives (1929), made on loan to Fox, was an experimental sound film featuring a synchronized music score, something the silent era attempted initially before trying out spoken dialog. *Two Weeks Off*, made for his home studio of Warner Brothers, was a silent that featured talking sequences, another level of the sound film's evolution. By the time he directed *Hard To Get* (1929), William Beaudine had made the transition to talking pictures, where the entire feature relied on spoken dialog.

Many actors lamented that by the time they got things just right, Hollywood cinema changed on them. This is true. The silent era of motion pictures had become a rather perfect visual medium as the 1920s ended, and produced enduring classics that really used the very depth of cinematic production. When sound movies ushered in and took over, they had primitive ideas of microphones hidden in bushes or in bowls of fruit on tables, forcing the actor to wander over near that area and speak his line. However, the new technology was so embraced by the public, the superior silent film productions were dismissed as archaic. The mainstream culture had fallen for sound movies, despite the limitations they had in comparison to what silent movies were able to offer. So, Beaudine made his transition. And so had Hollywood.

Marie Prevost and Wesley Barry in Heroes of the Street.

Cullen Landis in Watch Your Step.

George Pearce, Raymond Cannon, Patsy Ruth Miller, Cullen Landis in Watch Your Step.

William Beaudine with Welsey Barry on the set of The Printer Kid.

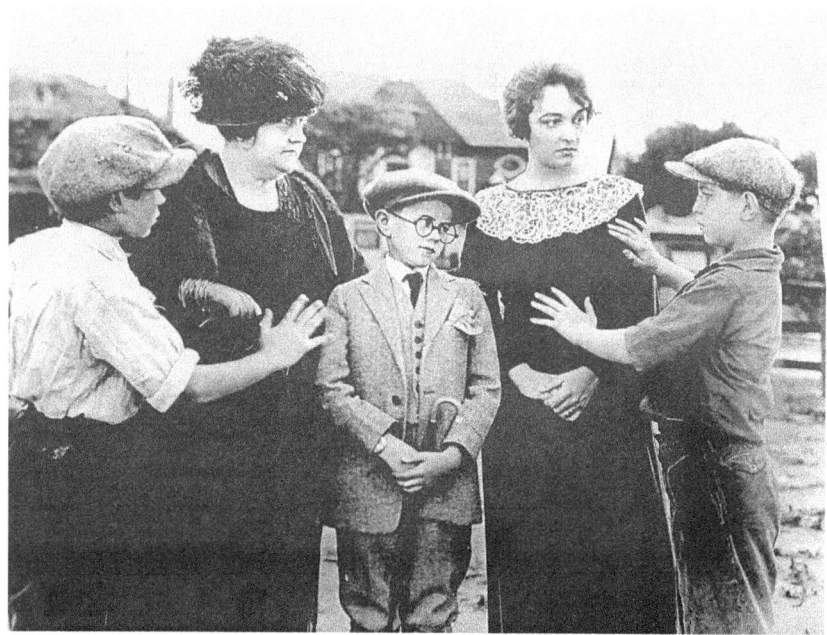

Buddy Messinger, (unknown), Newton Hall, Gladys Brockwell, and Ben Alexander in Penrod and Sam.

William Beaudine (standing), Lloyd Hamilton (seated on side of carriage), Patsy Ruth Miller, Matt Moore, Mary Carr, Ben Alexander, and Cameo the Dog in A Self Made Failure.

William Beaudine and Mary Pickford pose in a gag shot for Little Annie Rooney.

Mary Pickford and the kids in Sparrows.

Lobby card for Hold That Lion.

THE EARLY SOUND FEATURES

In 1925, the Vitaphone sound-on-disc system was introduced to Sam Warner of Warner Brothers studio. This system had been created by Western Electric, using the audion tube invented in 1906 by Dr. Lee DeForest and an electromagnetic photograph reproducer which had been invented in 1913 by Dr. Irving B. Crandall and F.W. Kranz. Upon seeing a demonstration of the sound-on-disc system, Sam Warner approved and the studio created the Vitaphone Corporation on April 20, 1926.

The first Vitaphone shorts were produced at the former Vitagraph studios in Brooklyn. Warner Brothers set up a program to be presented at New York's Piccadilly Theater on August 7, 1926 to introduce Vitaphone. The first feature to utilize the Vitaphone system was *Don Juan*"(1926) starring John Barrymore. The sound for this film was synchronized music and effects, but the accompanying shorts -- a speech by Will Hays, President of the Motion Picture Producers of America, followed by several musical pieces -- were all-talking subjects. Thus, the first fully talking pictures were short subjects. The release of *The Jazz Singer* starring Al Jolson the following year was heralded as the first feature to have spoken dialog.

When *The Jazz Singer* premiered at the Warner Theater in New York on August 6, 1927, it was immediately a tremendous sensation and ushered in a new era. The one sad note was that the man most responsible for seeing the potential of Vitaphone, Sam Warner, had died just the day before this triumphant premiere. While the story creaked even then, *The Jazz Singer* benefited greatly by Jolson's performance. It was essentially a silent film with the musical numbers and a brief dialog sequence done with sound. As indicated at the conclusion of the previous chapter, William Beaudine adapted to sound film as a director at the same time. He helmed a sound film that contained a music score on its soundtrack, and then one that featured talkie sequences. The evolution of the technology was central to his next few projects.

Once sound was established via *The Jazz Singer* and some experimental Vitaphone shorts, it allowed short subject producers to ponder the variety now possible with advances in the film medium. In their April 6, 1930 issue, *Film Daily* printed the results of a survey they conducted among 600 exhibitors throughout the nation. A vast majority believed that sound had added to the entertainment value of short subjects. The consensus was that short subjects of all kinds, and comedies in particular, had undergone such improvement since sound came along that they now constituted an indispensable part of the program, and were being demanded by patrons. Exhibitors stated that shorts were responsible for saving the program when the feature was weak, that not having a short with the feature was like a main course with no dessert, and some even went so far as to suggest feature pictures be made uniformly shorter, thereby allowing for shorts. Rita McGoldrick, then chairman of the Motion Picture Bureau, International Federation of Catholic Alumnae stated:

> In the ten years (we) have been previewing pictures, (we) have watched with the greatest interest the steady development of the short subject from the insignificant filler-in on the average program, to the high-class project which, in so many instances lately, have threatened to run away with the show. Sound gave new life, a new vigorous vitality, to the humble shorts.

The first all-talking feature, *The Lights of New York* premiered at the Mark Strand Theater in New York, on July 6, 1928, less than a year after the premiere of *The Jazz Singer*. In its 57-minute length, this crime melodrama presented, for the first time, dialog clichés like "Take him for a ride," but audiences were thrilled to see a 100% talkie. Between 1926 and 1929, hundreds of short films were produced by Warner Brothers at their east coast Vitaphone studios, featuring famous and lesser known Vaudeville performers doing songs, dances, novelty acts, and dramatic sketches. Producers filmed excerpts from hit Broadway plays that were currently running.

The death knell was sounded for silent pictures. Exhibitor H.E. Hoag stated in 1930: "A silent comedy is very flat now. In fact, for the past two years, my audiences seldom laughed out loud at a silent."

The bigger studios hastily transformed recently shot silent features into talkies by dubbing in voices and sound effects. The smaller studios did not have the funds to accomplish this, and thus their silents of late 1929 and early 1930 received very little distribution, save for small town theaters that were not yet equipped for sound. But by the 1930's sound was so firmly established in the cinema only someone with the status of Charlie Chaplin was able to pull off making a silent movie. William Beaudine had, by this time, established himself as fully capable of directing a talking picture. From *Hard to Get* in 1929, his films were all talkies.

One of the things that many studios believed necessary during the early sound era was to remake some of their hit silent movies as talkies. The silent film is, today, hailed as an art form, but at the time of the sound movie revolution, it was very quickly dismissed as archaic. This negligent attitude resulted in a lot of lost films, hampering our deeper appreciation of cinema's rich history. In fact, silent movies were dismissed so cavalierly, some studios would cut up film scenes from movies that had been hailed as triumphs only a few short years earlier, add a soundtrack that included snarky narration, and release these blasphemous creations as short subject novelties.

William Beaudine's career was enjoying great success and a massive workload. He made films with Fox, Universal, and his home studio First National. After the success of *Fugitives*, Fox wanted him under contract. However, in April of 1929, Beaudine signed a contract with First National to direct six films in one year. His pay was $15,000 per film with a seven-week production schedule. And since his previous studio, Warner Brothers, had purchased First National in 1928, the films were released as Warner Brothers First National productions.

So good was his transition to directing sound films, that William Beaudine toyed with the idea of writing a textbook for other filmmakers who were struggling with the new sound film production.

He went so far as to start compiling material based on his own work in talkies. Beaudine believed that a great deal of production costs would be saved if directors had knowledge based on the experiences of contemporaries who had successfully transitioned to sound films. However, his workload was such that he didn't have time to more fully investigate this idea.

One of William Beaudine's early assignments was to remake the Booth Tarkington story *Boy of Mine*, which had been a successful silent feature, into a sound version. *Father's Son*, as the talkie was entitled, featured Leon Janney in the role that had been played by Ben Alexander in the silent version. Lewis Stone plays the strict, cold-hearted father that had earlier been portrayed by Henry B. Walthall. The mother was played by Irene Rich, who had also played the role in the silent. The coming attractions trailer featured these three actors discussing the movie in order to promote it as a sound version of the Tarkington story. And while the film was completed in 1930 and reviewed in the December issue of *Photoplay*, it was not released until February of 1931.

Perhaps the most interesting project during this period was an independent film Beaudine made around this time for Liberty productions. *The Mad Parade* was a war film with an all-female cast; something that was quite unheard of in 1931. The story, under a different title, was originally going to be directed by Dorothy Arzner and feature Ruth Chatterton, Jean Arthur and Fay Wray in the cast. In fact, there was some footage shot that still exists. Apparently, Chatterton left the production and it was shelved until the studio resurrected for Beaudine and a new cast that included Evelyn Brent, Lilyan Tashman, Irene Rich, Louise Fazenda, and Marceline Day.

Also known as *Forgotten Women*, the narrative concerns women in the military dealing with the horrors of war. This was a particularly ambitious and courageous project that received a great deal of publicity while it was being shot. Once it was completed, Paramount bought the right to distribute, and cut the film to where little remained of Beaudine's original vision. The movie flopped at the box office and was dismissed as a misguided novelty by critics. It holds up much better in the 21st century as it presents another perspective of the horrors of war. Now there are historical as well as aesthetic reasons to appreciate *The Mad Parade*.

Beaudine returned to First National to complete the final film on his contract; a sound version of one of his biggest silent screen hits, Booth Tarkington's *Penrod and Sam*. Leon Janney, from *Father's Son* was cast as Penrod, with veteran child actor Frank "Junior" Coghlan as Sam. Beaudine was able to cast a few actors with whom he'd worked in previous movies, something he always tried to do with every production. For instance, Matt Moore, who had been in *A Self-Made Failure*, plays Penrod's father in this remake. Also, Cameo the dog is back in what would be the canine's last screen appearance. Beaudine cast his own daughter, Helen, as Penrod's sister Margaret. Interestingly, Beaudine also had a daughter named Margaret, who had appeared in his two 1929 features *Hard to Get* and *Two Weeks Off*.

Unlike the silent, which relied almost completely on the initiation of sissy Georgie Bassett into Penrod and Sam's exclusive club, the talkie opens up to more of the book. Dialog allowed Beaudine to expand not only the narrative, but also the characters. The sound remake includes scenes that rely on dialog and would have been less effective in a silent. In fact, the initiation of Georgie is not even shown. While it had been a focal point of the silent version, in this talkie it is planned and referred to but the circumstances are not shown on camera. This leaves more room for the conflict between Penrod and Sam over the affections of a pretty girl, some family conflicts, a few scenes in the school, the death of Penrod's beloved dog,

Leon Janney, who plays Penrod, had been in *Father's Son*. An excellent actor, it is interesting to note that one of his strengths is to convey a great deal with expression and no dialog. Of course, in early talkies, the lessons learned in silent films were enhanced not removed. However, later in his career, Janney became known for talking. A top-level radio actor, he was famous for being able to effectively do virtually any dialect. Frank "Junior" Coghlan, who played Sam, was already a veteran actor whose career dated back to silents. He recalled in his autobiography that despite his experience in pulling a punch during a fight scene, he actually connected with the actor playing his nemesis. Frank also remembered the fight between Penrod and Sam:[20]

> I hit Penrod back into a large stuffed chair and then charged into him. My drive made the chair fall over backward and we both landed in a heap on the floor. As I landed on top of him, I whispered, "are you all right?" When he whispered back that he was, the staged fight went on to its conclusion.

One of the strongest aspects regarding Beaudine's direction of this sound remake is his eye for visual presentation. His establishing shots are usually long-shots that take in the surroundings before we move to the action contained therein. The empty lot with the boys' fort shows a vastness that separates the kids from the adult world. The birthday party they attend shows boys and girls in attendance, but separate, with girls chattering with each other and boys wrestling. Despite his ability to direct dialog scenes, Beaudine did not overlook his keen visual eye. Beaudine told the press:

> Directing young actors in talkies is much more simple than it was in silent pictures. In the old days children lost their naturalness because we gave them every direction all through the scene. Grown-up actors, too, were cued. We didn't realize It then, but now we can see, with children In particular. It took away their individuality.

The young actors never come off as phony, but rather as how real children would actually behave. This is further evidence of how Beaudine was adept at directing children.

The success of *Father's Son* and *Penrod and Sam* showed that Beaudine continued to be a reliable director during the sound era. It also showed that he could be a company man and was not connected so completely to his own edgy vision, as per *The Mad Parade*, which was simply ahead of its time. As a result of

---

20 Coghlan, Frank. *They Still Call Me Junior*. Jefferson, NC: McFarland. 1993

this success, Beaudine's directorial services were beckoned by Columbia Pictures studio head Harry Cohn.

Columbia was, at this time, considered a lowly studio in comparison to Warners, MGM, or Paramount. Notoriously, a couple years later, Clark Gable and Claudette Colbert were sent there as "punishment," only to come up with *It Happened One Night* (1934) for director Frank Capra, which won Oscars in every major category and remains one of the best films ever made.

Beaudine was hired to direct a B movie programmer entitled *Men in Her Life*. The screenplay was by newcomer Robert Riskin, who would later write *It Happened One Night*. Thus, snappy, witty dialog and a fast-pace made *Men in Her Life* an especially well received B feature.

William Beaudine had no problem directing B movies. According to Wendy L. Marshall's biography:[21]

> He was still getting between $2000 and $2500 a week and it appeared all was forgiven with regard to going against the Hollywood establishment with *The Mad Parade*. Beaudine had the credentials to press for the opportunity to do bigger pictures, but he didn't. He considered himself lucky to be working when millions of others weren't.

This was borne out when Beaudine's vast background in comedy locked into the expert timing needed to make Riskin's sharp, witty dialog come off most effectively in *Men in Her Life*.

There were plans for Beaudine to the direct *The Guilty Generation*, a gangster drama featuring Leo Carrillo and Boris Karloff. But he was re-assigned to instead helm a feature starring Jean Harlow, in her first movie for which she'd be given top billing and essaying the star role.

Jean Harlow had done some bits in silent movies before being put under contract by Howard Hughes to star in his early sound epic *Hells Angels* (1930). Hughes had begun the film as a silent,

---

21 Marshall, Wendy L. *William Beaudine: From Silents to Television*. Lanham, MD. Scarecrow Press. 2002

but when the talking picture revolution happened during production, he had to scrap much of what was shot and replace actors whose accents did not translate well to movie dialog. Jean Harlow was hired for the sound version, replacing Norwegian-born Greta Nissen in the lead role. Despite little experience, Harlow caused a sensation, mostly due to her appearance rather than her performance. Serious about becoming a better actress, Harlow worked to do her best in subsequent films, but was frustrated by Hughes never securing a strong part for her, and instead profiting by loaning her out elsewhere.

In 1931, New Jersey racketeer Abner Zwillman took a liking to Jean, and arranged with Hughes, and with Harry Cohn, for a two-picture deal at Columbia. The first, *Platinum Blonde*, had been directed by Frank Capra and was well-received, but most of the accolades were reserved for leading man Robert Williams, who died suddenly shortly after the film's release. The second of Jean's two-picture deal had her in the lead role with support from Mae Clarke and Marie Prevost. Cohn needed an efficient, competent, patient director with a good track record. Thus, Beaudine was borrowed from Warner Brothers- First National to direct *Three Wise Girls*.

William Beaudine's work in *Three Wise Girls* once again shows his talent for establishing shots. The story deals with Jean Harlow as Cassie, a small-town girl working at a soda fountain who longs to make things better for herself and her mother. She travels to New York City where a home town friend is working as a successful model, but discovers that to get ahead in that field, you have to subject yourself to situations that are quite unsettling, especially to a small-town girl like Cassie.

There is a neat transition scene that depicts Cassie's leaving her home town and traveling to the Big Apple. Beaudine uses an overhead shot of busy New York to establish Cassie's arrival. He then cuts to a soda fountain where Cassie is employed, showing that while she upgraded to a larger city, she remains stuck in a low wage job doing exactly as she had been doing back home. However, the big city surroundings, result in a much different type of customer, and a much different type of boss. Cassie's employer continues to make advances to the point where she has to punch him before leaving the job.

William Beaudine's patience with, and support of, Jean Harlow helped with her performance. He arranged for a professional soda fountain dispenser to teach Harlow how to create sundaes and sodas, so she could be effective on camera during those scenes. It only took a few hours of instruction before Jean was proficient enough to look believable on camera. Beaudine also hired two expert models to teach Jean the "peacock strut" used to show off gowns to best advantage. These expenditures were minor and, coupled with Beaudine's efficiency as a director, did not cause the movie to go over budget.

Jean Harlow's ability to maintain a lead role in this Columbia feature led to her eventual hiring by MGM, igniting her career. Her films steadily improved and she remains an icon of 1930s American cinema, despite dying young before the decade ended. Thus, William Beaudine is a pivotal director in her career.

After *Three Wise Girls*, Beaudine was out of work. He blamed Sam Briskin, a Columbia head of production who worked with studio president Harry Cohn. Cohn wanted to make the Harlow film, but Briskin did not. Briskin felt that the expense to secure Harlow's services, the connection to gangster Zwillman, and the fact that she was under contract with Howard Hughes, and wouldn't likely do subsequent Columbia films, made it a bad deal. Beaudine was attracted to the project, and wanted to make *Blonde Baby* rather than *The Guilty Generation*. Because he sided with Cohn, it angered Briskin. Apparently, word went around that *Three Wise Girls* would have been more successful at the box office had it not been for Beaudine's direction, and it affected his ability to find work. Beaudine blamed Briskin. According to Wendy L. Marshall's biography, Beaudine had written in his personal diary: "October 17, 1931 - April 18, 1932 - No job for 6 months. First time in my career. Thanks to Sam Briskin, the SOB!"[22]

---

22 Marshall, Wendy L. *William Beaudine: From Silents to Television*. Lanham, MD. Scarecrow Press. 2002

After the six-month layoff, Beaudine was at Paramount to direct a sound version of the silent *Merton of the Movies*, which would be released under the title *Make Me a Star*. It was the perfect project for him, as it not only satirized show business it celebrated comedy. And Paramount had several people available with whom Beaudine had worked before, so he included actors like ZaSu Pitts, Charles Sellon, Ben Turpin, and Snub Pollard, having been familiar with their work.

Stuart Erwin plays Merton Gill, a small town boy who longs to be a cowboy star in the movies like his hero Buck Benson. Joan Blondell is Flips, an actress at Majestic Studios who feels sorry for the naive young man and gets him a bit part in a Buck Benson film. Merton is thrilled, but so inept that he can't get his one line right. Flips talks to a comedy producer and they concoct an idea where they would shoot a western parody and have Merton play it straight, realizing he'd be unintentionally funny. Merton dislikes comedies, believing they are beneath the great are form of cinema, so they keep their ideas from him. Merton often complains that he especially dislikes "that silly cross-eyed man" so Beaudine arranged to cast cross-eyed Ben Turpin to play himself. Beaudine had directed Turpin in the past, and Ben found the idea amusing and appealing.

The comedy sequences were effective in *Make Me a Star* because Beaudine knew how to stage a slapstick sequence, and he hired people who knew how to perform in them. Along with Turpin and Snub Pollard, Bud Jamison and Billy Bletcher, slapstick pros who date back to the silent era, were also involved. The dramatic sequences were heartfelt and sincere. Stu Erwin's closing speech to Joan Blondell is both triumphant and heartbreaking. Beaudine allowed Erwin to approach the role as he understood it, and Erwin appreciated the artistic freedom. Reviews pointed out that he had a great future in movies.

Unfortunately, it was over three months before Beaudine worked again. The Depression had finally hit Hollywood, and the type of programmers Beaudine directed were being cut back at a lot of studios, and the directors were usually people already under contract. Stuart Erwin suggested Beaudine as director of his film *The Crime of the Century*, which starred Jean Hersholt as a mentalist who reports crimes before they happen.

To make up for any time where he had trouble securing projects, Beaudine would return to the comedy shorts where he got his start. Earlier in 1930-1931 he helmed a few two-reelers for Sennett, including *The College Vamp* with Andy Clyde. And after *Crime of the Century* Beaudine directed a few more shorts, this time under the pseudonym William X. Crowley. One of these shorts was *The Big Idea* which starred Ted Healy and his Stooges.

A two-reel pastiche of musical numbers and absurdist comedy, *The Big Idea* had, as its center, Ted Healy trying to work on a scenario in his messy office. The camera is pretty much stationary, but William Beaudine's penchant for letting comedians improvise allows us to see Healy at somewhere near his best, with some silly and fun vignettes featuring his stooges, Moe Howard, Larry Fine, and Jerry (Curly) Howard. What is most interesting about this short is that it would be the final one in which the Stooges appear in support of Healy. Shortly after filming, the Stooges took an offer to do short comedies at Columbia Pictures. Jules White had just started a short comedy unit at that studio, and was hiring comedians to make two-reelers. In fact, the Stooges' first Columbia release, the musical short *Woman Haters*, was filmed and released before *The Big Idea* hit theaters. By the time *The Big Idea* was released in May of 1934, the Stooges were wrapping up the filming of their second Columbia short, *Punch Drunks*. Thus, William Beaudine has the historical significance of directing a transitional film in the Three Stooges' career.

William Beaudine's biggest break came along when Paramount asked him to direct the W.C. Fields feature *The Old-Fashioned Way*. Sam Hardy, a dear friend of Fields, suggested William Beaudine as the director. Hardy had worked with Beaudine on some First National silents in the late 1920s, and most recently on the film *Make Me a Star*. Fields was a comedian who needed to be left alone to improvise, and Hardy realized Beaudine was the perfect director for that situation. Fields trusted Hardy, Paramount summoned Beaudine, and *The Old-Fashioned Way* became perhaps Beaudine's best film of the 1930s.

The year 1934 was a good one for W.C. Fields. Not only did he release his masterpiece, *It's a Gift*, but also two of his best features, *You're Telling Me* and *The Old-Fashioned Way*. So, this was a particularly good assignment for William Beaudine, and promised to result in further ascension into directing A-level pictures.

Fields plays The Great McGonigle, the crooked manager of a 19th century acting troupe that arrives in a small town to enact the melodrama "The Drunkard." McGonigle's crookedness is more about cheating landladies and theater exhibitors, not his own people. A sub-plot involves McGonigle's daughter and her love for the lead actor in the troupe. The actor's wealthy father disapproves of his son's theatrical career, but when he sees him perform on stage, he is charmed. He allows his son to marry the McGonigle girl if they both stay away from her crooked father. Of course they refuse. But McGonigle finds out about it and makes a grand gesture. He leaves the troupe in the hands of others, and goes on the road with a small time medicine show, telling the couple that he has a great booking that is too good to pass up. William Beaudine recalled the scene in which McGonigle makes that sacrifice:[23]

> The audience was expecting a funny twist to the scene. And if Fields made the slightest false step, the whole tragedy of his parting would have gone to pieces in a burst of laughter. But he didn't make that false step. He acted with the pathos of a true clown. He held his audience and conveyed to them the sadness of the old man's parting from the only person that meant anything in his life. That was a great bit of acting.

Fields does offer some of his acting in *The Old-Fashioned Way* as well as some of his best comedy. Beaudine's ability to know when to step back and let a comedian improvise, and when to step in and avoid going too far off, was perfect for someone like Fields.

---

23 "Just a loveable old so and so" *Film Weekly* December 7, 1934

There are many comic highlights in *The Old-Fashioned Way*. Fields promises a role to a wealthy dowager who helps finance the show. He gives her one line: "Here comes the prince!" The woman rehearses the line back stage with every possible inflection, but is never put in the show. Fields just used that as a ploy to get her financial support. Jan Duggan, who worked with Fields a few times, is very funny in this role.

Another highlight is when the ill-mannered Baby LeRoy accosts the annoyed Fields at a dinner. McGonigle needs the people he is dining with to be supportive of his show, so he endures the child dropping his expensive watch in molasses, which ruins it. He also squeezes McGonigle's nose and throws food in his face. When the others at the table rush to the window to see a passing "horseless carriage," McGonigle reaches to strangle the child, but sees he has left too. He finds the child bent over, looking at something around the corner, sneaks over, and gives the kid a kick in his backside. Beaudine remembered:[24]

> The studio was in an uproar about that scene. They said, "You can't do that! People won't stand for it. You can't kick a kid!" It gets the biggest laugh in the picture!

To temper the scene, Beaudine had to insert a shot of the baby smiling after being kicked, to show he wasn't hurt. Neither he, nor Fields, were happy about having to do that.

Finally, a big highlight in *The Old-Fashioned Way* is that it captures Fields' juggling act on film; the one he performed in vaudeville and for the Ziegfeld Follies. Beaudine frames the action in a medium shot, allowing the entire stage to be visible, so all of Fields' performance is contained. Working with balls, and boxes, performing routines he had perfected over the decades, Fields offers a dexterous and nimble performance that continues to impress as late as the 21st century.

The Old-Fashioned Way was a hit at the box office, which was good for both W.C. Fields and William Beaudine. Fields' contract with Paramount was up, so the success of this movie allowed

---

24 "Just a loveable old so and so" *Film Weekly* December 7, 1934

him to make some demands before re-signing. For Beaudine, it was success in a top level A movie featuring a big star and from a major studio. This promised to not only make him in demand again, but would likely lead to more work in prestigious productions rather than programmers.

Unfortunately, Beaudine was impatient. While he should have waited for more offers so that he was able to build upon the success of The Old-Fashioned Way, he instead responded to a request from England to work there. Regarding what would transpire, it stands to reason that he would have achieved greater and more lasting success had he stayed United States to capitalize on the success of the Fields film. But as 1934 became 1935, William Beaudine was headed to England.

Mae Clark and Jean Harlow in Three Wise Girls.

Joan Blondell and Stuart Erwin in Make Me a Star.

W.C. Fields in The Old Fashioned Way.

THE FILMS IN ENGLAND

The British film industry of the 1930s was filled with interesting, often creative low budget movies that entertained moviegoers. But it also featured a lot important work by Alfred Hitchcock whose development helped further extend the language of cinema. Future notables like Michael Powell and David Lean were working in the industry, learning about the cinematic process and developing their own ideas that would later advance cinema. Actors like John Mills, Jack Hawkins, Robert Donat, and James Mason were on their journey to international stardom.

One of the top comedy stars in England was Will Hay, who was inspired to enter comedy after having seen W.C. Fields do his act in vaudeville. Hay had a long successful career on stage, including the English music halls, working under impresario Fred Karno, the man who discovered both Charlie Chaplin and Stan Laurel. Hay continued to laud Fields as his inspiration, so it would stand to reason that while *The Old Fashioned Way* was playing successfully in theaters throughout the world, its director would be considered to helm a Will Hay film.

Hay was reticent, as are most comedians, about anyone telling him what to do. And, like most directors, Beaudine had some concerns as to the comedian not accepting his approach as a filmmaker. However, once pre-production work began on *Dandy Dick*, both Hay and Beaudine were delighted to discover they were on the same page, creatively. Beaudine always liked to step back and allow the comedian to improvise. Hay was smart enough to accept a veteran filmmaker's technique and vision to make the comedy more visually impactful.

Dandy Dick featured Will Hay as a country vicar who is accused of drugging race horses. The comedy of situations, some slapstick, and Hay's reaction to embarrassment, were all elements Beaudine could work with effectively. Hay was comfortable with Beaudine's approach, and was delighted with the success of the finished film. Once the movie was released and achieved success, Hay requested Beaudine's services again.

Meanwhile, Beaudine followed up *Dandy Dick* by directing veteran comedian Monty Banks in *So You Won't Talk*. Banks had been a successful silent movie comedian, his 1927 feature *Play Safe* becoming a minor classic. He later left acting to concentrate on directing, but in the early 1930s, he did a bit of work on camera. Because of his veteran status in both areas, Beaudine recalled Banks being particularly easy to direct. Banks understood his screen character, and benefited from the creative freedom Beaudine gave all of his star comedians. Also, Banks never interfered with Beaudine's ideas as a director, realizing the proper respect for the position.

However, it was his next Will Hay production, *Boys Will Be Boys*, that would likely be Beaudine's most significant production during his British period. This film allowed Hay to utilize a schoolmaster character that he had developed on stage in the 1920s. The movie's success established that character on film and also made Hay a motion picture star.

In *Boys Will Be Boys*, Hay plays Dr. Alec Smart, an educator who works at a prison. He applies for a job as headmaster of a boys' school, but the governor writes a letter to the school recommending that they do not hire him. Smart's unscrupulous friend Faker Brown forges the governor's name on a positive recommendation and gets him the job. However Faker then blackmails Smart into getting him a job on campus, so he can steal a valuable diamond necklace from Lady Dorking.

A breakout film for Will Hay, *Boys Will Be Boys* benefited greatly from William Beaudine's long association with screen comedy. Along with knowing the rudiments of film direction -- proper establishing shots, keeping movement within the frame during action sequences, and knowing when to move from a medium shot to a close-up -- Beaudine also knew how to spotlight the central comedian. The screenplay had been written by Will Hay, so the comedian benefited greatly from Beaudine's penchant for allowing more creative freedoms.

In William Beaudine's opening shot, we hear Will Hay's voice but it looks like the classroom skeleton is speaking -- a clever and amusing way to introduce the character that nicely sets the tone for the film. Beaudine's success directing young people came in handy during sequences where students are involved, whether they are participating in a rousing welcome replete with practical jokes, or getting Dr. Smart involved in a card game for money. His background in slapstick was effectively utilized in such boisterous sequences as Smart being pulled on a rug by a taxi, or a wild rugby match that ends in a free-for-all. It was a grueling shoot for the middle aged comic, but he was game for all of the knockabout.

Throughout the film, Hay plays smart as misanthropic but likable, not quite in the same manner as W.C. Fields, but with enough basic similarity to cause the connection to be indicated in reviews. Perhaps the henpecked, good natured aspects of Fields in films like *It's a Gift* and *You're Telling Me* are closest to Hay's approach. Beaudine, naturally, knew how to work with that, and his collaboration with Hay was a huge success. Will Hay became one of the biggest stars in British cinema beginning with the success of *Boys Will Be Boys*.

Beaudine directed Will Hay in more films the following year, including *Where There's a Will*, which introduced Graham Moffatt in a Will Hay film, and *Windbag The Sailor*, in which Moffatt acted as straight man to Hay, along with Moore Marriott, both of them figuring prominently in subsequent Hay comedies.

Beaudine's other Hay films were a bit more situational and conventional than *Boys Will Be Boys* had been, but both were big hits and continued Hay's stardom in the UK. *Windbag the Sailor* features Hay as a saloon braggart who tells his tales of being at sea to a captive audience. When he is talked into being captain of an actual ship headed to the West Indies, he must try to back up his verbal claims with actual competence. Thrown from his ship by mutineers, Hay and two co-horts end up on an island in the West Indies and convince the natives that their radio has special powers. After establishing themselves in this new environment and winning the trust of the natives, Hay and company get even with the mutineers when they arrive on the same island.

Despite being more situational than the more slapstick-oriented, bombastic *Boys Will Be Boys*, *Windbag the Sailor* offers a lot of comedy on the ship, in the life boat that takes Hay to the island, and the eventual dénouement of the narrative.

In is unfortunate that the films Beaudine directed for comedian Max Miller are now lost. Miller was another popular UK comedian, said to be a major influence on Benny Hill, among others. Period critics indicated that Miller's fast talking stage act didn't always translate well to the screen. He was also quite ribald for the times and much of his material would have to be toned down for the movies. The films he did with Beaudine's direction were his most successful and best received by critics. The Beaudine-directed features included *Get Off My Foot* (1935), *Educated Evans* (1936) and *Take it From Me* (1937). *Get Off My Foot* was Max's first starring role, while *Take it From Me* had him playing a boxing manager to American fighter-actor Buddy Baer, brother of boxing champion Max Baer. Beaudine seemed to understand Miller and connect successfully with him, so it is unfortunate we have no access to their films together. Although Max Miller was primarily a stage performer, even his toned-down screen appearances should be available to evaluate, especially for those who study British comedy stars.

The other UK comedian William Beaudine directed was George Formby, who was already established when Beaudine helmed *Feather Your Nest* (1937). Formby was another stage star who decided to try doing film comedy, but was infamously told by a studio representative that he was too stupid to play the bad guy and too ugly to play the hero. He started out doing low budget review films, which biographers have lauded as significant to understanding Formby's work, and started to emerge in successful comedy features during the 1930s. *Feather Your Nest*, directed by William Beaudine, was one of his more successful efforts, and notable for including the song "Leaning on a Lamp-post," which became a hit for Herman's Hermits in 1966.

After three years and a dozen feature films, William Beaudine was established in England as a top flight director of comedians, who were pleased with his methods, and the eventual success of the finished films. Therefore, the actors whose movies he directed always welcomed his collaboration. William Beaudine was so happy working in the UK, he applied for permanent residency in England. However, his request was denied. Beaudine refused to pay income tax on the $80,000 he had earned since 1935. Beaudine had paid US income taxes on these wages in 1935, 1936, and 1937. He agreed to pay both UK and US taxes on all income after 1937, but refused to pay retroactive British tax. As a result, William Beaudine was ordered to leave England by December 31, 1937. An article in the *Los Angeles Times* stated:[25]

> William Beaudine, acknowledged by British movie experts to be "one of the most successful American directors who ever made pictures in this country," has been refused an extension of his labor permit by the Home Office, it was disclosed, and must leave England by December 31. Beaudine originally was ordered to leave September 15 but subsequently was granted permission to remain until the end of the year and wind up his affairs on condition that he does not work. Although Beaudine takes the ban philosophically, declaring he has "no grouch" against the Home Office decision, the British film colony sees the refusal to extend the labor permit as a boomerang. Beaudine, it was revealed recently, discussed with Alexander Korda a project to make a series of ten pictures involving the expenditure of about $2,000,000 and giving employment to many British players, writers and technicians.

William Beaudine returned to his homeland of America, only to discover that, in his absence, the industry had moved on. British cinema was growing and William Beaudine's comedies with the country's top comedians were very popular in that country. But in the 1930s, success in England did not mean the same in America. Not all of his films in the UK had a US release, and those that did weren't widely distributed. British cinema got compara-

---

25 American Film Director Must Quit England. *Los Angeles Times*. September 25, 1937

tively scant distribution in America during the 1930s. There were so many Hollywood movies being released, those from other countries were considered special attractions and usually only played the big cities. And even then, it would be a production like Jean Renoir's "Grand Illusion" (1937). Beaudine was directing mainstream comedy features whose massive popularity was limited to the UK market. They would play all over England, be seen in Australia, even Canada.

Beaudine didn't seem to realize this when he prepared his return to America. He felt that since he had, cinematically, built upon the success he had with *The Old Fashioned Way*, it would be enough to sustain continued interest in his home country. He also believed that because he also worked with the British counterpart of America's W.C. Fields, it could only help. He directed what was considered to be Will Hay's best and most successful feature film at that time. The problem was that since Beaudine wasn't immediately accessible in his own country, despite being active in filmmaking, studio heads who might have wanted his services could not connect with him because he was out of the country. When this inaccessibility goes on for years, the studios eventually forget about you.

Between the British taxes he was paying and the fact that a bank he bought an interest in had failed, taking away a good portion of his savings, Beaudine needed the money as much as he wanted the work. Beaudine left America as a top director with a salary that studios no longer wanted to match. This resulted in Beaudine spending almost the entirety of his first year back home looking for work as if he were a journeyman director who was new to the business. Beaudine had been a movie director since the teens. He had directed everyone from Mary Pickford, to Jean Harlow to W.C. Fields. He had enjoyed success overseas. But now he was out of work.

Will Hay in Boys Will Be Boys.

RETURNING TO AMERICA

William Beaudine's absence from America for four years was an absence indeed, and it didn't seem to matter at all that he had been continuing to work as a busy director whose movies were financially successful. During his absence, the top spots in cinema were filled younger filmmakers who established themselves years after Beaudine had. Despite over twenty years of experience, William Beaudine was considered a has-been whose last work of note had been *The Old-Fashioned Way* four years earlier.

As alluded to earlier in this text, this was an interruption of significant momentum after the success of Beaudine's "class A" Paramount picture with W.C. Fields, *The Old-Fashioned Way*. Films like the sound remake of *Penrod and Sam* and the Jean Harlow-starrer *Three Wise Girls* would seem to be top flight pictures now, in retrospect, while they were not considered major productions at the time. *The Old-Fashioned Way* was.

Hollywood was then, as now, a town of immediate cinematic gratification. If you're gone for a while, you can become forgotten, unless your impact is already at an enormous level (Charlie Chaplin and Harold Lloyd are good examples, although their spaced out talkies were less successful than their more consistently released silents had been). Beaudine had risen to the top and needed to act upon that momentum rather than leave Hollywood to make films overseas. The momentum of success was spent on the English films of Will Hay, Max Miller, and others, and while this has its own cinematic significance, it deeply hampered Beaudine's impact in his own country. William Beaudine understood, upon his return, the gist of his problem, stating that he couldn't get anywhere, and that people, meaning the studio heads with whom he once worked, hand forgotten about him. He put an ad in the trades, but there were no takers.

There were a few other theories that have been speculated upon. Some believed that Jack Warner of Warner Brothers thought Beaudine should pay the extra taxes in order to keep working in England. Warners had been profiting from Beaudine's overseas work, and things were tight in America.

Being out of work for ten months upon his return to America was difficult for Beaudine, who was happiest when he was busiest. He contacted Warner Brothers for which he directed several successful feature films during the silent era. They had nothing for him, but Bryan Foy, associate producer of the Warner "B" unit, thought he would be a good fit to direct a couple of entries in the studio's Torchy Blane series. Beaudine accepted the jobs despite the pay being far less than what he'd once earned at the same studio.

The Torchy films centered on the character of Torchy Blane; a courageous, wise-cracking female reporter played by Glenda Farrell. Her co-star was Barton MacLane, a big, beefy guy who specialized in playing heavies in the studio's gangster dramas. In the Torchy films, he played a police detective who was romantically linked with Torchy and on whom she relied for info to help her stories. They starred in one film, *Smart Blonde* (1937), which ran just about an hour in length, and was ready-made for the second spot on double feature programs. It was a huge hit with moviegoers, so Warners continued making Torchy Blane films. Glenda Farrell recalled for *Time* magazine in 1969:[26]

> So before I undertook to do the first Torchy, I determined to create a real human being—and not an exaggerated comedy type. I met those [news-women] who visited Hollywood and watched them work on visits to New York City. They were generally young, intelligent, refined, and attractive. By making Torchy true to life, I tried to create a character practically unique in movies.

Despite Farrell and MacLane being very popular in the roles, after three more entries, the studio recast the roles with Lola

---

26 Bubbeo, Daniel. The Women of Warner Brothers: The Lives and Careers of 15 Leading Ladies, with Filmographies for Each. Jefferson, NC: McFarland & Company.

Lane and Paul Kelly for one film. Moviegoers reacted negatively to the recasting, so Farrell and MacLane returned for three more films. William Beaudine was hired at that point, replacing series director Frank McDonald, and directed the next two films in the series: *Torchy Gets Her Man* (1938) and *Torchy Blane in Chinatown* (1939). After one more film, not directed by Beaudine, Farrell left Warner Brothers and the roles were again recast, this time with Jane Wyman and Allen Jenkins. Moviegoers once again reacted negatively, so no more films were produced. The one constant in the series, no matter who played the lead roles, was Tom Kennedy as the bumbling Officer Gahagan.

The Torchy Blane films directed by Beaudine were probably the best in the series. Beaudine's efficiency was just the right ingredient to bring this fast-paced 63 minute potboiler in on time and within its limited budget. While any director wants to have more money, and more time, at his disposal, there is also a real art to a director like Beaudine being able to creatively put together a low budget B movie shot on standing sets within a limited schedule.

In his first, *Torchy Gets Her Man*, Beaudine responds to the tight screenplay by Albert DeMond, who was experienced at writing for women, and had penned at least one other Torchy script. Despite being away from the series for one film, both Glenda Farrell and Barton MacLane settled comfortably back into the roles, having played them for four other movies (this was the sixth in the series, but the fifth in which they appeared). This makes it easy for Beaudine to direct the actors, allowing him to concentrate on how to best present the narrative. As with most of his films, *Torchy Gets Her Man* benefits from establishing shots, including stock footage of a race track that cuts to Barton MacLane standing in a crowd at that track, which was shot in the studio. Despite it being a crowd, Beaudine places MacLane in the frame so that he is noticed immediately. Also, the director's succession of shots, from close-ups to medium two-shots, are uniformly effective. It allows the film to keep up a pace that is akin to the other films in the series, and maintain its popularity with moviegoers.

During production of *Torchy Gets Her Man* the breezy attitude on the set extended to the filming. At one point, MacLane was seated at a desk and Farrell was sitting atop another desk on the set. Glenda jumped up and said her line, and everyone fell down laughing, including MacLane, Farrell, and the crew. Farrell had put her foot right into a brass cuspidor on the set. While filming another scene, the overzealous MacLane dialed a telephone so forcefully he sent it skidding across the desk, once again causing laughter on the set that Beaudine had to contain.

Situations like these extended to Beaudine's next film in the series, *Torchy Blane in Chinatown*. During a scene at a garden party, some extras in the background are playing bridge while the foreground features a scene with the principle members responding to the narrative. Suddenly an extra yelled out "I've got a perfect hand!" Of course this spoiled the scene and the extra was ordered off the set. Feeling sorry for him, Farrell talked Beaudine into giving him another chance. It was later revealed that the other extras at his table had stacked the deck and caused that perfect hand to happen, but they hadn't counted on him spoiling the scene.

Torchy Blane in Chinatown starts out slowly and builds its narrative in the usual manner as Torchy and her detective boyfriend each try to solve a murder regarding some jade tablets. Their friendly rivalry is stepped up, with more good humor coming from their likeable characters and amusing relationship. Once again Tom Kennedy's bumbling presence adds to the fun. It is a programmer, of course, but *Torchy Blane in Chinatown* is probably the best film in the series. This film felt more like a traditional mystery than the others, with twists and turns that invite the audience to try and figure it out for themselves.

The Torchy Blane films directed by William Beaudine were more comedic in tone than the Torchy movies that came before. That, combined with the fast-paced action and dialogue, definitely suits the directing style that Beaudine had developed. Barely over an hour each, these programmers never feel rushed because Beaudine was able to compose his shots in a way that moved the story along while also giving the audience the information they needed to follow it.

There was some talk of actually taking advantage of Beaudine's experience directing in the UK and filming the next Torchy Blane movie on location in Scotland. However, the next film turned out to be *Torchy Runs For Mayor* after which Glenda Farrell left Warner Brothers.

Beaudine went over to Fox studios to speak to Darryl Zanuck, who had not only worked with him in the past, he had also been a personal friend of his. Zanuck agreed to throw him some work, so he assigned Beaudine to direct the film *The Honeymoon's Over* for producer Sol Wurtzel at the studio's B department. However, Wurtzel had already chosen Eugene Forde to direct that film. As a result, when William Beaudine showed up on the set, he was told that Forde had already been assigned to that production, and thus Beaudine's services were not needed.

Figuring it was merely a mix-up -- something that could easily happen at a big studio, especially when dealing with the B unit under separate supervision -- Beaudine then tried to get back in to see Daryl Zanuck. However, this time the studio head refused to even see him. It was then that Beaudine realized that despite being a friend from the past on a personal level, from a business standpoint Zanuck dismissed him as a has-been the same as the other studio heads. As a result, Zanuck wasn't about to spend a lot of time finding a project for Beaudine. The director realized once Zanuck was told the film he assigned Beaudine already had a director, that was as much energy as he wanted to expend on his problem.

For a director who thrived on work, William Beaudine was becoming increasingly more frustrated at not being able to land a job in Hollywood. The Torchy series efforts sustained him slightly, but he was used to going from one film to another, having several projects lined up, working for several different studios from the top rank to the lower budget, and responding to each project accordingly. Beaudine had been a successful veteran director from silent shorts to silent features, from pre-codes to films in the UK, and now a couple of fast-paced B movies. He knew there had to be a place for him somewhere, but after the misunderstanding at Fox and Daryl Zanuck not really wanting to bother with him, Beaudine felt defeated.

Beaudine despondently walked out of the 20th Century Fox gates and sat dejectedly outside the studio, wondering what he should do next. At that point an event occurred, an omen of sorts, that made a tremendous impact on the director. For the rest of his life, Beaudine would recall seeing a legless man on a makeshift coaster struggling to get up and over a curb. Once he managed to do so, he looked up, noticed Beaudine, smiled and said, "I made it!" Beaudine would state, "If that guy could make it I could. I knew I'd be ok after that."

For the remainder of his life, William Beaudine would recall that incident as his inspiration to keep working after returning to the American film industry from England. So, this was the incident that inspired Beaudine to swallow his pride in regard to salary, and to take the jobs he could get. Beaudine realized that he could make even the lowliest low budget film appear better than its financial parameters would allow. Noted as being an efficient director who got the job done quickly, having even more limited time to complete a feature for the poverty row studios, it is likely that this period of his career is where the "one-shot" description happened. Not during the same time. Beaudine was never referred to as a "one shot" director in his lifetime. In fact, he was quite well respected until this gap in his career as an American director happened. As we now come to the next portion of William Beaudine's career, we will be exploring the B movies, the poverty row releases, the exploitation films, and other projects that have been unfairly dismissed. In fact, some of the films that William Beaudine directed from this point are good, solid entertainment that has effectively lived on.

Glenda Farrell and Barton MacLaine were stars of the Torchy series.

DIXIE NATIONAL PRODUCTIONS

Although William Beaudine did not work for many months after finishing the second and last of his Torchy Blane quickies, circumstances had been going on that would lead him to what would be the body of his career in low budget B movies.

Jed Buell was a theater manager in the late 1920s before joining Mack Sennett's studio as director of publicity in 1930. A creative man with an eye for edgy ideas, he started his own company in 1937 to produce an all-midget western, *The Terror of Tiny Town*. Picked up for distribution by Columbia Pictures on a lark, the movie proved to be remarkably successful as a curio and generated good box office results. Buell considered doing a series of films with little people, but a chance meeting brought him in another direction.

Herb Jeffries was a singer and musician who was in bands that played before the movie at small theaters in African American neighborhoods. He noticed large groups of young people coming to see the low budget westerns that would play in the "Blacks Only" theaters down south, as that accessible, inexpensive product from poverty row studios was all these theaters could afford. Jeffries understood African American moviegoers being attracted to the easy action and heroism of low budget westerns, remembering his own childhood admiration of Tom Mix and Jack Holt.

Jeffries contacted Buell and told him an idea he had for an "all-colored western" in which he would star as the movie cowboy. Along with being a fan of westerns, Jeffries himself had grown up on a farm. He was skilled in horseback riding and roping, and could easily handle a leading role in as a cowboy in a western movie. Buell liked the idea, but felt Jeffries, who was of mixed race, was too light skinned to play the lead. It took Jeffries some time to eventually convince Buell, indicating that makeup could be used to darken his tone.

Shot in only five days, *Harlem on the Prairie* (1937) was a big hit, especially in the segregated theaters down south, where young black youngsters who loved westerns all clamored to see a cowboy adventure with an all-black cast. Jeffries made more westerns, and also did personal appearances in full cowboy garb. In the north, the films would play as the second film in double features, and would sometimes headline as a B movie in theaters with mixed audiences.

Buell's idea of a series of films with little people inspired his idea to instead do films featuring African American casts as a result of these initial successes. Jeffries indicated to Buell that there were many black actors and actresses who played smaller parts in movies who would be very interested in the opportunity to expand their talents and play leads and more substantial roles. So Buell and his partners, Ted Toddy and Rev. James Friedrich, started Dixie National Productions, specializing in films with African American casts for the 400-odd Blacks Only theaters in the south. As with the Herb Jeffries westerns, the films also played in neighborhood theaters and secured second feature spots in the north. Noticing that many of the actors clamoring for roles in his films had a background in comedy, Buell needed a director who would be willing to do B level films but knew how to direct screen humor. He contacted William Beaudine.

Beaudine was intrigued by the idea and excited by the opportunity, even though the pay would only be $500 per movie, an amount the director used to make in just one day during the silent era. Also, low budget movies had a negative reputation, and anyone who directed them would not likely be hired by the major studios, as he would be dismissed as a poverty row director. The fact that these films were for a niche market, mostly Blacks Only theaters in the south, they had a further stigma. There was no way Buell would have gotten any other formidable director to take this job. However, Beaudine needed the work, he wanted the work, and so he agreed to direct these films.

At first William Beaudine didn't take any credit at all. Jed Buell is credited as director for *Mr. Washington Goes To Town*, even though it was Beaudine who directed. Otherwise, Beaudine was given permission to direct under the pseudonym William X. Crowley, which he had used back in the 30s when he was under contract with Paramount and took a couple of jobs helming short subjects for Sennett (where he first met Jed Buell).

William Beaudine directed several films for Dixie National, including *Four Shall Die, She Done Him Right, Mr. Washington Goes to Town, Up Jumped the Devil, Lucky Ghost,* and *Professor Creeps*. Most of these were comedies featuring Mantan Moreland, who became best known for playing Birmingham Brown the chauffeur to Charlie Chan in that series.

Mantan Moreland had been a vaudeville performer who first scored in the successful show *Blackbirds of 1928*. He then worked in Broadway shows and even toured Europe. Monogram hired Mantan to play opposite actor Frankie Darro in a series of films, elevating him to the status of co-star with equal billing and footage.

At the same time, Moreland was doing comedy relief in mostly low budget movies, and also appeared in several "race films" that were produced for neighborhood theaters. Because he was very talented, was pretty well known, and took direction well he was offered his own starring series by Jed Buell. The opportunity to star in his own films was an attractive proposition, and he gladly accepted the offer. Being a comedian, Mantan responded most favorably to the creative freedom Beaudine liked to give his actors, especially his comedians.

In *Mr. Washington Goes To Town*, Mantan Moreland stars opposite F.E. Miller, who had been instrumental in developing African-American musicals on Broadway. Long a part of the team Miller and Lyles (with Aubrey Lyles), Miller knew how to respond to the comedy team dynamic, which is how he was presented opposite Mantan Moreland.

The film opens with the two in jail, when Miller reads in the paper that Mantan has inherited a ritzy hotel from a deceased relative. They plan to check out the hotel the next day when they are released from lockup. Mantan falls asleep and dreams he is a bellhop in the fancy hotel, responding to all manner of weird guests. There is a headless man carrying his head in his hands. There is an invisible man who struggles with occasional visibility.

And there is a landlord who insists there is gold in the hotel and destroys the building in his manic search for it. When Mantan is awakened the next day as he and Miller are released, Miller suggests they check out the hotel. Unsettled by his nightmare, Mantan wants no part of it.

Mr. Washington Goes To Town premiered for black patrons at the Lincoln Theater in Los Angeles and, according to the *Motion Picture Herald*:

> Within a minute from the time the picture started, the audience was laughing so loudly as to drown out sections of the dialog, and this response kept up through the picture. Whites present in professional capacity joined in.

Much of *Mr. Washington Goes To Town* is slapstick and reaction humor, but there is also some funny dialog (Jack Benny being referred to as "that fella who's on Rochester's radio show"). The film was billed as the first "all-colored feature length comedy" (which is historically inaccurate, but that was the tag line). Later it was successfully previewed for white audiences, and it enjoyed some success as a second feature in theaters with predominantly white or integrated attendance.

Another one of Beaudine's films for Dixie National that proved quite popular but also stirred some controversy was *Lucky Ghost* (1942). This one featured Miller and Mantan down on their luck, walking endlessly down a country path. They come along a chauffeured car that has run out of gas. They entice the wealthy owners into a dice game, which Mantan wins. He and Miller drive off in the chauffeured vehicle, nattily dressed in new suits, and leaving the hapless losers behind, standing in the road in their underwear.

They end up in a nightclub where they run afoul of the big, imposing gangster who runs it, because Mantan dances with his girl. Just then, the gangster's descendants, ghosts from a nearby graveyard, come to haunt the place, causing slapstick havoc and a lot of reaction humor.

Lucky Ghost was filled with a lot of ingredients to appeal to its target audiences. Popular jazz numbers, jitterbug dances, slapstick, and verbal humor. At one point, Miller and Mantan are walking along complaining about being hungry, and having to drink water to keep full. Mantan quips, "I've drunk so much water my stomach thinks I'm taking in washing!" But most of the humor is reactive and physical, both areas that Beaudine, and the comedians, had solid experience, so they blended well when working together. Maceo Bruce Sheffield, who played the imposing gangster, also acted as associate producer of the film.

As popular as *Lucky Ghost* was with African American moviegoers of the period, some white audience members of the same time reacted negatively. In April of 1943, *Lucky Ghost* was scheduled to be shown at the University of Wisconsin's Union Play Circle in its new million dollar theater wing of the Wisconsin Union. However, after students previewed the film, members of the student committee agreed to withdraw it, believing it presented an erroneous and disparaging picture of African American life. In the April 3, 1943 issue of *The Capital Times* an article stated:[27]

> Showing of the film *Lucky Ghost*, which had been objected to as presenting an erroneous, disparaging picture of Negro life, has been cancelled by the university student film committee. *Lucky Ghost* was scheduled to be shown this weekend at the Wisconsin Union Play Circle. After viewing the picture Friday night at a private showing, members of the student committee agreed to withdraw it, feeling that it failed to meet artistic standards set for Play Circle pictures. Representatives of independent student groups protested showing of the picture. Merrill Pollack, New York, speaking for the group which asked that the showing be cancelled, said action of the film committee is a step towards better understanding among racial groups on the campus.

There was even a letter to the editor in which Merrill Pollack, who spearheaded the protest, claimed that a film like *Lucky Ghost* depicted black people as the "inferior race" Hitler claimed them

---

27 U.W. Cancels Film After Protests. *The Capital Times*. April 3, 1943

to be! Meanwhile, African American audiences in the Blacks Only neighborhood theaters were laughing and applauding.

Certainly, by today's more enlightened standards, *Lucky Ghost* does not portray African Americans in an entirely positive light. However, when we put it into historical context, it is at least noteworthy that this film does feature an all-black cast filling both lead and supporting roles. These actors all get to play off of each other, whereas had they been supporting players in a film led by white actors, they certainly would have been relegated to supporting roles, either as the comic relief and the butt of the jokes, or with little contribution despite their skills. In a film like *Lucky Ghost*, we get to see black actors here playing a variety of roles that aren't limited to butler, chauffeur, et. al.

Of course, in the post civil rights era, we look at these movies differently as to the way the actors are presented. But with lengthier roles in parts that were superior to those they would get in more mainstream movies; we get a better perspective of each actor's skill and ability to convey a more layered character. Finally, we must also take into account the massive popularity these movies enjoyed with African American audiences of the time. They approached the films as comedies with comedians, and expected the silliness that was presented. The historical context remains significant. We learn from the past.

After a few more films, Beaudine was pleased to be comfortably back to work as an active filmmaker, and no longer cared that he was not working in the majors. He enjoyed the creative challenge of working under a tight schedule with a limited budget, and gratified that the end product was successful.

Beaudine asked Jed Buell if he could branch out. Buell was also an executive with Producers Releasing Corporation, and although it was a low budget studio, its product was often popular and lucrative enough to where Beaudine felt he could once again use his own name in the credits. The next, and perhaps most noted phase in William Beaudine's directorial career, as a master of the low budget feature, as about to begin in earnest.

Poster for Lucky Ghost.

Trade ad for Mr. Washington Goes to Town.

Mantan Moreland, Margarette Whitten, Maceo B. Sheffield, Arthur Ray in Mr. Washington Goes to Town.

PRODUCERS RELEASING CORPORATION

As he was readying production on the first of his all-black features for segregated and neighborhood theaters, Jeb Buell also produced a film for Producers Releasing Corporation (PRC), one of the lowest of low budget studios. Because he secured silent comedy great Harry Langdon to appear in what would be his first starring role in a feature since talkies began, Buell hired William Beaudine to direct. Buell felt Beaudine's sense of comedy and knack for working with creative comedians would benefit the project despite its low budget.

Producer's Releasing Corporation was originally known as Producers Distributing Corporation in 1939 when it was formed by Ben Judell. But after seven productions, the company was going broke, so in 1940 producer Sigmund Neufield took it over as his own production company, with Harry Rathner, former sales associate, as its President. It was absorbed by the Pathe corporation by the end of that year, with Leon Fromkess hired in 1942 as production supervisor. PRC enjoyed some success with westerns featuring Tim McCoy, Bob Steele, and Buster Crabbe, as well as films featuring such notables as Bela Lugosi, Glenda Farrell, Erich Von Stroheim, and directors the caliber of Beaudine, Jean Yarbrough, Phil Rosen, Lew Landers, Joseph H. Lewis, and Christy Cabanne.

William Beaudine was hired to direct Harry Langdon in *Dummy Trouble*, which was eventually released as *Misbehaving Husbands*. Langdon had been one of the great stars of silent comedy. Developing his comic character through decades on stage, Langdon signed a contract to start in short comedies with Mack Sennett in 1924. Initially having the challenge of adapting his meek, slow moving, offbeat stage persona into the fast-paced slapstick of Mack Sennett productions, Langdon eventually gained more creative control and soon his films were created according to his vision. Some of his best short films for Sennett include *All Night Long*,

Saturday Afternoon, and *His Marriage Wow.* His short comedies were so popular, Langdon was hired by First National in 1926 to make feature films, resulting in classics like *Tramp Tramp Tramp, The Strong Man,* and *Long Pants.* Gaining momentum as a silent screen star, Langdon began directing his own films in 1927, and while films like *Three's a Crowd* and *The Chaser* are considered surrealistically brilliant today, his offbeat approach didn't connect with mainstream audiences at the time. Perhaps he would eventually have better established himself with ensuing films, as audiences got more used to his approach, but silent movies were concluding, and Langdon had to reinvent himself for talkies.

At first Langdon wasn't sure how to expand his screen character for sound films. His early talkie shorts for Hal Roach were hit and miss. But eventually Langdon established himself in talkies, with good two-reel efforts from Educational, Paramount, and Columbia.

Harry Langdon's silent screen persona was slowly paced, much moreso than the other comedians of the era. His character would ponder each scene, sit and blink as he pondered, and Langdon was such a good actor, he would make such sequences absorbing and fascinating. When he started in talkies, he eventually redirected this screen persona into one that used sound within the context of somewhat similar character. Rather than ponder and blink, Harry would respond with nervous stammering befuddlement. This worked well in short films, but to sustain an entire feature, even one at the B level running just about an hour, was a bit more daunting

Set up for a 12 day shoot on a very low budget, *Misbehaving Husbands* was Langdon's first starring role in a feature film since his self-directed 1929 silent *Heart Trouble.* Langdon co-starred in the early sound features *A Soldier's Plaything* and *See American Thirst,* and had supporting roles in some other features like *Hallelujah I'm a Bum, My Weakness, Atlantic Adventure,* and even a stint opposite Oliver Hardy in *Zenobia* while Stan Laurel was in contract negotiations. However, *Misbehaving Husbands* allowed Langdon to carry the film as the lead, with a good supporting cast.

The freedom that Beaudine was noted for giving his stars was beneficial to Langdon, who never needed a lot of direction

Harry Langdon plays an innocently fluttery dress salesman who owns a shop. When he is spotted maneuvering a store mannequin by a gossip, she mistakes him for flirting with another woman, and it gets back to his suspicious wife (Betty Blythe). But what is most significant about this innocent B-level feature is William Beaudine's allowing Langdon to carry the film on his own terms, which is why his performance is so amusing.

Beaudine got the movie made as a filmmaker, while Langdon added nuance to his character that might not have been captured as effectively by another director. Langdon bends and holds up his forefinger when making a verbal point. When he finds the mannequin's shoe has snagged inside his coat, his reaction is comically non-verbal. There are several seconds of non-verbal scenes as Harry tries to sneak home late at night because he missed an appointment, but the wife thinks his sneakiness is due to philandering. When Harry is trying to sneak into his room, he suddenly notices a string on his coat, and begins pulling it. It has nothing to do with the scene, just one of those Langdonesque tangents that would have fit comfortably in his silents. Beaudine stepped back and let him creatively explore in the same manner.

Langdon handles verbal comedy also. When questioned by the cops, he is talking about a mannequin while they believe he is discussing an actual woman. When his wife's lawyer confronts Harry at his office and reveals the wife wants a divorce, his double take is from the silent era, as are the fluttery hands as he speaks, but Beaudine blocks the scene so that Langdon rises from the couch and goes directly to the phone to call his wife. The camera follows him. It is Langdon's movements that guide the film's visual structure. Langdon even gets to play tried-and-true fear and confusion when a woman (due to a setup) comes to his house and starts amorously flirting with him. His reaction reminds one of similar scenes in his classic silent feature *The Strong Man*.

Misbehaving Husbands comfortably rested in the second spot in double features, and was even top-billed at some of the neighborhood movie houses, the Langdon name still holding some weight. *The Hollywood Reporter* called it "a strikingly good little picture," further stating:[28]

> A rollicking, high-speed domestic comedy, so well done and played with such zest that the laughs stumble over each other to provide 65 minutes of unadulterated entertainment. *Misbehaving Husbands* is worth a spot on any bill.

Critics also pointed out that Beaudine made the low budget feature look like a more expensive production, something he would have a knack for as he continued working on poverty row.

The success of *Misbehaving Husbands* resulted in Jed Buell also hiring William Beaudine to direct another of his productions for PRC, *Emergency Landing* (1941). Beaudine once again recalled his start in short films, when he had little time or money to work with, and once again used expediency and brought the film in on time and on budget. Beaudine's direction of the flying and some of the more action-heavy scenes helped make *Emergency Landing* a slightly more interesting movie, at least visually.

Because of his success with the two Buell-produced films, other PRC producers hired him to direct their projects. This gave Beaudine more work, but the pay remained meager. *Federal Fugitives* (1941) starred Neil Hamilton, who had been a pretty notable name in silents and as a leading man in romantic pre-code dramas. He would later redefine his career as Commissioner Gordon on TV's *Batman* in the 1960s.

Hamilton played a military intelligence officer who tracks down a group of foreign agents. He is poisoned by them but rescued just in time. Unfortunately, *Federal Fugitives* did not represent William Beaudine at his best. It was only a fair film, interesting in that it used notable actors from the silent era like Hamlton, Betty Blythe, and Frank Shannon. Using silent film actors who had once been notable, but were now having trouble finding work, was a standard practice for PRC, and it worked better in another of Beaudine's efforts for the studio.

One of Beaudine's better PRC films during this period was the first for producer Martin Mooney. *Mr. Celebrity* (1941) is about a

---

28 "Misbehaving Husbands." *The Hollywood Reporter*. December 9, 1940

young boy who lives with his uncle. The uncle is always gambling on horses and is considered unfit by the child's grandparents, so they try to take custody. The uncle and nephew travel to Kentucky to Celebrity Farm, and stay at a place run by silent movie stars Francis X Bushman and Clara Kimball Young.

With greater substance than *Federal Fugitives* offered, *Mr Celebrity* was more notable for giving roles to silent movie era stars. In fact, Hedda Hopper's newspaper column garnered the film some publicity, stating that this hiring was actually patriotic:[29]

> Ever since the news got out that Director William Beaudine was giving the old-timers a break in the picture *Mr. Celebrity* Bill's office has been swamped with letters from fans all over the country. One enthusiast wrote: "Thank God for one American director who still has work for Americans." Well, Bill's an old-timer from way back and he agrees with me that to shove our own people out of parts, extra and bit work to make room for Europe's refugees is, attempting to right one injustice with a much greater one. We wouldn't think much of a mother who shoved out into the cold and starved her own children, so that she could take in and feed the neighbor's. But that's what's been happening on a big scale out here, despite the thousands of dollars collected over and over again from film people for the benefit of those very refugees' home countries.

Mr Celebrity was another second feature or one for neighborhood movie houses, the appearance of the silent actors merely a novelty and not a real selling point. It was, however, a big success. *Showman's Trade Review* raved:

> Here's one made for peanuts that equals the product turned out by some of the majors for sheer entertainment volume. It shows that a smart director, William Beaudine, has what it takes when given the proper material. It also proves that entertainment can be made for much less than a million dollars.

---

29 Hedda Hopper's Hollywood. *Los Angeles Times*. October, 10, 1941

The Motion Picture Herald was equally impressed with this production, despite it being a low budget second feature:

> One of the most substantial supporting program films to come out of Hollywood regardless of budget. *Mr. Celebrity* contains just about everything from heart tugs, comedy, and action to nostalgia, all neatly wrapped up and aimed at every type of audience.

But perhaps it was *Film Daily* that was most praiseworthy about *Mr. Celebrity*, stating:

> Here is a challenge to the producers who spend a fortune making a motion picture and wind up with six reels of film lacking those essentials so necessary to the protection of their own investments. Made at a cost below the budget usually alotted for extra people in the average picture, this film is a standout in all departments. It is alive with action, drama, and first-rate performances. It is beautifully cast, expertly directed, and where they got all that production on such a limited budget is a mystery even to those who claim this sort of thing can be done all the time. *Mr. Celebrity* can stand on its own as good solid entertainment.

O. Henry Briggs, president of PRC, was so impressed with *Mr. Celebrity*, he sent a telegram to Beaudine thanking him for directing the studio's best movie of that year.

Blonde Comet (1941), a race car drama, is notable as having a subject matter that gives the viewer the sort of female lead that isn't as frequent in movies made during the 1940s. Virginia Vale plays the daughter of a tire manufacturer who becomes a race car driver that enjoys success in Europe and the United States. Barney Oldfield, a notable racer, is cast in an acting role to add authenticity, although his acting isn't exactly at the level of Ms. Vale or co-star Robert Kent, who plays her rival/love interest.

The plot features Vale as Blondie Comet who races frequently with Kent's character and each wins roughly the same number of races, with the other coming in second. They connect when a mutual friend is killed during a race, and when they both qualify for the prestigious Indianapolis 500. Kent's car fails, and Blondie offers hers. *Blonde Comet* was a well-directed action drama that was popular in neighborhood theaters. A theater in Dallas promoted *Blonde Comet* by having a mock race car on the sidewalk out front, along with an easel containing photos of various races that took place in that city.

William Beaudine seemed to have a bit more time to be creative on his next PRC film, *Miracle Kid* (1942), which featured Tom Neal as a prizefighter. Neal is best known for Edgar G. Ulmer's 1945 PRC film *Detour*, which has become a cult classic among low budget films. Neal had been a member of the boxing team at Northwestern University, had debuted on the Broadway stage in 1935 and had received a law degree from Harvard, also in 1938. So, he had quite a background. *Miracle Kid* is a quirky little film with Neal playing a fighter whose opponents believe he has mind-related powers that cause them to lose the bouts. A group of health nut promoters represent the fighter, and try to sell the idea that these powers come from their diet and nutrition ideas. Of course, at the end, the fighter proves that it is his prowess in the ring that matters.

Tom Neal has an impactful presence as the fighter, and Carol Hughes comes off well as his girl. They sustain the narrative and both respond well to William Beaudine's direction. Beaudine is allowed to have some creative ideas in *The Miracle Kid*, such as a health nut promoter eating sausages and pancakes, but when he has a visitor, he hides this breakfast and brings out a bowl of fruit.

Perhaps the best film Beaudine made at PRC was the prison drama *Men of San Quentin* (1942). PRC increased the budget and production time for this film, and arranged to shoot on location in the prison, the first film to do so. Because of his successful track record at the studio, William Beaudine was chosen to direct.

The story is about a new warden coming to the prison with ideas for reform that offer respect and a progressive trajectory rather than the brutality that had ruled the past. It is generally based on the prison's actual warden at the time, Clinton E. Duffy. The new warden believes the punishment is the confinement and works on respect and offering opportunities for the men to learn and grow in preparation for life outside of the prison walls. In one of the film's most stirring scenes, a prisoner gets hold of a gun and the warden walks into the crowded prison yard, unarmed, and takes the gun from the prisoner without incident.

William Beaudine was the perfect director for this movie, as it was a solid story with strong performances by actors who were best known for playing supporting roles. Actors like Charles Middleton, Dick Curtis, and George Breakston were given roles they could creatively explore, and Beaudine allowed them the freedom to do so. Curtis was often the bad guy in western films, and a comic villain in short comedies, including several with The Three Stooges. Third-billed in this feature, Curtis turns in what may be the finest performance of his long career, playing perhaps his most layered character.

Despite still being an obviously low budget picture, *Men of San Quentin* is both entertaining and occasionally powerful, although the second half of it feels like the entire movie was made solely to sing the praises of the warden. The message of treating prisoners like humans, not animals, is one that still resonates today. There are some shots that effectively capture the claustrophobia of confinement.

A preview of *Men of San Quentin* was held in the mess hall of the prison for around 500 convicts and 400 guards and their families. It was later shown to the prison's 4300 other inmates over the next week. Several newspaper journalists were also in attendance. The prisoners were impressed at the film's authenticity and told the journalists. The warden proclaimed the film to be a true story of prison life in a major institution. Critics called the film authentic and entertaining. *Film Daily* stated:

> *Men of San Quentin* has lots of action for a regular theater audience. William Beaudine's direction is smooth and colorful. The players, throughout, give an excellent account of themselves. This is an authentic picture, but also an exciting, lively and gripping yarn with all the story elements of a good movie.

Running 80 minutes instead of the usual hour length, *Men of San Quentin* remains one of the better films to be released by PRC.

There were certain actors Beaudine worked with repeatedly during his tenure with PRC, including Ralph Byrd who is best known as the movies' Dick Tracy. He reconnected with actors he'd directed in silents, like Spec O'Donnell. And between the PRC productions and those for Dixie National, he was getting a lot of work, even if the money was far less than he'd gotten in earlier years. Beaudine didn't care. Although he still hoped to get back into working at major studios, with more time and better budgets, for a director who was most interested in being active and engaged in film production, he was happy to be working so consistently. Once again, William Beaudine was going from one film to the next, and had projects lined up.

Due to his consistent success with Dixie National and PRC, William Beaudine's services were summoned by Monogram Pictures producer Sam Katzman. It started a very long and successful relationship with that studio, including most of the features with the very popular Bowery Boys (so much so that they have their own chapter in this text), as well as entries in the Charlie Chan and Philo Vance series, and films in the horror and western genres. Beaudine was not under contract, as he would continue to also direct films for PRC, as well as Republic and other low budgets studios that specialized in B product. Settling into directing B movies, William Beaudine took pride in being the most active and successful B movie director currently active.

Beaudine was philosophical about his status. He was no longer the up-and-coming maverick director of the silent era. He wasn't beginning to establish himself with A pictures at top studios like before he went to England. He was considered, by some studio heads, as a has-been whose more noted work was behind him. So, as he continued with B movies, he focused on the challenges they offered, such as the limited shooting days and threadbare budgets. Beaudine himself accepted the situation and refused to listen to producers who told him he was "washed up." he considered himself a filmmaker and he had no intention of stopping.

Harry Langdon in Misbehaving Husbands.

Silent movie stars Francis X. Bushman and Clara Kimball Young appeared in Mr. Celebrity.

Poster for Men of San Quentin.

MONOGRAM STUDIOS AND AN INCREASE IN PRODUCTIVITY

William Beaudine's long, illustrious career that included silents, pre-code talkies, and movies overseas, is perhaps best identified by the work he did at Monogram Pictures. Now that he had found a niche directing B movies, William Beaudine discovered with Monogram the perfect fit among the poverty row studios. Throughout the wartime years, Beaudine directed some of the best films for the studio, featuring the likes of Bela Lugosi, The East Side Kids, and John Carradine. He would freelance a bit during the post-war years, including a return to PRC (discussed in a separate chapter), and when The East Side Kids became The Bowery Boys, he directed nearly all of the films in that series (also discussed in a separate chapter). But from the early 1940s into the mid 1950s, most of William Beaudine's massive output was for Monogram.

Monogram's beginnings date back to Rayart Pictures, founded by Ray Johnston in the 1920s. In 1928 it became the Syndicate Film Exchange, then, as sound films happened, Continental Talking Pictures. In 1931, the name Monogram studios was adopted with Johnston as President and Trem Carr in charge of production. During the early 1930s, a young John Wayne had a series of westerns at Monogram, while other noted films released by the studio included the literary adaptions *Oliver Twist* (1933), *Black Beauty* (1933), and *Jane Eyre* (1934).

In 1935, Herbert J. Yates of Consolidated Film Industries merged with Monogram and with Mascot Pictures to form Republic Pictures. However, after a year, Johnston and Carr withdrew from the company due to conflicts with Yates, and, by 1937, had reformed Monogram as a separate studio. Republic flourished on its own, becoming synonymous with many classic B western series, including top stars like Gene Autry and Roy Rogers. Monogram had their own western series, giving work to veteran silent stars in series like The Rough Riders (Buck Jones, Tim McCoy, Raymond Hatton), and The Trail Blazers (Ken Maynard, Hoot Gibson, Bob Steele).

Monogram was very interested in producing a lot of product, including as many as 40 feature films per year. They also wanted to cover all genres and sub-genres, not only westerns, but also comedy, musicals, melodrama, and horror. Thus, it was the perfect situation for William Beaudine. He was a director who could master different genres. He worked quickly and expediently. He respected his actors and gave them much-desired creative freedom. He was patient and good humored on the set, making the production a happy experience for those involved. And he had a knack for making poverty row films look better than their low budgets and brief shooting schedules would seem to allow. Monogram would become Allied Artists in 1953, and Beaudine would remain semi-active with them at that date. All told, Beaudine would direct over 70 feature films for the studio. This chapter focuses on some of the features Beaudine directed for Monogram during wartime, 1943-1945.

William Beaudine's first film for Monogram turned out to be not only one of his best, but also one of that studio's best. *One Thrilling Night* (1942) is a delightfully appealing, fast-paced romantic comedy about a young couple trying to enjoy their wedding night at a hotel before the husband returns to military service the next morning. With every turn, they are beset by the sudden appearance of dead bodies that disappear just as quickly, and other shaky goings-on. They enlist the aid of a dimwitted house detective, but, despite his best efforts, only complicates things. John Beal and Wanda McKay are delightful as the couple, and Warren Hymer is his oafish best as the house detective.

John Beal had worked with the likes of Katharine Hepburn, William Powell, and Myrna Loy by this point in his career, and in later years he would fondly recall *One Thrilling Night* as his favorite of all of his films. Certainly it was not the greatest movie in which he appeared from a cinematic perspective, but Beal responded well to the creative freedom Beaudine allowed him as an actor, and the opportunity to work with such a strong cast. Wanda McKay had played smaller roles until given the opportunity to shine in *One Thrilling Night,* and she rises to the occasional most effectively. Beaudine was able to draw out perhaps her greatest performance.

Warren Hymer came from an acting family, and was theatrically trained. By 1942, he had developed something of a niche playing the amiable dumb ox. An actor like Hymer responded perfectly to director Beaudine's penchant for allowing actors to assume some level of creative control. With his squinty eyes, rugged verbal delivery, and flustered double-takes, Hymer truly makes the role his own. His background and firmness of character also responded to the creative freedom Beaudine's direction allowed. Hymer also turns in one of his finest performances.

Beaudine's direction works perfectly because he effectively uses the limited sets and maintains a quick pace without anything inessential. As a result, there is no time wasted. Once again his long ago training working in cheap, quick shorts, sometimes shot in one day, helped to benefit him with the direction of a feature films. *Film Daily* stated, in a July 6, 1942 review of the film:[30]

> Director William Beaudine could probably have had the smash hit of th e the season if major money had been available for the production of *One Thrilling Night*. Not that this number lacks anything. *One Thrilling Night* is great stuff for all types of audiences -- it's a feather in the Monogram cap.

The Monogram brass was quite pleased with Beaudine's first film with them and made sure he got plenty of work thereafter.

William Beaudine followed up this auspicious debut with another murder mystery, *The Phantom Killer* (1942), starring Dick Purcell, Joan Woodbury, John Hamilton, and a returning Warren Hymer from *One Thrilling Night*. While essentially a more serious film, Beaudine's approach to the material offered a breezy, lighthearted presentation even with the more sober subject of murder. William Beaudine was pleased to find Mantan Moreland in the cast, and Moreland was also happy to be working with the

---

30 One Thrilling Night" *Film Daily* July 6, 1942

director again. They had enjoyed a good connection with the Dixie National productions on which they collaborated, and Moreland once again responded well to Beaudine's direction.

Moreland is allowed to be central to the narrative's development. He is a custodian on duty, when a well-dressed man, while leaving, asks him the time. Later, when Mantan discovers a man has been murdered, he contacts police and tells them what he knows. Mug books at the police station are of no help to Mantan, but he then sees the man's photo in a newspaper. However, the identifying photo is a deaf mute businessman whose presence is accounted for. Dick Purcell plays an assistant district attorney that believes there is indeed something to Mantan's story, and sets out to prove it. It is eventually revealed that the killer has a twin brother who is a deaf mute, and he assumed that identity to commit his crimes.

It is established early on that the characters—and the audience—are very sure that Hamilton's character committed the crimes, and the mystery derives from figuring out not who did it, but how they are going to prove who did it.

Beaudine keeps the pace brisk, with Purcell's fast-talking character sustaining most of the narrative, anchored by John Hamilton (best known for his later role as Perry White on TV's "The Adventures of Superman") as the suspect. Joan Woodbury is an attractive, appealing presence, while Warren Hymer assists with the comic element of the production as a concerned and befuddled police sergeant. Warren Hymer has a standout bit where he is talking to his wife on the phone, and her voice heard from the other end of the line is of a fast, high-pitched, cartoonish quality. The scene doesn't flip back and forth between her and Hymer, it just focuses on him and we only hear her voice, which makes it funnier via his reactions.

Monogram was again pleased with Beaudine's handling of *Phantom Killer*, and arranged for a premiere in Hollywood of both that film and *One Thrilling Night* in a double feature, attended by cast members of each movie. Meanwhile, the August 21, 1942 issue of

Film Daily called the film a "swell mystery drama," further stating in their review:[31]

> Replete with a finely twisted screenplay by Karl Brown, a tightly welded sequence of situations milked but not draggy, that carries full suspense under the very capable direction of William Beaudine. Enactments by the cast are of the finest quality, with Dick Purcell, Joan Woodbury, John Hamilton, and Mantan Moreland earning their spurs for fine performances. Balance of the cast perform ably. The plot's unwinding cleverness, plus the absolute tightness of William Beaudine's direction, are mostly responsible for its satisfying qualities as a mystery thriller. Not to be overlooked, however, are the very fine portrayals.

Beaudine effectively established himself at Monogram right out of the box. But his continued work would further define his directorial career at this point. And while Beaudine remained happy with his work and was gratified by the good reviews, box office success, and accolades from producers and studio heads, he still hoped this level of success might get him back with the majors.

At around this time, Beaudine signed with an agency in hopes that his agents could secure work for him at the major studios. After several months they were not successful, so he Beaudine left them and signed with another agency. The new agents were also unsuccessful. Again, Beaudine was pleased with the amount of work he was getting, and the creative freedom he was enjoying, but he still sought the money and budgets that the major studios would allow. These unsuccessful attempts forced Beaudine to realize that his place in Hollywood was in B movies, so he decided to retain his full focus on the work he was getting.

Actor Bela Lugosi made an enormous impact in the 1931 Universal feature *Dracula*, so much so that his approach to the character is how it continues to be defined. Even though Lugosi only played Dracula in two movies (the other being the 1948 parody *Abbott and Costello Meet Frankenstein*), it is his style and delivery that is invariably used when anyone acts out the character, even in a

---

31 "Phantom Killer." *Film Daily*. August 21, 1942.

comedy sketch. By the early 1940s, Lugosi was working in a lot of low budget B movies, bringing up their quality with interesting, edgy performances. William Beaudine had the opportunity to direct Lugosi in the 1943 Monogram feature *The Ape Man*.

Lugosi plays Dr. James Brewster whose experiments have resulted in his becoming half human and half ape. His only cure can happen if he injects himself with human spinal fluid. Wallace Ford plays a typical fast-talking reporter named Jeff Carter, and Louise Currie his pretty photographer Billie Mason. They are investigating Brewster's disappearance, which leads them to his sister Agatha (Minerva Urecal), who hunts ghosts. A series of murders take place, and Brewster needs continual injections, as they wear off. He goes on his killing spree with the help of an actual ape. The photographer gets captured, is rescued by the reporter, and Brewster is killed by the ape.

Beaudine understood the campiness of this horror movie and tried to keep it light and amusing. In fact there is a running character who seems to be detached from the immediate narrative, but looms about in several scenes. At the end, the reporter asks who he is, and the man says, "I'm the author of the story - screwy idea, wasn't it?" He then rolls up the car window to reveal "The End" on its surface. Ending the film on a gag does not negate the actual mystery and horror elements that precede it, but it does offer the sort of light approach that Beaudine would continue to add to any film he did that neared the horror genre.

Louise Currie lived to be 100 years old, and in later interviews would fondly recall working with Bela Lugosi and with William Beaudine. She recalled Beaudine's calm temper, his readiness for each day's shooting, his giving the actors a lot of creative leeway, and his ability to do a lot with a little. *The Ape Man* was shot in 15 days. *Film Daily* called it "a thrill-packed shocker" stating: "Here is an offering that should appeal to horror fans. It has Bela Lugosi doing his usual good work in the title role, able direction by William Beaudine, and good production values supplied by Sam Katzman and Jack Dietz."

Beaudine's direction and the actors did a good job cultivating an eerie atmosphere that endured. The cutting back and forth between all the characters and what they were up to raise the tension somewhat.

Beaudine would direct Lugosi in another horror film, *Voodoo Man*, the following year. That would also boast the talents of John Carradine and George Zucco. Phil Rosen was originally slated to direct, but production delays resulted in his being assigned elsewhere, so Beaudine was given the assignment. Along with the actors already cast, Beaudine also requested the services of both Louise Currie and Wanda McKay for the leading female roles, as he liked to work with the same actors when possible. *Voodoo Man* was shot in only seven days.

Zucco is helping Bela capture young women so he can transfer their energy into his dead wife. He uses a gas station as a front. Carradine plays a helper in this process. Beaudine once again ends on a gag with a would-be screenwriter planning to transfer this experience into a movie, and telling his producer Bela Lugosi should be its star. It's rather curious that this film ends on a gag, because up until that point it is rather creepy. Beaudine keeps that creepy factor intact up until the end after everything is resolved, rather than playing the entire film as comedy.

In-between these two Lugosi features, Beaudine directed the actor in an offbeat role for *Ghosts on the Loose* (1943), featuring The East Side Kids. Beaudine would direct several films in this series and it would become a rather important part of his career during this period.

This idea's genesis was the 1937 film version of Sidney Kingsley's play *Dead End*, produced by Samuel Goldwyn and directed by William Wyler. A group of actors from the stage production who played teenage gang members were hired for the movie. The antics of Billy Halop, Bernard Punsly, Gabe Dell, Leo Gorcey, Huntz Hall, and Bobby Jordan proved to be so popular with moviegoers, they were hired by Warner Brothers to appear with Humphrey Bogart in *Crime School* (1938), and were billed as The Dead End Kids. The group, with that billing continued to be very popular in films like *Angels With Dirty Faces* (1938), a classic with James Cagney, and other Warner movies like *Hell's Kitchen* (1939), featuring a young Ronald Reagan, and They Made Me a Criminal (1939) with John Garfield.

Sam Katzman saw the success of The Dead End Kids, and produced a juvenile delinquent drama called The East Side Kids, featuring Hal E. Chester, Harris Berger, Frankie Burke. Burke was best known as the James Cagney lookalike who played Cagney's character as a boy in Angels With Dirty Faces. The film was a hit, so Katzman decided to produce a low budget series, and managed to add original Dead End Kids Leo Gorcey and Bobby Jordan to the cast of the second film, Boys of the City (1941), playing the characters Muggs and Danny.

By the time William Beaudine first directed The East Side Kids in Clancy Street Boys (1943), another Dead End original, Huntz Hall, was also included in the cast as Glimpy, along with former Our Gang original Sunshine Sammy Morrison as Scruno, as well as veteran child/teen actors Benny Bartlett and Billy Benedict.

William Beaudine realized the comedy potential in the East Side Kids series, something that was touched upon in the earlier films, but not pursued as fully until The Clancy Street Boys. Beaudine went over his ideas with the actors, and they responded favorably. Huntz Hall recalled in a 1993 interview with Wendy L. Marshall:

"I loved the guy. He was like a father to us."

Screenwriter Harvey Gates had scripted several East Side Kids films, and had prepared a script where Muggs' mother reveals she has been telling a wealthy relative that she has seven children (Muggs is her only child). The relative, Uncle Pete, is a Texas cattle man and has been sending birthday money to each child. Apparently her late husband first bragged about his large family, and when he died, she couldn't bring herself to make him out a liar. To help his mother out, Muggs enlists the gang to pretend to be his siblings, and has Glimpy play the sister he's supposed to have.

Beaudine huddled with the actors and came up with some gag ideas that would work in context. First, he opened the film with the rest of the gang, as well as a rival gang, looking for Muggs, who is hiding because it is his birthday and he doesn't want to suffer the expected spankings. Drawing from his background in silent comedy, Beaudine has Muggs sneaking quietly behind a large, heavy set pedestrian, but when the man turns a corner, Muggs is revealed sneaking along. The gang spot him and sneak along behind him in the same manner. It is all done visually and comes off as very funny. This sort of humor adds another layer to the Kids, giving them more depth than merely rowdy characters on the streets.

Some of the business Beaudine added once Huntz Hall was in costume as a girl, was for his rolled up trousers to keep falling down below the hem of his skirt, causing the others to quickly help push them back up. Glimpy, the "sister," is expected to connect with Uncle Pete's daughter, played by the very attractive Amelita Ward (she later married Leo Gorcey).

Gorcey and Hall had fun with the comedy and added some ideas of their own. Sunshine Sammy, whose career dated back to silent comedy, and had worked with Harold Lloyd, easily slipped into a more comedic role. Hall told Marshall about Beaudine's direction:

> He knew all the tricks. We worked Saturdays and some nights until midnight. This man had energy. He was so unbelievable. He used to start at eight in the morning and eight at night he'd say "let's get another shot. It was hard work but fun.

The critics noticed the emphasis on humor, calling *The Clancy Street Boys* the best film in the series.

Beaudine recruited Bela Lugosi to play a Nazi villain in the then-topical *Ghosts on the Loose*, his followup to *Clancy Street Boys*. The script was by the inexperienced Kenneth Higgins who offered a rather meandering haunted house story with Nazi spies and the Kids. Beaudine, with the help of the actors and their ideas, tried to inject some life into the weak script, but were not particularly successful. Still, *Ghost on the Loose* had enough attractive elements to be a moneymaker in neighborhood theaters, pleasing the Monogram brass.

From this point, Beaudine directed several other East Side Kids movies, including *Mr. Muggs Steps Out, Follow the Leader,*

Bowery Champs, and *Come Out Fighting.* Beaudine maintained the formula of using humor to carry the narrative, and the actors continued to develop their comedy skills. In 1946, Leo Gorcey's agent took over as producer of the series, and revamped it as The Bowery Boys. At the actors' insistence, Beaudine directed many of the entries in that series, so much so that these films have their own separate chapter in this study. By using humor as early as 1943 in the East Side Kids series, Beaudine helped develop the format that would later work as the construct of the Bowery Boys series.

Beaudine continued to be successful directing productions for Monogram throughout the war years. Monogram's productions benefited greatly from Beaudine's experience and vision as he exhibited his versatility. Drama, romance, and mystery were all covered outside of the comedies Beaudine was helming for The East Side Kids. He even directed an upbeat musical, *Hot Rhythm,* with Robert Lowery and Dona Drake. Beaudine particularly enjoyed being reunited with Harry Langdon for a few films. The first was *Spotlight Scandals,* which Beaudine co-wrote (as William X. Crowley) with Beryl Sachs. The musical comedy review featured Billy Gilbert, Frank Fay, and such acts as singer Wee Bonnie Baker, and The Radio Rogues. Langdon is a lot of fun as a comic stage manager. The other Beaudine-directed films in which Langdon appeared were the musical-comedies *Hot Rhythm* and *Swinging on a Rainbow.* The latter was, sadly, the comedian's last film and was released posthumously.

In 1944, Beaudine had another opportunity to helm a comedy, this one featuring veteran performers Billy Gilbert, Shemp Howard, and Maxie Rosenbloom. *Crazy Knights* (aka *Ghost Crazy*) was amusing silliness, but has more camp value now because of Shemp's association with The Three Stooges. Comedy buffs connect also with Gilbert, who appeared in films with Laurel and Hardy, The Marx Brothers, and the Stooges. Rosenbloom, a prizefighter-turned-actor, played the likeable dumbbell in dramas and comedies. He had innate talent as an actor and was good in his roles. Shemp especially has been noted in other studies as being good with ad-libbing and improvising comic ideas on the set of his films. So he responded well to the freedom Beaudine gave his actors.

Shemp and Gilbert work well as a team and did a few more similar comedies for Monogram, but this, the best of them, is the only one Beaudine directed. He took advantage of his own freedom by requesting the services of actors he liked working with in previous films, including Minerva Urecal and John Hamilton.

Producer Lindsley Parsons requested Beaudine to direct a film for a proposed series about Kitty O'Day, a telephone operator who became an amateur detective. Parsons had worked with Beaudine on the film *The Mystery of the 13th Guest* (1943), and was impressed with the director's command of the set while retaining his good humor, as well as for his efficiency. Parsons wanted Beaudine to bring out the comic possibilities for each effort, and a series was expected to continue over several films. Jean Parker, best remembered for the Laurel and Hardy movie *The Flying Deuces* (1939), was hired to play the title role in *Detective Kitty O'Day* (1944).

The film was an amusing trifle with the typical setup of a female detective and her supportive boyfriend dealing with murder, crooks, and false accusations by dimwitted cops. Beaudine did what he could with the material, but a series never materialized.

Only one sequel was made, *The Adventures of Kitty O'Day* (1945), and the series was discontinued due to lack of interest from moviegoers. Monogram understood what was popular, especially with The East Side Kids, and the newly acquired Charlie Chan series from Fox studios. The Kitty O'Day films were not pulling those numbers in the neighborhood theaters, and weren't sought after as second features in the bigger houses.

By 1945, William Beaudine found himself in much the same position as he had begun to develop before leaving for England in 1935. He was established as a reliable director with a strong background whose films enjoyed both critical and commercial success. Thus, Beaudine was once again in demand by several other studios. It just wasn't Warner Brothers and Paramount anymore. It was Monogram, PRC, and Republic. While he continued to work for Monogram, he was not specifically under contract, so other B level production companies sought his work, giving him further opportunities to explore other genres.

When referencing Beaudine's expediency, and the fact that he was connected quite specifically to B-level productions at this time, it does not, in any way, give any substance to the "one-shot" moniker that Beaudine has been unfairly given by snarky latter day film geeks. Beaudine's expedience refers to his ability to work under budget and get a complete feature film made in one week. And it wasn't due to shooting just one take on most scenes. Beaudine came to the set fully prepared, with the script memorized, the camera angles worked out, and his approach all set. He would work well into the night, getting in just one more sequence shot. Even though he failed to in his attempts to return to the bigger studios and more lucrative productions, Beaudine was not a bitter man and did not spend the remainder of his career breezing through low budget movies with disdainfully few takes. William Beaudine came to every project with the full intention of making a good movie within whatever parameters he had to observe.

By the post-war period in filmmaking, William Beaudine had understood, and accept, his status as a director of B movie product. He accepted the fact that his pay wasn't as high as it had been before he went to England. He instead was pleased that he was getting so many opportunities to direct, with no layoff periods. William Beaudine thrived on work. And work he did.

Wanda McKay and John Boles in One Thrilling Night.

Trade ad for Ghosts on the Loose.

Louise Currie and Bela Lugosi in The Ape Man.

Mantan Moreland and Dick Purcell in Phantom Killer.

POST WAR FREELANCING AT MONOGRAM, PRC, AND ELSEWHERE

William Beaudine maintained his association with Monogram studios during the post-war years, mostly concentrating on the Bowery Boys series which will be covered more extensively in a separate chapter. However, Beaudine also sought work at other studios. While continuing at Monogram, Beaudine also did films for Universal, Republic, and back to PRC.

Girl on the Spot (1946) is a very unusual film that Beaudine directed for Universal studios. Lois Collier plays a woman who has witnessed a murder, so she helps police trap the culprit. He is a Gilbert and Sullivan fan, so Collier, whose father (George Dolenz) heads an opera company, arranges to perform several songs in a show, hoping to expose and trap the killer. While the narrative is standard, the method of presentation is something different in that it is a musical. It comes off remarkably well. It is worth noting that George Dolenz is the father of Micky Dolenz, whom Beaudine would later direct on TV in *Circus Boy* and who later played the drummer for The Monkees.

One Exciting Week was made for Republic Pictures and features radio comedian Al Pearce as war hero Dan Flannery. Flannery is heading home to be honored by the townsfolk, but is attacked by gangsters and suffers amnesia. The criminals then convince him he is a fellow crook and a wanted man. Beaudine had a lot of fun with the casting of this comedy, with Shemp Howard and Pinky Lee among the crooks.

Beaudine then went over to PRC to direct a couple of detective films. First, he helmed *Philo Vance Returns* which turned out to be the last film featuring S.S. Van Dine's detective. Perhaps the best Philo Vance film was *The Kennel Murder Case* which was made for Warner Brothers and featured William Powell in the lead role. *Philo Vance Returns* starred William Wright as the detective. Wright was an effective character actor and occasional star of B movies, his promising career curtailed by his death at age 38. His turn as Philo Vance is not bad, but the film was shot in only seven days. Beaudine fared better directing a Michael Shayne detective mystery entitled *Too Many Winners*. At this time, Hugh Beaumont was starring as the sleuth. Of course Beaumont would later define his career as Ward Cleaver on TV's *Leave it to Beaver*.

One of the more interesting movies Beaudine directed at PRC during the post-war years was *Gas House Kids Go West*, which was a lot like the Bowery Boys films he had been helming at Monogram. The popularity of films like the Bowery Boys, and The East Side Kids, inspired PRC to create their own series of mischievous younger men. The first film *Gas House Kids* even featured one of the original Dead End Kids, Billy Halop. It also included Carl Switzer who had been in Our Gang (The Little Rascals) as Alfalfa. Both were having trouble finding work, Alfalfa as an adult, and Halop after coming out of the army (in fact, the working title for the film was *East Side Rascals*). The first film was successful, so Beaudine was asked to direct the second.

Gas House Kids Go West had Switzer returning, and added former Our Ganger Tommy Bond as well as Bennie Bartlett, an East Side Kid who would later become a Bowery Boy. Billy Halop was in none of the sequels.

The film opens with the boys having roughed up a new neighbor who is a stuffy ballet dancer that speaks condescendingly to the boys. Beaudine cast dancer Ronn Marvin in the role, and, extending beyond his actual dancing skill, Marvin was able to play a comically stuffy character who was at odds with the boys. When the Gas House Kids are told by an understanding police sergeant that they can win a trip to California in a basketball game, they enter to compete. When they get there, the Kids are surprised to discover the stuffy ballet dancer is a part of the opposing team.

The Gas House Kids exhibit genuine athletic ability during the first part of the game, but when the ballet dancer gets in, his spins and pirouettes baffle the boys and his team catches up. It has already been established that when the ballet dancer hears music, he has to dance, so when an audience member cheerfully starts playing a harmonica, the dancer starts dancing, and this distraction is enough for the Gas House Kids to score the winning basket.

What is most impressive about this scene is how William Beaudine shot it. He places the camera overhead in order to keep all of the action on the frame, but does not have the camera pull back enough to reveal how small the set is (likely a high school gym, with almost nothing for an audience). Special effects show that Alfalfa has a trick shot that bounces on the backboard three times and then plops into the basket. So Beaudine edits to medium shots and closeups effectively from his long shots. His cameras follow the action with rhythm and cohesion. The scene is funny, exciting, and very well directed. It is also a good example of how Beaudine was able to make a cheap film appear as though it had much better production value. Audience noise is added, and the shots are such that it appears there are far more people watching the game. Beaudine's prowess with comedy direction is also evident during this scene, as he cuts away to the police sergeant, acting as referee, and reading a rule book as he goes.

Once this scene concludes and the Gas House Kids head west, it becomes a bit more standard, while still remaining sincere and enjoyable. There is a pleasantness to the entire production, but not enough to attract sustainable moviegoers. Taking the boys out of their element from the city streets to a western town was able to lead to a lot of humor, and the relationship these rough kids had established with the police sergeant was commendable. After one more film, not directed by Beaudine, the idea for a Gas House Kids series was jettisoned. Beaudine would remain with the much more successful Bowery Boys.

While at Monogram during the post-war years, William Beaudine was busy with the Bowery Boys series, but that isn't all he was doing at the studio. Beaudine also helmed a few of the last entries in the Charlie Chan series and a couple of the Jiggs and Maggie films.

The Charlie Chan series began at Fox studios in the early 1930s, with Warner Oland playing the Chinese detective based on Earl Derr Biggers' stories. Keye Luke played Number One Son Lee Chan. When Oland died in 1938, Sidney Toler took over the role, and Victor Sen Yung played Number Two Son Jimmy Chan. Fox dropped the series in the 1940s, but Toler brought the property to Monogram where it was given new life. Chan was now a low budget B movie series, with comedy relief by Mantan Moreland as Chan's chauffeur Birmingham Brown. When Toler died in 1947, the films were still popular, so Roland Winters was hired to play the detective. William Beaudine was hired to direct *The Chinese Ring* (1947), Winters' first film as the Chinese sleuth.

Screenwriter Scott Darling dusted off the script for his 1939 feature *Mr. Wong in Chinatown* and rewrote it for the Charlie Chan character. Mantan Moreland was pleased that Beaudine was hired to direct the film, having worked with him more than once, and having responded favorably to being allowed some creative input. *The Chinese Ring* had a new star and a new director, but it still comes off as a solid debut for Winters, and for Beaudine. Being given a bit more money to work with was also helpful, so Beaudine had the opportunity to improvise.

Beaudine also directed the Charlie Chan feature *The Shanghai Chest*. This was an original script by newcomer Samuel Newman, who would later work in television, notably the *Perry Mason* TV series. Beaudine was once again able to get a lot of production value out of a low budget B movie. His choice of shots, use of darkness, and making the most of the limited settings, all combine to offer an effective presentation.

Beaudine continued to work effectively with *The Golden Eye*, and his last film in the Chan series, *The Feathered Serpent*. The latter is a significant effort in that Keye Luke returned to play number one son Lee Chan for the first time in ten years, making this the only Charlie Chan film to feature both Luke and Victor Sen Yung playing the two noted son characters. The Charlie Chan series ended with the next film, *Sky Dragon* (1949), which was not directed by William Beaudine.

The Jiggs and Maggie series was based on the George McManus comic strip *Bringing Up Father*, which was the title of the first film, directed by veteran comedy director Eddie Cline who is noted for having worked closely with Buster Keaton during the silent era. Cline also directed the first sequel, *Jiggs and Maggie in Society*, after which he retired from directing movies (he did some work with Keaton in television). Cline did continue to work on the scripts for the Jiggs and Maggie films. Beaudine directed the next three efforts; *Jiggs and Maggie in Court, Jiggs and Maggie in Jackpot Jitters*, and *Jiggs and Maggie Out West*. The popularity of the comic strip resulted in a ready-made audience.

The title roles were played by Joe Yule and Renie Riano. Yule was the father of Mickey Rooney, but had been estranged from both him and his ex-wife, Rooney's mother Nellie Carter, after their divorce in 1924. He enjoyed a solid career in Burlesque. When Rooney achieved film stardom, Yule showed back up in his son's life, but his Burlesque background was an embarrassment to MGM studio head Louis B. Mayer. Rooney himself was proud of his father's work, and ignored Mayer's request that the two stop publicizing that they were father and son. To keep him out of Burlesque, Mayer put Yule on the MGM payroll and gave him small roles in films like *Boom Town* with Clark Gable, *Woman of the Year* with Katharine Hepburn, and *Air Raid Wardens* with Laurel and Hardy. By the time Yule was at Monogram, Rooney was no longer with MGM.

Renie Riano had been playing minor roles in scores of Hollywood movies since the late 1930s, and would continue to do so into the television era. The Jiggs and Maggie series was her only opportunity to play a starring role. Riano played over the top and with a real comic flourish, and this served the Maggie character well.

Jiggs and Maggie Out West, the last film in the series, is typical as to how each of them was mounted. It features the family going west where Maggie's grandfather has left her some property in his will. They search for the treasure, with the help of grandpa's ghost, but hindered by some outlaws. The film has an odd conclusion with cartoonist George McManus playing himself and revealing that he is the creator of the characters and the entire story was fictional.

This ending is very reminiscent of the closing gags of Beaudine's horror features Beaudine for Monogram. But since the entire movie is a wacky comedy it doesn't feel too out of place. *Jiggs and Maggie Out West* was shot on the Gower Gulch western studios that would later be purchased by Gene Autry.

The Jiggs and Maggie movies were each shot in about a week, and enjoyed popularity in the neighborhood theaters and as second features in the bigger houses. The films probably would have continued being produced had Joe Yule not died of a heart attack in 1950, before what turned out to be the last film in the series was released. There was some discussion about replacing him, but he had been so popular, and his status as Mickey Rooney's father such a saleable point, they decided to simply end the series with his last movie.

One of the more interesting, and prestigious, productions William Beaudine directed during the post-war years at Monogram was a screen adaption of Robert Louis Stevenson's *Kidnapped* starring 19 year old Roddy McDowall who also co-produced the film. The novel had been filmed before in 1938 for Fox, but Beaudine's version for Monogram is, arguably the better screen adaption. Despite the film's low budget, Beaudine's penchant for placing the camera carefully and making more out of his budgetary limitations was notable. It was also notable that his screen version of *Kidnapped* was much more faithful to Robert Louis Stevenson's original source material than the bigger budgeted Fox picture.

McDowall stars as David Balfour, who has his birthright stolen, is kidnapped, and sold into slavery. McDowall recalled in his later years that Beaudine was a very congenial director who never lost his temper, and did a good job directing *Kidnapped*. Because McDowall liked Beaudine and appreciated him, their connection during filming was very positive, and it was a happy and productive experience.

This was a transitional film for McDowall who was moving from child actor to adult actor and had to secure his career for grown-up roles. *Kidnapped* was successful and especially significant to the continued success of Roddy McDowall's career. A sequel was considered but never produced.

Another interesting project had William Beaudine traveling over to the low budget Lippert Pictures at the request of noted cowboy star Don "Red" Barry. Barry had started his own production company with the idea of expanding his range as an actor. It wasn't a successful venture, and only lasted a few films. But Barry requested Beaudine to direct his movie *Tough Assignment* in which the cowboy actor takes on the role of a crusading newspaper reporter in a movie that is considered to be film noir. Barry was known as a very difficult actor to work with. William Witney and John English both refused to work with him. Beaudine had no such misgivings and agreed to direct his film. Barry, as executive producer, wanted a director who was efficient and could work quickly, and Beaudine's reputation preceded him.

The most interesting thing about *Tough Assignment* is that it was shot with the Garutso Balanced Lens which allowed for deep focus at a wider apeture, offering what was advetised as a 3-Dimensional effect. It made everything in the forground and the background, appear in perfect focus. Some of the more noted films that used this lens include *Cyrano De Bergerac* (1950), *The Member of the Wedding* (1952), and *The Wild One* (1953), but its use in Hollywood movies was short lived. However, the fact that William Beaudine was one of the few directors to make use of the Garutso Balanced Lens is worth noting, even if it happened to be on a rather lackluster production.

William Beaudine was now quite established as a B movie director at the poverty row studios. It was commendable that indie filmmakers attempting to expand into low budget production, like Don "Red" Barry, would summon his services. And, tt was a natural for him to do most of his work for Monogram, as that was one of the better low budget companies during the 1940s and 1950s. Beaudine directed westerns, musicals, horror movies, comedies, and literary adaptions, but the biggest impact he made was on one of the most popular film series of the post war era.

As indicated earlier, The Bowery Boys had evolved from The East Side Kids, which had itself evolved from The Dead End Kids. This new revamp of the series was produced by Jan Grippo, Leo Gorcey's agent. It was essentially a comedy series with elements of dramatic narrative structure as the East Side Kids had been. The emphasis, however, was on comedy, and the characters were better drawn than they had been in the East Side Kids series, especially Huntz Hall.

William Beaudine had been, as previously noted, responsible for the adding of more humor to the East Side Kids films, an idea which led to Jan Grippo reformatting the series once he took over as producer. So, naturally, Jan Grippo wanted Beaudine to be the regular director for the Bowery Boys films, and the actors wanted him as well. However, due to other projects, Beaudine could not begin directing the films in this series until their fourth release. And, as with the East Side Kids films, once William Beaudine began directing Bowery Boys movies, it was his vision that helped define the series.

Because William Beaudine directed so many entries in the Bowery Boys series, and because he was so instrumental in the structure and success of the films, they have been given a separate chapter of their own.

Poster for Ghost Crazy.

Poster for Gas House Kids Go West.

Victor Sen Yung, Byron Foulger, Mantan Moreland, and Roland Winters in "The Chinese Ring."

The Feathered Serpent *is the only Charlie Chan film in which Keye Luke and Victor Sen Yung appeared together.*

Trade ad for Jiggs and Maggie Out West.

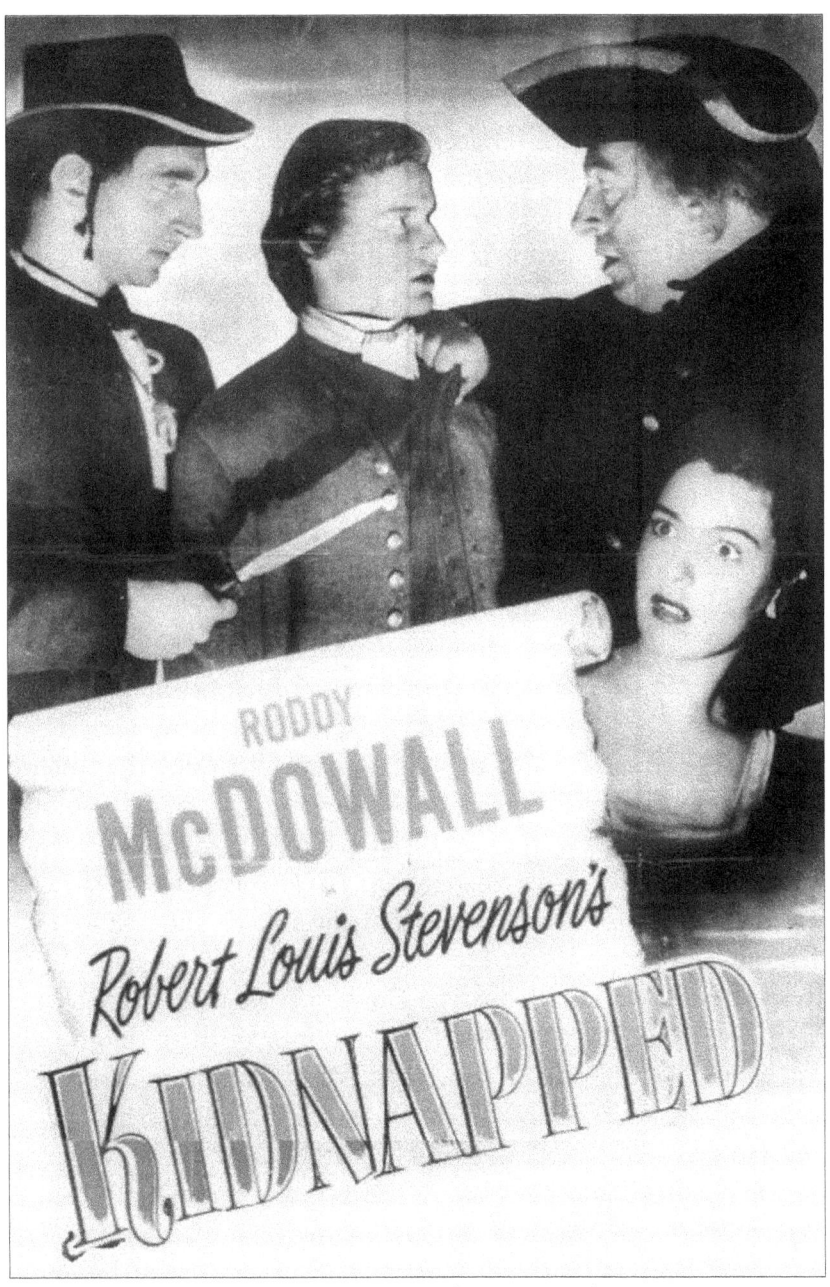

Kidnapped had Beaudine directing a film version of classic literature.

THE BOWERY BOYS

As discussed in the chapter on Monogram studios, William Beaudine first began directing The East Side Kids, spawned from the Dead End Kids, with their 1943 feature *Clancy Street Boys*. His approach was to focus more on the inherent humor in the series, which was effective for the next several East Side Kids films Beaudine directed.

In 1946, Leo Gorcey's agent Jan Grippo took over as producer of the series and Beaudine would direct over 20 features among the 48 in this series, which would last until 1958. This was mostly due to the series stars, Gorcey and Huntz Hall, who liked working with Beaudine and felt the results were some of the better efforts in the East Side Kids series.

However, as discussed in the previous chapter, Beaudine was active on other projects, so he was unable to start directing The Bowery Boys until their fourth feature, *Spook Busters*. The first few films were, like the earlier East Side Kids movies, basically dramatic narratives with some humorous touches. Beaudine's first Bowery Boys film featured the boys as ghost exterminators who get mixed up with crooks that are manipulating the effects in the house they are investigating. While this premise is taken seriously in performance, it is essentially a comic idea rather than a dramatic narrative.

The actors who made up The Bowery Boys at this point were all veterans of The East Side Kids, and four of them dated back to the first Dead End Kids movies at Warner Brothers. Along with Gorcey and Hall, Bobby Jordan was again a part of the group. Jordan was an original Dead End Kid, and one of the leading players in The East Side Kids, but left to serve in the military, returning after World War Two was ended. However, his part in The Bowery Boys was greatly diminished and he only stayed for about a year. Gabe Dell, another original Dead End Kid, was an outsider in most of the East Side Kids films, sometimes as a rival who was involved with gangsters, other times someone who made good and had a status outside of the gang. He continued in this role with The Bowery Boys. In later interviews, Leo Gorcey would refer to Gabe Dell as the best actor of the group. *Spook Busters* was his first Bowery Boys movie, and he plays a former member of the gang who is returning from the Navy. The gang is rounded out by Leo's brother David Gorcey, and actor Billy Benedict, both of whom were in several East Side Kids films.

An especially amusing addition was another member of the Gorcey family, Bernard Gorcey, as Louie Dumbrowski, owner of the Sweet Shop where the gang congregated. He was a veteran of Jewish theater, and appeared in Charlie Chaplin's first sound film *The Great Dictator* (1940). The diminutive Louie was loud and aggressive, and always frustrated by the Boys as he wound up in the middle of their schemes. Bernard Gorcey the actor was similar, and, in later interviews, Leo would fondly remember how five foot tall Bernard would stand up to Beaudine, over six feet tall, and demand more screen time.

The idea of exterminating ghosts was, of course, the premise for the 1984 feature *Ghostbusters*, which was also this film's original title. So, William Beaudine's first of many films with The Bowery Boys was not only a hit, it helped inspired one of the most financially popular movies of all time.

Beaudine's next Bowery Boys film created a concept that would be used frequently in the group's subsequent films. Hypnosis turns Sach into a championship prizefighter. Naturally, at the wrong moments, the power wears off. This idea would be used in other Bowery Boys comedies such as *Master Minds* when Sach is able to predict the future if eats too much sugar. In *Blues Busters* a tonsillectomy turns Sach into a singer. A concoction in a chemistry lab turns Sach into a college football hero in *Hold That Line*. A magic spell makes Sach a wrestler in *No Holds Barred*. An electric shock allows him to predict winning numbers in *Crashing Las Vegas*. All of these, other than *Master Minds* and *Crashing Las Vegas*, were directed by Beaudine.

Billy Benedict, who appeared as Whitey in many of the Bowery Boys features, recalled how, despite their affection for Beaudine, both Leo Gorcey and Huntz Hall were difficult to corral on the set and get to work, which was a challenge for William Beaudine:[32]

> A lot of other actors who worked with them went crazy too. They get a script and most of the actors they used learned their dialog, came on the set, and were ready to shoot. Leo would speak and the other actor doesn't hear his cue because they changed the dialog so much. Finally all they did was wait for Leo to stop and then they'd say something. Huntz would be trying to upstage Leo. Beaudine wouldn't let him mug too much. Huntz was the type who had to have somebody hang on him and not let him go overboard, and Beaudine was good for doing that. He had a great sense of comedy.

Despite the challenge of working with Gorcey and Hall, the relationship was professionally fruitful. The Bowery Boys comedies remained exceptionally popular and sometimes held the top spot on double feature programs at major theaters. In fact, Beaudine's 1950 Bowery Boys effort, *Blues Busters*, is considered by many to be the best film in the entire series.

Blues Busters opens with Sach in the hospital after getting his tonsils out. Louie put up the money, and wants to be paid back. The gang has no idea how they can raise money, until suddenly Sach starts singing along with the radio in a beautiful crooning voice (dubbed by John Laurenz[33]). The gang attempts to get Sach a gigs in a nearby nightclub, and eventually opens their own, turning Louie's Sweet Shop into a club where Sach performs exclusively. Of course the film concludes with Sach losing this power and returning to his old self.

What sets *Blues Busters* apart is that it is an unusual talent for Sach to have. Usually his prowess is in a physical medium which allows him success in the wrestling ring or on the football field. He croons the sort of pleasant pop songs that were quite popular at this time (Laurenz's delivery is not unlike Perry Como or

---

32 Marshall, Wendy L. *William Beaudine: From Silents to Television.* Lanham, MD. Scarecrow Press. 2002

33 *The Hollywood Reporter* review credited Bob Carroll as the singer who dubbed for Huntz Hall, but this appears to be in error.

Dean Martin, both hit singers at the time). *Variety* stated in their review:[34]

> Monogram's Bowery Boys have a somewhat different entry. In *Blues Busters* they take to song to bolster the usual pattern of rowdy mugging, and it all comes off successfully for their market. It's a good twist for this standard series. Producer Jan Grippo gives the picture a smarter looking mounting than entries in the series are usually accorded. William Beaudine's direction is able.

While Beaudine's being singled out was hardly a rave, the fact that the director of a B movie that was part of a series got any mention at all was of some significance.

Hold That Line is another one of their best efforts, with the Bowery Boys going to college and Sach becoming an athletic star after mixing a concoction in chemistry class that gives him special powers. The film opens with a group of elderly scholars sitting quietly in a common room; reading, playing chess, etc. At an appointed time they all get up and sing the school song, then return to their quiet situation. The sudden song is the sort of absurdity that Beaudine always enjoyed doing. He slowly pans the room, showing the men quietly seated and reading, playing chess, or doing some other activity that requires no sound or movement. He cuts to a closeup of a man's watch, which shows 12 noon. The man gets up walks over to a gong and hits it. The sudden noise causes the men to get up and sing, then cheer, then return to their quiet activities. Beaudine's succession of shots is perfect. This opening scene makes us think of how much The Bowery Boys will be disrupting these proceedings.

The film is a variation on George Bernard Shaw's *Pygmalion*, which had been used by The Three Stooges in *Half Wits Holiday* a few years earlier. In the Stooges film, a wager has two refined men attempting to turn the trio into gentlemen. In *Hold That Line*, a couple of high level professors have a wager that a young man from the lowest strata in life can respond to higher education.

---

34 "Blues Busters." *Variety* October 25, 1950

This leads The Bowery Boys into the college experience, and Sach's prowess on the football field. This is a variation on the 1938 Joe E. Brown feature *The Gladiator*, and the basic concept would be used again for *Trading Places* (1983).

Beaudine's direction is also significant in its use of setups. The narrative introduces, and establishes, John Bromfield as Biff Wallace, the school's All American athlete. Biff's smugness is taken down a few notches by Slip's matter-of-fact reaction: "we're all Americans, what has he done after that?" Sach shocks a math class by solving a difficult equation, but he has an adding machine under his desk, which he is working with his toes. Slip's malaprops are perfect for English class. And before he creates the concoction that makes him invincible, Sach unwittingly creates TNT, throws it out the window of the chemistry lab, and causes it to explode on the Dean.

Taking the Bowery Boys out of their element and placing them in a college setting is sort of situation that rankled Bernard Gorcey, who realized in these situations his screen time might be reduced. So, it was arranged, via the narrative, for Louie to see an article in the newspaper about an old man who returned to college, and does so himself, claiming he missed the gang. He doesn't share many scenes with them, but does get his own bit where girls are fawning over him for being "cute," and when the boys have to dress as girls and return to their old neighborhood as part of a fraternity haze, Louie laughs uproariously. Slip gets even by putting the ladies duds on Louie while the gang laughs at him.

Ghost Chasers has the gang dabbling in spiritualism, and are aided by a ghost who helps them capture gangsters. Of course Sach is the only one who can see the ghost. And while such an idea was pretty standard for any comedy act (and was one that Beaudine would investigate often), it turned out to be another one of the best Bowery Boys efforts, and among their most popular.

Robert Easton, a dialect coach, appeared in Beaudine's 1952 Bowery Boys entry *Feudin' Fools*, as he specialized in hillbilly roles. Easton recalled:[35]

---

35 Marshall, Wendy L. *William Beaudine: From Silents to Television.* Lanham, MD. Scarecrow Press. 2002

Beaudine was meticulous. He gave you guidance. Gave you latitude on one had to improvise and try new things, but on the other hand, gave you a clear idea of what he wanted. Then all you had to do is look at him and you knew if it worked because he was very appreciative.

Changes were happening with Monogram studios in 1953 when they transitioned to Allied Artists. They had begun using that name for its more expensive productions (although still low budget by comparison to the big studios) in 1946. In 1953, the Monogram name was retired all together. However, since The Bowery Boys movies were the studio's most profitable, it was one of the productions retained during the transition.

Another change, specific to The Bowery Boys series, was the retirement of Jan Grippo. He was replaced by Ben Schwalb, who wanted to emphasize the comic element of The Bowery Boys even moreso. Even in the Beaudine-directed films produced by Grippo, there is a dramatic element to inform the comedy, such as Sach being kidnapped by gangsters in *Hold That Line*, because they have bet against the odds on the opposing team.

Jalopy was William Beaudine's first Bowery Boys film under the Allied Artists banner and produced by Ben Schwalb. There was a scene where Huntz Hall was supposed to run through several race cars to go pick up his hat. Huntz's stunt man refused to do the scene. Huntz didn't want to do it himself, but Beaudine talked him into it. Hall agreed, due to his respect and admiration for Beaudine, but the scene was a very tense situation and Hall was quite agitated afterward. He went to the producer and asked that Beaudine be replaced as the series director. Schwalb, having no allegiance to Beaudine, having just come onto the project, wanted to make the stars of his top series happy. Beaudine was replaced by Edward Bernds.

Edward Bernds had been a sound man at Columbia, working on many of Frank Capra's early features. Bernds began directing short comedies in 1946, helming several very good Three Stooges shorts. He also directed a few of the later features in Columbia's Blondie and Dagwood series with Penny Singleton and Arthur Lake, and based on Chic Young's comic strip.

Bernds' approach was much different from William Beaudine's. While Beaudine allowed creative freedom and sought the ideas of his actors, Bernds stuck to the script more carefully, especially when it was he who wrote or co-wrote it. As a result, even though some of the Bernds-directed Bowery Boys features are among their best, it was not a happy collaboration. Leo Gorcey and Huntz Hall had slowly been singled out in the films as a veritable comedy team, Edward Bernds really focused on that concept. This was ok with the actors up to a point, but they didn't like that they were no long part of an ensemble (in some films, actors like David Gorcey and Bennie Bartlett have almost no lines at all). Gorcey and Hall also disliked the infusion of Stooges level slapstick taking the place of the underlying serious stories. They were used to a certain format, as established by William Beaudine, and realized that another director would have his own approach.

Edward Bernds wasn't happy either, and in later years recalled the experience negatively. In the 1980s, Bernds told Ted Okuda for *Filmfax:* "Leo Gorcey was a pig. A miserable person. Huntz hated Leo. Leo didn't hate Huntz, he just put him down."

Of course it is not this book's intention to be negative toward Edward Bernds. He was a good director and successfully helmed many comedies, both shorts and features, as well as westerns and science-fiction films. It's just that his understanding of the characters and approach to the series structure differed from Beaudine's

After only one film with Bernds, the funny and successful *Loose in London*, Hall went to Ben Schwalb and begged him to bring William Beaudine back. Beaudine had accepted many other projects, so he only came back randomly, with Bernds directing most of the films at this time.

Among the films that Beaudine directed for The Bowery Boys during this period include *Paris Playboys, Jail Busters*, and *High Society*, even though Edward Bernds and Ellwood Ullman continued to write the screenplays. All of these films took the Boys out of the Bowery and investigated other possibilities in expanding the structure and parameters of the series. Of course a film like *Paris Playboys* would still be shot on a studio lot, and not actually on location. It would be the same set that was used for a prison in *Jail Busters*. The latter film does have something of a straight narrative to back up the bombastic comedy, and supporting Bowery Boy Bennie Barltett is given a bit more to do.

High Society is the only Bowery Boys movie to be considered for an Academy Award. The Academy had wanted to nominate the writers of the Frank Sinatra musical *High Society*, released that same year, but in error awarded the nomination to Bernds and Ullman, writers of the Bowery Boys movie. While things were corrected before the ceremony happened, Bernds retained the letter announcing the nomination framed on his office wall for the rest of his life.

Beaudine then got involved in other projects and Bernds returned to directing the Bowery Boys series. However, Beaudine was not finished with the Boys. Shortly after filming the Edward Bernds-directed Bowery Boys feature *Dig That Uranium*, Bernard Gorcey died after sustaining injuries in an auto accident. Leo was so distraught, he had trouble carrying on.

While filming the next Bowery Boys film, *Crashing Las Vegas* directed by Jean Yarbrough, Leo was drinking heavily. Character actor Emil Sitka, who had a role in *Crashing Las Vegas*, recalled for this author, "Bernard was a friend of mine. Everyone liked him. Leo was devastated by his death. We all were. But on *Crashing Las Vegas* he was so drunk that there were times he had to be carried on and off the set."

Leo Gorcey left The Bowery Boys after that film, but the series continued in order to fulfill Huntz Hall's contract. Stanley Clements was added to the act that also included Huntz, David Gorcey, and Eddie LeRoy by the time William Beaudine once again directed them. Clements had worked with Hall and both Gorceys in some East Side Kids movies years earlier. Once he finished some other projects, William Beaudine agreed to return to the Bowery Boys series to direct what turned out to be their last two movies: *Up in Smoke* and *In The Money*. Both of these were among the better of the later films of the series. The former has Byron Foulger as the devil, who tricks Huntz Hall into selling his soul in order to get sports stats to bet on ahead of time. The last film in the series has the Boys hired to accompany a pampered poodle overseas, not realizing that he is owned by smugglers who have diamonds hidden on the pooch. Once Huntz Hall's contract had been fulfilled, the series concluded.

As indicated, during his time with The Bowery Boys, William Beaudine was also busy with other projects. Throughout the 1950s, Beaudine directed religious films, exploitation movies, had a stint with Disney, and started to helm some television shows as TV became more and more popular. All of these will be discussed in ensuing chapters.

One of the films Beaudine directed, in 1952, was *Bela Lugosi Meets a Brooklyn Gorilla*, a particularly odd film that later achieved cult status. The ingredients for this film were quite simple: take a couple of low-rent nightclub comics who patterned their act after the wildly popular Dean Martin and Jerry Lewis, add a drug-addled Bela Lugosi whose career was at low ebb, a threadbare budget lower than even most of Beaudine's recent movies, and a typically limited shooting schedule and you have *Bela Lugosi Meets a Brooklyn Gorilla*.

The producers were quite aware of William Beaudine's background working with comics, working with Bela Lugosi, and being able to make very low budget movies seem like their production values were better than they actually were. Thus, they figured that this movie would be perfect for his skills as a director. Beaudine accepted the challenge.

The Bowery Boys movies were actually very good training for this cheap, exploitative concoction, as its "comedy" owes more to that superior series than it does to the far superior Martin and Lewis. *Bela Lugosi Meets a Brooklyn Gorilla* is such of an oddball, it gets a chapter all its own.

Trade ad for the Bowery Boys comedy Spook Busters, *which influenced the 1984 hit movie* Ghostbusters.

Huntz Hall and Lloyd Corrigan in Ghost Chasers.

Gabe Dell on the piano accompanies Huntz Hall in Blues Busters.

Huntz Hall, Amanda Blake, and Leo Gorcey in High Society.

BELA LUGOSI MEETS A BROOKLYN GORILLA

As indicated at the end of the previous chapter, it is because it is among the strangest and most cult-beloved movies in William Beaudine's entire filmography that *Bela Lugosi Meets a Brooklyn Gorilla* has been given a chapter of its own. Certainly not because it is a good movie. It is not. But it is a very curious one.

Dean Martin and Jerry Lewis were the hottest thing in show business in 1952. Their films, TV appearances, radio appearances, and nightclub gigs had a level of popularity that could only be compared to the likes of Elvis Presley and The Beatles in later years. Sammy Petrillo was a tall, gangly teenager with an aptitude for silly humor, who looked uncannily like Jerry Lewis. When the resemblance resulted in his being introduced to Lewis, Jerry hired him to play his baby on an episode of TV's *Colgate Comedy Hour*. Petrillo would later recall he received sixty dollars for the appearance.

Petrillo eventually studied Lewis's delivery and mannerisms to the point where he could parlay his resemblance as a mimic and perform his act in a few of the smaller nightclubs. He teamed with a young singer named Duke Mitchell who cut his hair like Dean Martin. As Mitchell and Petrillo, they essentially copped Martin and Lewis's act and played a few smaller clubs around the Las Vegas area. This wasn't a problem, as they made little impact even within the confines of their region. They were really no more than an oddball novelty act.

However, Mitchell and Petrillo, along with their manager Maurice Duke, made a deal with Jack Broder, president of Realart pictures, for the duo to perform in their own low budget movie as its stars. The idea was that because Mitchell and Petrillo were riding on the coattails of Martin and Lewis' massive success in small clubs, they might be able to do the same in a series of low budget movies.

Jack Broder's company had been re-releasing older Universal productions, including the horror films, so he had a connection to Bela Lugosi. He had also produced his own low budget horror film *Bride of the Gorilla*, so he had that idea established. Discussions eventually resulted in their planning a horror comedy with a jungle setting, featuring Bela Lugosi along with Mitchell and Petrillo. While the comedians would be performing in much the same manner as Martin and Lewis did in their movies (with Mitchell getting a couple of songs, playing straight, and being the romantic lead, while Petrillo handled the crazy comedy), the film itself would be closer to what The Bowery Boys had been doing at Monogram.

William Beaudine was, at the time, directing the Bowery Boys films, so he was considered by producer Howard Cohen to supervise this movie. Of course what attracted Cohen was that Beaudine had notably developed a really solid reputation for efficiency. He was known for being able to get a lot done on a low budget and limited shooting schedule. Also, Beaudine had already worked successfully with Bela Lugosi on a few projects and it was a happy collaboration. Thus, Bela not only agreed to the hiring of Beaudine, he encouraged it. Of course Beaudine was also known for his ability to handle comedians, so that would jibe well with Mitchell and Petrillo. Finally, the screenplay for *Bela Lugosi Meets a Brooklyn Gorilla* was being written by Tim Ryan, who wrote for The Bowery Boys movies and had been working comfortably with Beaudine as well.

The reason this movie, of all the films Beaudine directed, gets its own chapter, is because it really can't fit in any other category. It stands alone as one of the most bizarre low budget films in the annals of B movies. Some have called it one of the worst movies ever made. Others have embraced it as a cult item. While it is by no means a great movie, it is not the worst, and it benefits significantly from Beaudine's direction.

It isn't clear how few days it took to shoot *Bela Lugosi Meets a Brooklyn Gorilla*. Research indicates anywhere from six days to nine days, which is roughly the same amount of time it took Beaudine to helm a Bowery Boys feature. And the budget has been claimed to be anywhere from $12,000 to $100,000. Bela Lugosi, suffering from morphine addiction at the time, was said to be pleasant and friendly on the set, and comfortable with Beaudine's direction. Mitchell and Petrillo, when they didn't rely so completely on mimicking Martin and Lewis, and settled into the narrative as actors, come off reasonably well despite having limited skills and being in their first movie. Both also benefited from Beaudine's guidance and patience. Finally, William Beaudine's genius for shooting to make the budget look higher was an asset.

Mitchell and Petrillo play nightclub comics who crash on a jungle island en route to a gig entertaining the troops in Guam. Nona, a native girl, tries to help the duo get off the island, introducing them to Dr. Zabor. Zabor is in love with Nona, who also has designs on Mitchell. To get him out of the way, Zabor turns Mitchell into a gorilla.

Much has been made about Petrillo's annoying mimicking of Jerry Lewis, but he actually comes off best when he gets away from that imitation. He is a silly, amusing presence in a low budget horror comedy not unlike Huntz Hall in the Bowery Boys features. Duke Mitchell, however, is not only a far cry from the talent and presence of Dean Martin, his two song numbers are pretty awful. Dean Martin's smooth style as both a singer and an actor, his ability to make a great deal out of his role as Jerry Lewis's partner, is nowhere to be found in Duke Mitchell's performance.

What makes the film work at any level at all is Beaudine's approach to the material. The limited indoor trappings really do look like a low budget jungle set, Beaudine knowing how to choose the right camera angles to make what little he has to work with most effective. Along with being able to reach Lugosi during a real low ebb in the actor's life and career, he was able to take the limited skills and inexperience of Mitchell and Petrillo and make it work as well as it does. Beaudine doesn't just point the camera and print the first take without any ideas or approach. Even when Mitchell is warbling his lousy song numbers, Beaudine cuts from close-up, to medium shot, to reaction shots of Charlita, playing Nona. He offers a nice visual contrast of the actors in native garb with a suit-clad Lugosi sitting cross-legged in the hut with them.

There is a delightful absurdity when Lugosi strolls in formal attire, and a cane, through the jungle with his native manservant (played by Mickey Simpson).

Beaudine uses darkness effectively to disguise the cheapness of the set's background. He tracks his actors, holds his shots to let the dialog carry the narrative, and uses a nice succession of shots to enhance the comedy. It all works effectively as good low budget B-level cinema for which William Beaudine was an expert.

However, because the Martin and Lewis movies are enduring classics, this film comes off as a cheap imitation with a comedian who isn't as funny, and a straight man who is pretty awful at every level. Viewers balk at the comparison and don't accept the film on its own merit. Conversely, *Bela Lugosi Meets a Brooklyn Gorilla* has generated a cult following because of how much worse it is than any Martin and Lewis movie. There are those who celebrate badness for its own sake and embrace the film at that level. Truly, the film is a mildly amusing trifle among low budget cinema of the post-war era and nothing better or worse.

Perhaps the most interesting thing about *Bela Lugosi Meets a Brooklyn Gorilla* is the story of its production. Jerry Lewis told this author:

> Oh god, Duke Mitchell and Sammy Petrillo! I created my own monsters! I remember Dean and I were aware of what they were doing in some of the smaller clubs. But they didn't go beyond that so we didn't pay a lot of attention. Then we found out they were going to make a movie. Dean said to me, "we have to stop these guys." They were stealing our act. We weren't going to let that happen. Dean was never confrontational so I went to see Jack Broder and gave him hell. Then Hal Wallis went to see him and gave him hell. But they made and released the movie anyway. It wasn't successful at all, but you'd be surprised at how many people have told me how much they liked the movie Dean and I made with Bela Lugosi! Well, we never made a movie with Lugosi. So I say to those people, "my god, you can't tell the difference?" (laughs)

What happened was, Jack Broder offered to allow Hal Wallis and Paramount Pictures to buy the film and destroy it. He wanted more than the amount of the film's budget. Wallis refused and eventually their talks broke down. Not wanting to take a complete loss, Broder had to release the film.

Duke Mitchell told interviewer Bill Cappello in a 1980 interview that he believes the lawsuit was planned all along:

> I think the concept was to get involved in a lawsuit in the first place, then sell it back to Martin and Lewis and Paramount for big numbers. A lawsuit was filed while we were shooting the picture so I figure Broder tried to sell out to Paramount and they told him, "we don't want it." His asking price must have been too high.

Bela Lugosi Meets a Brooklyn Gorilla played a few neighborhood theaters like a lot of B product at the time. While a series was considered, Mitchell and Petrillo made no other films together. In 1954, Broder re-released the film under the title *The Boys from Brooklyn*, but it played even fewer theaters than before.

Critic Seraphino Alaimo reviewed *Bela Lugosi Meets a Brooklyn Gorilla* for the *New York Daily News*, stating:[36]

> In *Bela Lugosi Meets a Brooklyn Gorilla*.we're introduced to a couple, Duke Mitchell and Sammy Petrillo, who are an outrageous imitation of the comedians, Dean Martin and Jerry Lewis. Just in case some faithful fans of the famous pair might be tempted to compare the teams, don't waste your time. The comedy presents Petrillo and Mitchell performing their pranks against a jungle background, replete with a tribal chief, some sorry looking natives and a beautiful native princess. In addition, they've thrown in Bela Lugosi as the mad scientist. A character one is very likely to meet in the bongo-bongo country. Come to think of it, Ramona the chimp was the only authentic actor among the crew.

---

36 Bela Lugosi Meets a Brooklyn Gorilla. *New York Daily News*. September 2, 1952

The lawsuit generated a lot of publicity in the trades, and that killed the Mitchell and Petrillo partnership. Nightclubs became reticent about booking the act, fearing that Martin and Lewis would never consider playing there if they did. So Duke and Sammy pursued separate careers.

Legend has it that while Martin Landau was preparing for his Oscar-winning role as Bela Lugosi in Tim Burton's film *Ed Wood*, he screened *Bela Lugosi Meets a Brooklyn Gorilla* more than once, stating: "It makes Ed Wood's actual films look like *Gone With The Wind*."

And there is a bit of final irony regarding Jerry Lewis as well. In an appearance on television's *Today* show, an interview with Lewis opened with several clips of him appearing on that same network, NBC's, *Colgate Comedy Hour*. Except one of the clips featured not Jerry, but Sammy Petrillo. An amused Lewis pointed this out to humiliated host Bryant Gumbel stating, "I was never that good looking."

Trade ad for Bela Lugosi Meets a Brooklyn Gorilla.

Trade ad promoting a showing of the movie and an appearance by Mitchell and Petrillo, using the Martin and Lewis lawsuit as publicity.

Bela Lugosi ignores a mugging Sammy Petrillo.

RELIGIOUS AND EXPLOITATION FILMS

William Beaudine was already comfortably working outside of the Hollywood establishment in the profitable B movies for poverty row studios, when he accepted an offer to venture further away. Exploitation producer Kroger Babb needed someone seasoned and efficient to helm his independent feature *Mom and Dad*, and was delighted when Beaudine accepted the job and agreed to finish the film in six days.

Kroger Babb had been a busy, active individual even from childhood. He even appeared in *Ripley's Believe it or Not* for having refereed a record number of sporting events. He worked as a sportswriter before being hired as a publicity man at a local theater. His stunts to promote the movies increased attendance greatly, even if the movie itself wasn't very good. So he built upon that and joined the Cox and Underwood company that was notable for making controversial movies about then taboo subjects. Cox and Underwood made so much money on their film *High School Girl*, with the help of Babb's promotion, they both retired. Babb then started his own company, Hygienic productions. *Mom and Dad* was produced in 1945 and because of its controversial topic resulting in lawsuits wherever it played (over 400 total), it became one of the most popular films of the 1940s.

Mom and Dad deals with a young girl whose parents never gave her any information about sex and sexuality, so she gets involved with a boy and succumbs to his charm. The result is a pregnancy, which she keeps quiet while the boy is away on business for his father's company. The boy dies, and the girl must face her dilemma alone.

With a cast that was filled out by veteran supporting actors like George Eldredge, Hardie Albright, and Lois Austin in the cast, and an old hand at low budget quickies like William Beaudine at the helm, *Mom and Dad* comes off as a regular Hollywood B production. The only difference is its subject matter, which was a big taboo at the time. They would refer to the situation as "personal hygiene," and anything lurid was dismissed by publicity as having a concluding moral that is against pre-marital teenage sex.

Kroger Babb sold the film as a roadshow attraction, where theaters would pay a specific price to run the film. Lawsuits in various cities caused the film to generate more publicity and interest, with Babb losing only three of the over-400 cases that made it to court. It became the third highest grossing film of the entire decade of the 1940s, returning, to its investors, $63 for every dollar invested. William Beaudine's connection to the film as a director was to guide the actors, some of whom he'd worked with on other projects, and complete the film with patience and efficiency. His professionalism is shown via his choice of shots to enhance the drama. He was comfortable with using Marcel Le Picard as his cinematographer, someone he'd worked with on many other films.

But the true success of *Mom and Dad* was the promotional events surrounding its release. According to John Wooley for *The Land*:[37]

> Each screening of Mom and Dad featured the live appearance of a lecturer, whose job involved a frank little talk, winding up with a pitch for booklets that explained sex-related topics in easy-to-understand terms. The newspaper ad for its Oklahoma City premiere noted that the lecture topic was "Secrets of Sensible Sex," to be given at each performance of the movie by "Radio's Hygiene Commentator Elliot Forbes."

Of course several different people played this "Elliot Forbes" throughout the nation's screenings of the films.

One of Babb's publicity ideas for *Mom and Dad* was to segregate his audiences. In many markets, the film would be shown for men only on one night and for women only on the other night. This simply added to the offbeat interest in this unusual production.

When Kroger Babb changed his company's name to Hallmark and switched to religious movies with *The Lawton Story*, he sought Beaudine's help again. Apparently, footage that was already shot

---

37 Wooley, John. "Jesus in the Witchitas" *This Land*, Vol. 5, Issue 7, April 1, 2014.

in color of passion plays was utilized with newly shot footage helmed by Beaudine and featuring character actor Forrest Taylor, whose career dated back to the silent era. Taylor had appeared in scores of westerns, usually as the bad guy. Babb also brought in a 6 year old girl named Ginger Prince. Ginger was Babb's protege and she was billed as "the next Shirley Temple." Babb associate David F. Friedman told John Wooley:[38]

> (Ginger's) father was named Hugh Prince, and he was a booker for a little four-house (movie theater) circuit out of Toccoa, Georgia. Hugh was a nice little guy, but Ginger's mother was the stage mother of all time. From the time this child was conceived, her mother had ideas of grandeur for her. Every year, from the time she was three until she was six or seven, Ginger Prince was the featured attraction for the banquet of the Georgia-Alabama Theater Owners Association, and she did all of the Shirley Temple routine -- "The Good Ship Lollipop," all that. And she was awful. Of course, Kroger knows all about her, so he signs this little girl to a big Hollywood contract.

Ginger Prince was signed to do 15 feature films, but only appeared in two more exploitation movies and then left, because she wanted a normal childhood. And she did, enjoying an ordinary life as a successful high school student, which included cheerleading. When she was an adult, she returned to acting, and performed in over 80 plays, including on Broadway. She died in 2015.

The Lawton Story was a hit at its premiere, but flopped in general release. So, Kroger Babb gathered his thoughts, retitled it *The Prince of Peace*, and it succeeded slightly better, but it was nowhere near the success *Mom and Dad* had been. According to the trades, William Beaudine was set to direct Babb's exploitation movie *One Too Many* which deals with alcoholism, and once again features Ginger Prince. But somehow things must have broken down, because Erle C. Kenton is the credited director.

---

38   Wooley, John. "Jesus in the Witchitas" *This Land*, Vol. 5, Issue 7, April 1, 2014.

Beaudine's work on *The Lawton Story* was noticed by producer Paul F. Heard who made films for the Protestant Film Commission. He hired Beaudine to direct *Again... Pioneers*, which was another religious drama with a positive message. Although Beaudine was not a religious man himself, he was able to guide the cast that included such familiar names as Colleen Townsend, Tom Powers, Regis Toomey, Sarah Padden, Evelyn Brent, and Jimmy Hunt. These films were used for church screenings, but still managed to hire decent B stars, a top B director, and pay them well. Beaudine continued directing films for Paul F. Heard whenever he was between jobs. His other religious-based films include *The Congregation, For Every Child, The Hidden Heart, The Beginning,* and *Each According to His Faith*.

William Beaudine thrived on work, so if he could get jobs between assignments on his Bowery Boys features, he always took them. This was especially true when Huntz Hall complained about a dangerous scene he had to do in the film *Jalopy* and requested a new director to replace Beaudine. While Edward Bernds was directing Bowery Boys films, Beaudine branched off into other projects at Monogram studios, freelanced at the other studios, did an exploitation film, and a few religious movies. This is why he was too busy to return to the Bowery Boys series when Hall realized he acted impulsively and preferred working with Beaudine over Bernds. Now it was the Bowery Boys features that he accepted between assignments. But after directing them in *Jail Busters* (1955) he was far too busy to direct anymore until a couple years later when Leo Gorcey left the series and they needed Beaudine to helm a couple of films with Huntz Hall in the lead, so they could fulfill Hall's contract.

What made William Beaudine busier is the continued popularity of television. First investigating TV by doing some directing for the small screen as early as 1953, Beaudine decided to expand his workload and do more in this new medium. His efficiency, patience with actors, openness to creative expression, and general friendly demeanor lent itself well to television. It was also a very fast paced production situation and Beaudine was very good at working under pressure.

Although he was long past expecting a steady gig at one of the majors, being able to helm big budget productions, or win any awards, William Beaudine was firmly established as a top level B movie director. This prepared him for television much better than working at the bigger studios would. He now set out to be a top level TV director as well.

Kroger Babb with Ginger Prince.

Trade ad for Mom and Dad *showing segregated audiences.*

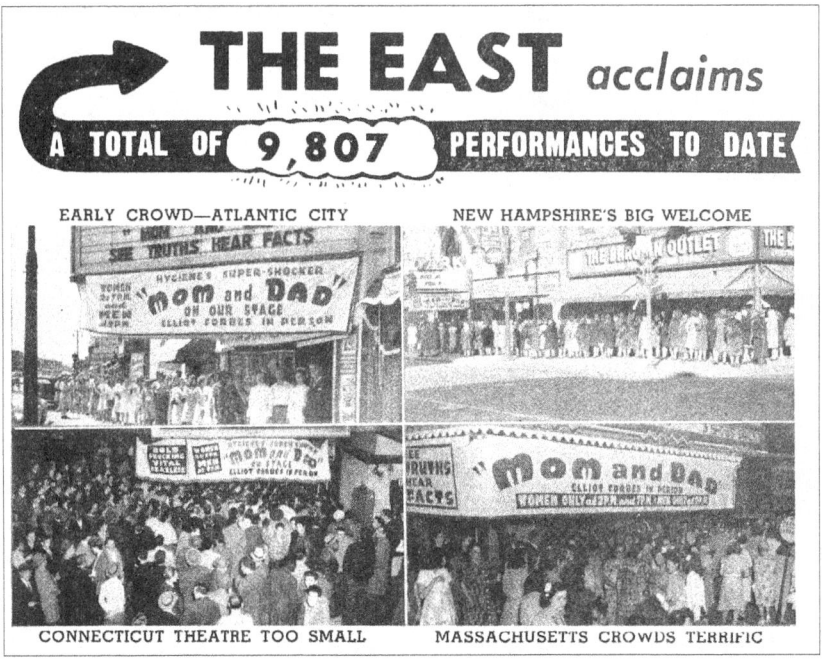

Trade ad promoting the success of Mom and Dad.

INVESTIGATING 1950s TELEVISION

While the concept of television dates back to the 1920s, the pivotal year for TV was 1948. Before that, it was a series of experiments, and, by around 1940, a luxury item that projected Presidential addresses and sporting events. In 1940, a new car cost around $1000. A TV cost nearly $700. The idea of spending that much money on a luxury item when there was little being broadcast seemed silly to most Americans. However, by the end of the war, there was a strong effort by the three radio networks - CBS, ABC, and NBC - to make commercial television a reality. More shows were broadcast, more TV's were produced, making them more affordable. But it still had not taken off with middle America.

On June 8, 1948, NBC hired comedian Milton Berle to host his own TV show, *The Texaco Star Theater*, and it was such a sensation, by the end of that year there were a quarter million televisions in American households. This caused more radio comedians to start TV shows, including Jack Benny and Red Skelton. The Colgate Comedy Hour was a variety show that rotated hosts like Abbott and Costello and Martin and Lewis.

By the dawn of 1950, television was certainly becoming a major force in culture. Filmed shows had joined news events, sporting events, and the comedy and variety programs. Dramas, situation comedies, and westerns soon proliferated, especially after the premiere of *The Cisco Kid* in 1950 and *I Love Lucy* in 1951.

At first, the bigger studios saw television as a threat, and refused to allow even their older movies to be played on TV. The smaller studios, however, saw TV as a way for their older movies to generate more income. Of course the big studios eventually came around (and even produced some TV shows later on), but, for instance William Beaudine's 1942 Monogram feature *The Phantom Killer* was on TV as early as 1947, while *Casablanca*, which came out that same year didn't get on TV until 1956.

Too busy with his film projects to get into TV right away, by 1951 William Beaudine was given the opportunity to direct some episodes of the new drama series *Racket Squad*. Even some two-reel producers and directors found television to be daunting. For instance, Jules White, who headed Columbia Pictures' shorts department, responsible for The Three Stooges and other comedy shorts, directed only one episode of the Wierre Brothers TV show *Oh Those Bells,* and quit, stating "who needs such a rat race." William Beaudine, however, adapted well to television production. Recalling his having to complete a silent short comedy in only one day, and noted for his efficiency, Beaudine responded to the tight TV production schedules and his work in the small medium soon became as sought after as in B movies.

Racket Squad was a dramatic anthology series that began with Captain John Braddock (Reed Hadley) introducing a case, and then narrating it as it played out with actors. He would open with the dialog, "What you are about to see is a real-life story, taken from the files of the police racket and bunco squads, business protective associations and similar sources around the country. It is intended to expose the confidence game - the carefully worked-out frauds by which confidence men take more money each year from the American public than all the bank robbers and thugs with their violence." The episodes concluded with Hadley marking the case folder with a rubber stamp that indicated "Case Closed," and stating, "I'm closing this case now - or rather, the courts will - but there'll be others, because that's the way the world is built. There are people who can slap you on the back with one hand and pick your pocket with the other. And it could happen to you." Beaudine actually directed a few of the intro and outro segments while not directing the actual body of the episode, whereas in other cases he would direct the narrative but not the intro-outro. And, sometimes he would direct both.

William Beaudine was not the series' only director for *Racket Squad*. The show was produced by the Hal Roach studios, which had gotten into TV production early, first in syndication (in 1950) and then for the CBS network from 1951-1953. Beaudine directed a lot of the episodes during this two year period. Hal Roach jr, who was in charge of the studio's TV production, was pleased at the many seasoned B directors who were available and interested in exploring television. It makes sense that so many B movie directors would have success in television. Many B movies ran about an hour in length, which isn't much longer than most TV episodes.

Westerns because exceptionally popular on TV during its early years. Many of the low budget B westerns found their way to television as early as the late 1940s, and William Boyd, who starred as Hopalong Cassidy, spent his life savings on securing all rights to the character and created a new Hopalong Cassidy TV series in 1947. Boyd was a shrewd businessman, exploiting his character by marketing drinking glasses, lunch boxes, T-shirts, and other such items. Then, when the Jimmy Stewart movie *Winchester 73* was released in 1950, westerns became popular once again on the big screen. TV westerns at this time were most marketed to youngsters, the Hopalong Cassidy idea inspiring similar shows like *The Lone Ranger* and *The Cisco Kid*.

One of the popular western TV series was *The Adventures of Wild Bill Hickok*, featuring handsome movie leading man Guy Madison as the title character with long time supporting actor Andy Devine as his sidekick Jingles. This series premiered in 1951 and lasted until the end of the decade. Madison and Devine liked each other and liked the roles they were playing, so they enjoyed the steady work the series provided. It was sponsored by Kellogg's cereals, which resulted in marketing similar to what William Boyd had succeeded in doing with Hopalong Cassidy. William Beaudine directed around 13 of the 112 episodes produced, all of them in 1953. This series was an especially rewarding project for Beaudine, as his son, William Beaudine jr., was the assistant director, and it was produced by Wesley Barry, a child actor Beaudine had worked with in the silent era.

Directing westerns for television was particularly daunting in that there was a great deal of location filmmaking, using standing westerns sets from older movies at various outdoor locations. The time it took to move the equipment, and the actors, took away production time, sometimes leaving Beaudine only a couple of days to shoot an entire western story. This is where his past experience with silent shorts came in especially handy. Another assistant director, Bob Rosenbaum, told Wendy Marshall:[39]

> He had a wonderful way about him, and he was much loved by the cast and crew. Guy Madison and Andy Devine just loved him. It was just a well-groomed and organized company. Everyone was delighted to come to work because Bill made the show so pleasant.

While continuing to direct movies, including a sporadic return to the Bowery Boys series, William Beaudine remained active in television, helming episodes of *Broken Arrow, Naked City, Circus Boy,* and *The Adventures of Rin Tin Tin.*

William Beaudine had caught the attention of independent producer Bert Leonard, who was behind several TV series. After Beaudine's success directing several episodes the children-oriented circus adventure *Circus Boy* (featuring a young Micky Dolenz, later of The Monkees, in the title role), Leonard hired Beaudine to helm *The Adventures of Rin Tin Tin.* Directing over 20 episodes of this popular series, Beaudine had now garnered the same strong reputation in television as he had established in movies. Because he was now past 60 and one of the older directors active in TV production, the crew and actors gave him affectionate nicknames like Pops or Pappy, which Beaudine enjoyed. He always corrected anyone addressing him as Mr. Beaudine, preferring to be called by his first name.

In 1958, Bert Leonard sent William Beaudine to New York to direct a handful of episodes for his series *The Naked City*, which was shot on location in the Big Apple. It was a much more sophisticated drama series than Beaudine was used to directing, and New York TV crews were often more literate in their approach. There was even an underlying prejudice against California directors. Beaudine, however, was quite successful, winning over the crew with his experience and his approach. He returned to California after spending several months directing in New York.

---

39 Marshall, Wendy L. *William Beaudine: From Silents to Television.* Lanham, MD. Scarecrow Press. 2002

While he was enjoying continued success directing B movies and enjoying success in the new medium of television, William Beaudine came up with a story that he felt would be perfect for Walt Disney. Disney had just gotten into TV production and Beaudine sought a meeting with the producer. He got one.

Reed Hadley was the star of Racket Squad.

Andy Devine as Jingles and Guy Madison as Wild Bill Hickock.

BEAUDINE AND DISNEY

William Beaudine's timing could not have been more perfect when he met with Walt Disney in 1955 just after finishing work on the Bowery Boys feature *Jail Busters* over at Monogram. Disney had gotten into weekly television production in 1954, after a few experiments dating as far back as 1950. Disney mostly did weekly series like *Disneyland* and ran clips from his features in an effort to use TV to promote them.

In the Spring of 1955, Disney was busily producing a children's variety show, *The Mickey Mouse Club* which he planned to premiere that Fall. Hosted by actor-songwriter-musician Jimmie Dodd and staff artist Roy Williams, the show featured a group of talented boys and girls who sang, danced, acted in skits, and introduced vintage Disney cartoons.

Disney also arranged for a series featuring his young Mouseketeers to air episodically. William Beaudine was hired to direct *The Adventures of Spin and Marty* due to his long history working with young people and also his ability to get things done quickly as per the pace of TV production. The short films had a $600,000 budget, so Beaudine was to use the Golden Oak Ranch, where the episodes were shot, and open up the visuals. Disney was pleased when viewing the rushes. Actor Harry Carey jr, who appeared in the series, recalled in an interview with Charles Tranberg, "Bill Beaudine was one of those old-time directors who liked to get the job done quickly and efficiently. I liked him. He knew what he wanted and was thoroughly prepared."

While in production with the Spin and Marty shorts, William Beaudine met with Walt Disney and pitched a story about a girl and her dog, entitled *Corky and the White Shadow*. Disney bought the story on the spot and gave Beaudine a 12 week shooting schedule. He thought it would be a perfect episodic series for *The Mickey Mouse Club*, along with *The Adventures of Spin and Marty*. When production finished on the Spin and Marty shorts,

Beaudine began filming *Corky and the White Shadow*, which premiered on *The Mickey Mouse Club* in February of 1956, after *The Adventures of Spin and Marty* had run its course.

When hired for *The Mickey Mouse Club*, each of the young cast members did a screen test to determine if they'd be effective in narrative drama. Beaudine chose fourteen year old Darlene Gillespie to star as Corky. Her co-star was Buddy Ebsen, who was currently appearing in Disney's very popular *Davy Crockett* TV series, but was a few years away from his career defining role as Jed Clampett on television's *The Beverly Hillbillies*.

Corky and the White Shadow is the story of a teenaged girl and her dog getting mixed up in a robbery, much to the chagrin of her sheriff father. At one point, during a ten-day shoot on location at Big Bear Lake in California, a scene where a tied-up Corky is confronted by a rattlesnake put Darlene Gillespie in a scary situation. The scene called for the snake to be shot before it struck, but the snake lunged at the girl during the first take. Darlene would recall that although the poison venom was removed from the snake, it was still terrifying.[40]

The Corky series was not as popular as Spin and Marty had been, mostly because it came second. But it was popular enough, and Walt Disney was pleased with the results. Disney decided to film new Spin and Marty episodes, called *The Further Adventures of Spin and Marty* with Beaudine at the helm, and also pegged Beaudine to direct a new ambitious project. Walt Disney wanted to make a live action feature length western movie for family audiences. He chose the novel *Children of the Covered Wagon* by Mary Jane Carr, and hired Tom Blackburn to write the screenplay. Blackburn had been writing scripts for Disney's *Davy Crockett* series for television and seemed like the perfect choice to adapt Carr's book.

As preparations were underway for the western feature, Beaudine traveled to Wisconsin with Disney actors Sammy Ogg, Annette Funicello, Tommy Cole, and Kevin Corcoran to film *Adventures in Dairy*, a series where the Disney kids visit a Verona

---

40 "Disney Films New TV Series at Big Bear Lake." *The San Bernardino County Sun.* October 10, 1955

dairy farm and are shown how it is run. Produced with the cooperation of the American Dairy Association, *Adventures in Dairy* was an eight episode segment for *The Mickey Mouse Club* during the 1956-1957 series, after which Disney sold the rights to the American Dairy Association, who distributed it to schools as an educational film.

An article in the June 17, 1956 issue of the *Wisconsin State Journal* discussed the filming in nearby Verona, Wisconsin, offering some insight into Beaudine's approach to directing the segments:

> To tell the story takes 55 persons from Hollywood and about 65 persons from the Madison area. When you get such a group of people on one dairy farm, it is perhaps a little difficult to determine just what kind of production is going to result. But the guiding genius of a tall, lanky director, William Beaudine, puts all the seeming confusion into a logical pattern of rehearsal and scene shooting that does have the realism of just what would happen on a farm. Beaudine, a man who practically lives each role in the scene he is getting to perfection, had the principles of the movie make at least six exits from the house for one scene before he was satisfied with the timing, conversation, and acting.

Articles like these, now read as history, help put to rest the claim that Beaudine only shot one take.

William Beaudine then began shooting *Children of the Covered Wagon*, which was eventually retitled *Westward Ho, The Wagons*. This was a much more expensive production than the Monogram B movies he had been helming. This feature was a Cinemascope and Technicolor production. Its cast included Fess Parker, who had scored with Disney in the *Davy Crockett* series, Kathleen Crowley, Jeff York, Sebastian Cabot, and George Reeves, then popular as TV's Superman.

Several popular Mouseketeers had small roles in the film, including Cubby O'Brien, Karen Pendelton, and Tommy Cole, along with David Stollery from *The Adventures of Spin and Marty*. Beaudine was disappointed when Darlene Gillespie became ill and was unable to appear in the film as George Reeves' daughter. She was replaced by fellow Mouseketeer Doreen Tracy.

Beaudine was quite pleased that Disney spent the money to borrow Yakima Canut from MGM to work as his assistant director. This became a problem when the Indian attack set to appear in the film was about to be staged by Canut who had years of experience in this area. Disney wanted nobody killed in the scene so as not to upset children attending the movie. Canut protested, but to no avail. He shot the scene as ordered. However, when Disney saw the rushes, he agreed that without anyone killed it looked phony, so he ordered retakes, despite the expense involved.

Westward Ho, The Wagons was unusual in that it wasn't a linear narrative throughout, but was instead a series of episodes within the framework of a feature film, probably with the intention of serializing them for television later. It was also believed that the changing stories all within the same context would keep children from becoming bored.

A syndicated columnist visited the set of *Westward Ho, The Wagons* and had this to say:[41]

> An Indian attack minutes away when I arrive on the set. Director William Beaudine is shooting the scene inside one of the big sound stages at the Walt Disney studio. It is dusk on the old Oregon trail. A group of covered wagons has been drawn up in a circle to await the first onslaught of a Pawnee war party. In the background a cyclo-rama creates a realistic illusion that the wagon train has been trapped in a valley surrounded by rolling hills. The Indians are somewhere out in the gathering darkness toward the hills. Director Beaudine has his camera focused upon a single wagon to catch a tense moment between Fess Parker, Kathleen Crowley and boy actor David Stollery. Fess lifts Kathleen up to the seat of the wagon and tells her to get In the back and lie prone. Then he turns to the boy, who is lugging a rifle almost as long as he Is. "Better

---

41 "With Fess Parker on the Westward Ho Set" *Lancaster Eagle-Gazette*. February 20, 1956

leave the fighting to men," he says. "But I am the man of this wagon," argues the boy. Fess gives him a long look. "I guess you are," he concedes. He takes the rifle and shows the boy how to exert the leverage to cock it. "Stand over here behind this wheel," he orders, "and keep your finger off that trigger until you mean business." Director Beaudine decides to try a take. In the middle of it, he calls for a cut. "Fess," he says, 'don't hesitate quite so long. I think you should be more under pressure." They try another, and Fess gets tangled up with the rifle. The next time, he omits a line. On the fourth try, everything is going fine until a chicken in a crate hung from the bottom of the wagon sticks its head through the slats, faces the camera and goes: "Ka, Ka, Ka, Ka, Ka!" "Oh, shut up," shouts Beaudine. Finally, they get the shot. "Isn't this the first picture you don't get killed in?" I ask Fess. "I'm not supposed to," he drawls, "but if I keep on messing up takes like that, they may do it to me after all."

With the expanse of widescreen cinematography and sharp Technicolor, *Westward Ho, The Wagons* is one of the most impressive productions in William Beaudine's long career. Variety stated in their review: "Cinemascope treatment allows a vast panorama against which to limn the simple, yet stirring, narrative, and there's the marquee lure of Fess Parker for the younger trade particularly."[42] Harrison's Reports wrote, "Set against highly impressive outdoor backgrounds and beautifully photographed in CinemaScope and Technicolor, this Walt Disney live-action western should go over well with the family trade, particularly the youngsters, for children play an important part in the proceedings."[43]

With a cast that included popular Mouseketeers, TV's Davy Crockett, and TV's Superman, *Westward Ho, The Wagons* was guaranteed to be a box office success. The Disney name also

---

42 Westward Ho the Wagons". *Variety*. December 19, 1956

43 "'Westward Ho the Wagons' with Fess Parker and Kathleen Crowley". *Harrison's Reports*. December 29, 1956

helped secure top bookings. Released at the end of 1956, it became one of the top grossing films of 1957.

In 1958, William Beaudine busied himself with other TV assignments, and helped wrap up the Bowery Boys series by directing their last two films. In 1959 he was summoned back to the Disney studios to direct *Moochie of the Little League* featuring Kevin Corcoran, whom Beaudine cited as the best young actor he'd ever worked with --- pretty high praise for a man who'd been directing children since the silent era. Kevin Corcoran recalled for Wendy Marshall how effectively Beaudine would help him through any especially emotional scenes:[44]

> He would talk you through stuff like that. He would come in and explain to you, in little people terms, what was going on, what my mindset would be, what the environment should be, and how the emotions should be. Then he would get you through it.

Corcoran also recalled how much William Beaudine would praise him for a job well done:

> You'd think you had won the Irish Sweepstakes. He would be turning cartwheels he was so happy. He was very affectionate, very emotional, and he would get emotion from you like you couldn't believe.

William Beaudine celebrated his 50th year in the movie industry while directing this series, and was given a party on the set. Buddy Mason's syndicated "Behind The Movie Sets" column discussed the event:[45]

> When young William Beaudine started working in the motion picture industry he hoped it would offer steady employment. As director William Beaudine, he celebrated his 50th anniversary in the business this July. And, from all indications, he can expect the job to offer regular

---

44 Marshall, Wendy L. *William Beaudine: From Silents to Television.* Lanham, MD. Scarecrow Press. 2002

45 Behind The Movie Sets with Buddy Mason. *The Algona Upper Des Moines.* July 30, 1959

employment! The cast and crew of the Walt Disney telefilm, *Moochie of the Little League,* for the 1959-60 season of ABC TV's Walt Disney Presents which Beaudine is currently directing, honored him with a surprise party on the set. Bill Beaudine began his career at The Biograph Studio in July 1909. He started as a "general helper," sweeping up the sets, getting coffee and sandwiches for the actors and crews and moving cameras around the makeshift stages for the famed D. W. Griffith. Kevin Corcoran presented William Beaudine with a gold tinted megaphone "from Moochie and the gang." and William H. Henderson, Vice President-Studio Operations, represented the Disney Studio in honoring the veteran director. Also attending the anniversary were stars Stu Erwin, Alan Hale, Frances Rafferty, and Jim L. Brown. During the past half-century, director Beaudine has lent his talents to a wide variety of film productions. His versatility is attested to by a long credit list of comedies, dramas, documentaries, westerns, serials, mysteries action features, period pictures, historical films, and just about any kind of film you can mention.

Walt Disney continued to be pleased with William Beaudine's work and assigned him to direct another western feature, *Ten Who Dared,* about the first exploration of the Colorado River, led by one-armed John Wesley Powell. It starred John Beal as Powell, along with Brian Keith, James Drury, Ben Johnson, and L.Q. Jones. Disney sold it as an authentic version of the events, but, as with most Disney productions of that era, it is a rather sugarcoated look at the history. Sadly, it is frequently cited as one of the worst movies made by Walt Disney studios. In his book *The Disney Films,* Leonard Maltin stated:

> *Ten Who Dared* is rock bottom Disney. In fact, it's hard to think of another Disney film so totally bad. Even a winning team (and this certainly was) is entitled to a few losses. But it's still difficult to understand how they could miss the mark so completely.

It is not known if the fact that *Ten Who Dared* turned out to be a weak movie was the reason Beaudine no longer directed for Disney after its release. Beaudine still had plenty of work, and his experienced direction continued to be sought. He did not realize that the 1960s would be his final decade.

William Beaudine continued with movie and television work throughout the 1960s. Two of his most notorious features were a couple of low budget efforts for producer Carroll Case that combined the horror and western genres. They were as offbeat and unusual as *Bela Lugosi Meets a Brooklyn Gorilla* had been, except this was 14 years later so even low budget films were often in color and were shot in widescreen. The very titles of *Billy The Kid Versus Dracula* and *Jesse James Meets Frankenstein's Daughter* seem too unusual to be actual movies. But they were. And they were also to be William Beaudine's final theatrical films.

BILLY THE KID VERSUS DRACULA & JESSE JAMES MEETS FRANKENSTEIN'S DAUGHTER

When producer Carroll Case, through Joseph Levine's Circle Productions, set up a couple of super low budget films that combined elements of the horror and western genres, he knew William Beaudine would be the perfect director. His efficiency was a factor in that each feature length film was to be shot in eight days. Also, he was well known and well liked by most of the B-level actors in Hollywood and could easily assemble a cast. Finally, he was without pretension, and would be willing to lend his name to these projects, despite their being crafted very quickly and with practically no budget in order to sell as a Drive-In double feature.

In June of 1965, William Beaudine began filming *Billy The Kid Versus Dracula*. He managed to secure the services of John Carradine for the Dracula role, Carradine having played the Count in the Universal classics *House of Frankenstein* (1944) and *House of Dracula* (1945). Harry Carey jr, whom Beaudine had worked with on the Spin and Marty series at Disney, signed on, as did his mother Olive Carey. Other familiar names included Virginia Christine, Roy Barcroft, and Charlita, all of whom had worked with Beaudine on other projects. Beaudine wisely chose former stuntman Chuck Courtney as Billy The Kid, his experience allowing him to exhibit the sort of adept horsemanship necessary for certain scenes.

When considering the circumstances -- a ridiculously low budget and an eight day shooting schedule -- *Billy the Kid Versus Dracula* is better than it should be. Taking advantage of the wide screen image and the colorful location cinematography, Beaudine puts together a remarkably handsome looking production that belies its budget. The special effects are mostly nil, with a rubber bat on strings and a red light beaming against a closeup of Carradine's menacing face, but then the visual imagery of Dracula unable to be seen in a reflection and his eventual fade into skeletal remains are comparatively impressive.

Essentially a horror film set in a western backdrop, *Billy The Kid Versus Dracula* plays mostly as a western with actors who are more noted for the genre, and conflicts that adhere to the western movie clichés (a reformed outlaw, conflict between ranch hands over a girl, an Indian attack). Dracula comes to town and convinces everyone that he is the uncle of a beautiful young girl, but his actions, and the accusations of some travelers, arouse suspicion in her boyfriend, the reformed gunslinger Billy the Kid. The narrative is simple and maintains viewer interest, while the cast play their roles earnestly, letting the story, title, and low budget represent the campiness. While Carradine would later claim this to be the worst movie in which he appeared (it isn't, by a longshot), he chews the scenery with gusto, making his oddball Dracula as outrageous as the original concept.

Billy the Kid Versus Dracula has enjoyed a certain cult status in the annals of bad movies, but it is the sort of bad movie that is nevertheless fun in a disarming manner. Olive Carey rises to the occasion in her small part as the town doctor, exhibiting a brashness and toughness that perfectly befits a seasoned veteran of such westerns as *The Searchers* and *Gunfight at the O.K. Corral*. Carey's career dates back to the early silent era. Roy Barcroft was elderly and overweight by the time he essayed the sheriff role in this movie, but he still offers a solid presence. Virginia Christine is delightfully flustered as one of the settlers who realizes Dracula's identity. And Melinda Casey as the central young blonde ingenue who nearly succumbs to Dracula's curse is competent for the role.

The same cult status has been given to *Jesse James Meets Frankenstein's Daughter*, although it isn't nearly as good. Shot on as low of a budget with as few shooting days, there is less opportunity for Beaudine to take advantage of the western settings. This film is also dotted with familiar western character actors, including Jim Davis, William Fawcett, and Nestor Paiva, but they don't have the same impact as those who appeared in *Billy The Kid Versus Dracula*.

First off, it is Dr. Frankenstein's granddaughter who figures prominently in this story, not his daughter. Jesse James is currently hiding out from a Marshall who is after him. He is traveling with a muscular, slow-witted friend, Hank Tracy. When Hank is wounded while the duo is evading a posse, they seek refuge at the only doctor in town, which is Maria Frankenstein, who works with her brother Rudolph. Maria decides to use Hank in her experiments, turning him into a powerful undead monster whom she names Igor. Perhaps the most interesting aspect of *Jesse James Meets Frankenstein's Daughter* is the use of Kenneth Stickfaden's laboratory equipment, which was also used in the original Frankenstein films, as well as TV's *The Munsters* and Mel Brooks' *Young Frankenstein*. *Jesse James Meets Frankenstein's Daughter* is one of the few times we get to see it in color.

Despite the western actors in the cast, *Jesse James Meets Frankenstein's Daughter* had much less of a western feel than *Billy the Kid Versus Dracula*. A lot of the action takes place in the Frankenstein home and lab which retains a lot of the gothic elements we typically associate with that concept. Perhaps the lack of a big name actor like John Carradine also made this film appear even more lackluster by comparison.

The films were paired up in the Spring of 1966 and released to the Drive-In movie theaters, running throughout the nation all summer long. Because of their low budget and campy titles, the pair of films turned an impressive profit, and were considered a success within the realm of period low budget cinema. Assistant producer Sam Manners told Wendy Marshall:[46]

> They were made for fun. Carroll Case felt Bill would do the best job on them and I'm sure they felt they could make money with them. Levine expected to clear more than $5 million on each film. This was not serious stuff and Pappy enjoyed every moment of it. Everybody did.

---

46 Marshall, Wendy L. *William Beaudine: From Silents to Television*. Lanham, MD. Scarecrow Press. 2002

These movies continued to enjoy campy popularity when released to home video, often with cheeky commentary as a special feature.

Jesse James Meets Frankenstein's Daughter has the distinction of being the last theatrical film directed by William Beaudine. He would continue to direct television until the end of the 1960s. Perhaps the tight shooting schedules forced Beaudine to actually have to rely on the first take on some scenes, and that likely caused latter day film buffs to assume he maintained that function throughout his long career, which is not at all accurate.

William Beaudine ended his career directing the *Lassie* TV series for many years, including several cast and storyline transitions. While directing *Lassie* he not only took time to direct the features mentioned here, but also a handful of *Green Hornet* TV episodes. This closed out his directorial career.

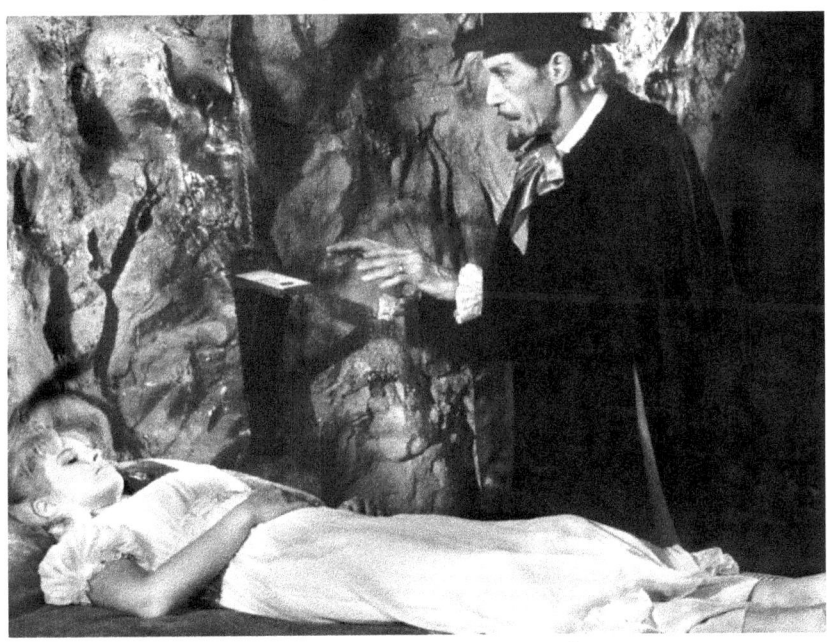

Melinda Casey and John Carradine.

Ad for Billy The Kid Versus Dracula.

Ad for Jesse James Meets Frankenstein's Daughter.

In many markets, the films were issued as a double feature.

LASSIE AND THE FINAL YEARS

The 1960s was William Beaudine's final decade directing films, and also his final decade in life. Along with the aforementioned efforts discussed in previous chapters, Beaudine also directed some 80 episodes of the TV series *Lassie*.

Lassie the collie dog was first depicted in Elizabeth Gaskell's short story *The Half Brothers"* in 1859, and further found its way into literature with Eric Knight's novel *Lassie Come Home* in 1940, which was later made into a 1943 MGM movie. A TV series began in 1954 with Tommy Rettig playing Jeff, Lassie's young owner and master, with Jan Clayton as his mother and veteran character actor George Cleveland as his grandfather.

In 1957 both Clayton and Rettig wanted to leave the series, and George Cleveland died, so a new cast was hired. Jon Provost played Lassie's new young owner Timmy, and his parents were played by Jon Shepodd and Cloris Leachman, while George Chandler played his grandfather. In 1958, Jack Wrather productions bought the rights to the series. Shepodd, Leachman, and Chandler were dropped as they didn't click with viewers and ratings had been plummeting since the transition. Provost was kept, and his parents were recast with Hugh Reilley and June Lockhart. Andy Clyde was added to the cast as Cully, an elderly neighbor.

William Beaudine jr. was hired as the production assistant, and recommended his father as one of the series' rotating directors. Beaudine sr. directed one episode, and his ability to get a lot done within the limited parameters of a TV production impressed the producers. He would direct more episodes per season than any of the other directors.

William Beaudine began directing Lassie episodes in 1960 just as this new cast was beginning to click, and helped guide the series back to greater ratings status. It was often a daunting and frustrating situation for Beaudine. While he had a lot of experience working with children and dogs, this series was set up with a specific boy-and-his-dog formula where Timmy would get into a jam and Lassie would get him out of it. Lassie had some specific reactions that were necessary. To get the dog to bark, a trainer would be positioned out of camera range on a ladder and would wave meat after Timmy delivered his line. The dog would bark at the meat, but look like it was looking at Timmy. Beaudine referred to Lassie as "meat hound," much to the chagrin of trainer Rudd Weatherwax, who referred to Beaudine as "that SOB."

Jon Provost recalled for the author: "I remember the Mr. Beaudine getting pretty cranky a lot of the time. He also would shout out directions while we were shooting, like directors did during the silent days. The sound crew would have to erase it afterward. But he directed many of the episodes and got the job done. He knew Andy Clyde from the silent days, so Andy could always cheer him up." Beaudine had directed Andy Clyde in the Mack Sennett comedies *Step Forward* and *The College Vamp*.

These accounts are curious in that one of the real constants in William Beaudine's long career is that his sets were always happy ones, be they television or movies, big budget productions or low budget quickies. Beaudine was always thought of as relaxed, prepared, friendly, and supportive. He allowed creative input from the actors, even when the shooting days were tight. He came prepared and was ready for any possible setback or challenge. But now, as he was coming to the end of his career, the set of *Lassie* was nothing like what has been describe about Beaudine's other productions. Suddenly he was "cranky a lot of the time."

Perhaps, despite all his experience, the changing culture of TV and film that was occurring in the mid-60s was beginning to affect the way others perceived Beaudine's methods. Maybe it also affected his attitude toward his work. Or perhaps just the way a show like Lassie had to specifically be shot was creatively stifling. In any case, as William Beaudine's long career was closing, the filmmaking he always loved doing was unfortunately less attractive and fulfilling on this particular project.

This does not mean that Beaudine's direction of the *Lassie* series was in any way below par. He still came prepared, still gave the actors freedom, and continued to approach each episode with the creative vision that had sustained him successfully for 50 years.

William Beaudine directed most of the best episodes during this period of the series. One of the most ambitious directorial feats that Beaudine accomplished with the *Lassie* series was a five-part episode arc called *The Journey*. Timmy and Lassie are caught in a runaway hot air balloon, and when they finally reach land, they have further adventures trying to make it home. It kept viewers riveted to their TVs, coming back each week to see what happens next, not unlike the old movie chapterplays. It was even compiled into a feature length film and released to theaters for the family trade in 1963. Even though most had seen it on TV, to see all of the episodes together and in color (most people had black and white TV sets back then), still generated interest.

By 1964 the *Lassie* series was achieving its highest ratings since its debut ten years earlier, and at least some of it had to with the creative input and guidance of William Beaudine's direction. The producers were very pleased with how the series was going, especially since they could make even more money off already telecast episodes because Beaudine gave them enough to string together as a feature film.

However, Jon Provost was losing interest in continuing with the role. He told the author, "It was several adults, me, and a couple of dogs. Everyone looked at the show as another job. I bonded with Andy Clyde, who was the adult who gave me the most attention. He was a funny, friendly little guy."

Once Provost left the series, it was revamped to feature Robert Bray as Corey Stuart, a forest ranger and Lassie's new owner and master. Stuart remained with the series for the next four seasons, as did Beaudine. Stuart left the series in 1968 due to his battles with alcoholism, and although he lived another 15 years, he never acted again, choosing to retire and enjoy his hobbies.

While directing the *Lassie* series, Beaudine was asked, in 1966, to direct four episodes of *The Green Hornet*, a TV series that featured Van Williams in the title role and Bruce Lee as his martial arts expert sidekick Kato. These aired during the 1966-1967 TV season. The TV series *Batman* had premiered the year before and was an enormous hit. Banking on the popularity of the *Batman* series, *The Green Hornet* was equally fun and campy, but not as successful.

William Beaudine's final episode of the *Lassie* series was wrapped on August 2, 1968. He didn't quit, but at 76 years old, and after 60 years in the movie business, he finally stopped receiving calls. Younger directors were sought -- certainly younger than Beaudine. The massive and versatile experience a veteran director who dated back to the silent era would be able to offer new TV and movie projects was not as attractive to producers as the young up-and-coming filmmakers with progressive ideas.

Jon Provost as Timmy with Lassie.

REDISCOVERY OF "THE CANDADIAN" AND BEAUDINE'S FINAL YEAR

By the time talking pictures came in and took over the movie industry back around 1929 and 1930, silent films almost immediately were dismissed as archaic. Studios were dismissive of their old silent product, allowing them to languish in vaults and decompose. Sometimes they would be cut up and joined by obtrusive music and corny comic narration to make fun of them. Fires in vaults destroyed entire silent screen legacy for some former great stars.

However, in the 1960s, film historians studying the silent era attempted to preserve what was left from the period, after decades of poor care left us with only a fraction of the silent movies that had been produced.

The American Film Institute joined up with the Library of Congress in an attempt to gather a comprehensive collection of American films to preserve for future study. The library wouldn't accept nitrate prints of films during the 1912-1942 period so preservationists like Kevin Brownlow and David Shepard set out to find silent and early sound movies to preserve on safety film. While there are indeed plenty of William Beaudine's silent movies that remain lost, one particular feature was rediscovered over 40 years after its initial release.

In 1969, a 35 mm nitrate print of William Beaudine's 1926 silent feature *The Canadian* was donated with a group of other films to the National Film Collection by Paramount studios. *The Canadian* was discovered in this group by Kevin Brownlow and David Shepard. The British born Kevin Brownlow stated:[47]

> The original nitrate print, knife-edged in its clarity, unseen for forty years, was as exciting an archeological discovery as film historians can hope for.

---

47   Brownlow, Kevin. *The Silent Films of William Beaudine*. American Film Institute. 1972

Having associated Beaudine with the raw comedy of Will Hay, I was totally unprepared for a film like *The Canadian*. The first sweeping long shot of the wheat fields, a spectacular cloudscape accentuated by panchromatic film, brought gasps from both of us. Beaudine has been sadly underrated. His wonderfully vivid and naturalistic style makes him a far more skillful director than many of those who were in the top bracket.

The story was based on the Somerset Maugham play *The Land of Promise* and had been filmed under that title in 1917. The story deals with a young woman in England whose aunt dies, leaving her destitute. She travels to Canada to live with her brother, a poor Ontario farmer who has his own challenges. The city-bred Nora, used to another way of life, is of no use on a farm, and has frequent conflicts with her brother's wife. She marries another, more successful farmer, and learns how to eschew her old city ways and adapt to farm life. This strengthens her relationship with her husband.

The lead was played by actress Mona Palmer, who made very few films, but turns in a remarkable performance. The biggest name in the film is Thomas Meighan, a leading star of the 1920s. He plays the husband, and had essayed the same role in the 1917 film.

The Canadian was screened at the Los Angeles Museum of Art in February of 1970 and an ailing Beaudine, in a wheelchair, was in attendance, having been brought to the event by his son, Bill jr.. After the film was screened, Beaudine was given a microphone to address the audience:[48]

> You know, before tonight I had never seen this picture. In those days, you shot it and went on to the next one. Seeing it now, maybe I wasn't such a bad director after all. In fact, I was quite good in spots, and it's a damn good film.

---

48 Brownlow, Kevin. *The Silent Films of William Beaudine*. American Film Institute. 1972

William Beaudine phoned Kevin Brownlow the next day and stated that the screening "did a hell of a lot for my ego." Beaudine was quite pleased when *The Canadian* received the New York Film Critics Award as one of the best films of the pre-sound era.

About a month later, on March 18, 1970, William Beaudine died. He was 78 years old. And since his passing, more of his silent films have become available. His B movies have been telecast on television, released on home video, and available for streaming. A classic like the W.C. Fields film *The Old Fashioned Way* has retained its status well into the 21st century. The Bowery Boys series was still being telecast into the 21s century, and all 48 films were released to DVD. Social media has even given new life to a movie as bad as *Bela Lugosi Meets a Brooklyn Gorilla!*

Unfortunately, another, far unfortunate development, also happened in the years since William Beaudine's passing. Snarky books have dismissed his work derisively, which has sadly permeated his legacy. Nearly any time he is mentioned anywhere, for any reason, he is referred to as "One-Shot," the inaccurate nickname that he was never referred to in his lifetime. He is defined by his weaker films like *Bela Lugosi Meets a Brooklyn Gorilla* or *Jesse James Meets Frankenstein's Daughter* by those who have likely never heard of, much less seen, *The Canadian, Sparrows, The Old Fashioned Way,*or even *One Exciting Night* and *Phantom Killer*.

As this study has spent time explaining, William Beaudine was a skillful, creative, prolific, and versatile director. And, as Kevin Brownlow has so eloquently stated, William Beaudine's work is underrated and deserves to be respected alongside the noted great directors in motion picture history.

Lobby card for The Canadian.

APPENDIX A: FILMOGRAPHY

Information for each film is provided as well as existing records allow. This filmography corrects errors from other sources, omitting films that should not have been listed, and adding those that should.

KALEM

Diana of the Farm (1915)
Bud Duncan, Ethel Teare, Charles Inslee, William Beaudine
Kalem. Two Reels. Released November 2, 1915

Minnie the Tiger (1915)
Written by Lloyd Hamilton...
Bud Duncan Charles Inslee Ethel Teare Harry Griffith
Kalem. One Reel. Released December 7, 1915.

Almost a King (1915)
Written by William Beuadine
Bud Duncan, Ethel Teare, Charles Inslee, Charles Mulgro, Merta Sterling, Martin Kinney, Giovanni De Rosa. One Reel. Released December 14, 1915.

The Bandits of Macaroni Mountain (1915)
Bud Duncan, Ethel Teare, John McDermott, Merta Sterling, Lillian Savage, William Clarke. One Reel. Released December 21, 1915

The Caretaker's Dilemma (1915)
Bud Duncan, Ethel Teare, John McDermott, William Clarke, Lillian Savage. One Reel. December 28, 1915

The Missing Mummy (1916)
Bud Duncan, Ethel Teare, Charles Inslee, John McDermott, Gus Leonard, Charles Mulgro. One Reel. Released January 4, 1916

Guardian Angels (1916)
Written by Howard Irving Young
Bud Duncan, Ethel Teare, John McDermott, Charles Mulgro
One Reel. Released January 11, 1916

Tale of a Coat (1916)
Bud Duncan, Ethel Teare, Charles Mulgro, John McDermott, Gus Lenoard.
One Reel. Released January 18, 1916

Snoop Hounds (1916)
Bud Duncan, Ethel Teare, Gus Leonard, John McDermott
One Reel. January 25, 1916

Artful Artists
Bud Duncan, Ethel Teare, John McDermott, Gus Leonard
One Reel. February 1, 1916

Wurra Wurra
Bud Duncan, Ethel Teare, John McDermott, Charles Inslee, Gus Leonard
One Reel. February 8, 1916.

Ham Takes a Chance
Lloyd Hamilton, Bud Duncan, Ethel Teare, Gus Leonard, John McDermott
One Reel. February 15, 1916

A Molar Mixup
Bud Duncan, Ethel Teare, John McDermott, Gus Leonard, Merta Sterling
One Reel. February 16, 1916

Ham the Diver
Written by Bud Duncan and Lloyd Hamilton
Lloyd Hamilton, Bud Duncan, Ethel Teare, John McDermott, Juanita Sponsler
One Reel. February 22, 1916

Winning a Window
Written by Frank H. Clark
Lloyd Hamilton, Bud Duncan, Adoni Fovieri, John McDermott, Gus Leonard, Martin Kinney. One Reel. February 28, 1916

A Riddle in Rascals
Written by Beaudine
Ethel Teare, John McDermott, Victor Rodman
One Reel. March 1, 1916

Maybe Moonshine
Written by Beaudine
Lloyd Hamilton, Bud Dancan, Adoni Fovieri, Porter Strong, Gordon Griffith, Wesley Barry, Ninon Fovieri. One Reel. March 7, 1916

When Hubby Forgot
Written by Ray Hertzberg
Ethel Teare, Victor Rodman, Roy Zell, Corinne Griffith.
One Reel. March 8, 1916

Ham Agrees with Sherman
Written by Beaudine
Lloyd Hamilton, Bud Dancan, Porter Strong, Norma Nichols
One Reel. March 14, 1916

The Eveless Eden Club
Written by Beaudine
Ethel Teare John McDermott, Gus Leonard
One Reel. March 15, 1916

For Sweet Charity
Written by Beaudine
Lloyd Hamilton, Bud Duncan, Porter Strong, Norma Nichols, Julie Cruze, Albert Edmondson, Juanita Sponsler, Ed Valentine.
One Reel. March 21, 1916

At Bachelor's Roost
Written by Howard Irving Young
Ethel Teare, Gus Leonard John McDermott, Charles Mulgro, Al Fretas, J. North, Roy Zell.
One Reel. March 22, 1916

Ham and the Hermit's Daughter
Written by Beaudine
Lloyd Hamilton, Bud Duncan, Porter Strong, Norma Nichols, Julie Cruze, Victor Rodman
One Reel. March 28, 1916

The Trailing Tailor
Written by Howard Irving Young
Ethel Teare, Gus Leonard John McDermott, Victor Rodman
One Reel. March 29, 1916

From Altar to Halter
Written by Beaudine
Lloyd Hamilton, Bud Duncan, Norma Nichols, Merta Sterling
One Reel. April 4, 1916

Trapping the Bachelor
Written by Beaudine

Ethel Teare, Victor Rodman, Milla Davenport, John McDermott
One Reel. April 5, 1916

Millionaires By Mistake
Lloyd Hamilton, Bud Duncan, Norma Nichols,
One reel. April 11, 1916

Fashion and Fury
Ethel Teare, John McDermott, Victor Rodman Harry Davenport, Merta Sterlin
One reel. April 12, 1916

Ham and Preparedness
Lloyd Hamilton, Bud Duncan, Norma Nichols, Junaita Sponsler
One reel. April 18, 1916

Their Taking Ways
Ethel Teare, John McDermott, Victor Rodman, Lilliam Clark
One reel. April 19, 1916

Counting The Count
Written by Sam Taylor
Ethel Teare, John McDermott, Victor Rodman, Alice Davenport, Gus Leonard, Merta Sterling
One reel. April 26, 1919

Romeo of the Coal Wagon
Written by S.A. Patten
Ethel Teare, John McDermott, Victor Rodman, Gus Leonard, Freddie Fralick
One Reel. May 3, 1916

UNIVERSAL

Musical Madness
Written by Harry Wulze
Gale Henry, Billy Franey, Heinie Conklin, Milburn Morante, Lillian Peacock
Shot in 1916, released in 1917

The Inspector's Double
Written by Charles Wilson, Harry Wulze
Billy Franey, Gale Henry, Harry Mann, Henie Conklin, Lillian Peacock, Milburn Morante.
One reel. Released September 30, 1916

Beans and Bullets
Written by Barney Furey and Harry Wulze
Heinie Conklin, Lillian Peacock, Milburn Morante, Bill Franey, Gale
  Henry, Jack Francis
One reel. Released October 21, 1916

A Crooked Mix-up
Written by W.M. Baker and Charles J. Wilson
Milburn Morante, Gale Henry, Heinie Conklin, Billy Franey
One reel. Released October 28, 1919

A Shadowed Shadow
Written by Jack Byrne
Milburn Morante, Gale Henry, Heinie Conklin, Billy Franey, Lillian
  Peacock, Dan Duffy
One Reel. November 4, 1916

In Love with a Fireman
Written by Walter Newman
Milburn Morante, Gale Henry, Heinie Conklin, Billy Franey, Lillian Peacock
One Reel. November 11, 1916

Their First Arrest
Written by Smythe Addison
Milburn Morante, Gale Henry, Heinie Conklin, Billy Franey, Lillian
  Peacock
One Reel. November 18, 1916

A Jailor's Vendetta
Written by Harry Wulze
Milburn Morante, Gale Henry, Heinie Conklin, Billy Franey, Lillian
  Peacock
One Reel. November 25, 1916

Scrappily Married
Written by William Beaudine and Harry Wulzw
Milburn Morante, Gale Henry, Heinie Conklin, Billy Franey, Lillian
  Peacock
One Reel. December 2, 1916

The Tramp Chef
Written by William Beaudine and Charles J. Wilson
Milburn Morante, Gale Henry, Heinie Conklin, Billy Franey, Lillian
  Peacock
One Reel. December 9, 1916

Their Dark Secret
Written by Sheba Canne and Harry Wulze
Milburn Morante, Gale Henry, Heinie Conklin, Billy Franey
One Reel. December 16, 1916

Jags and Jealousy
Written by Karl R. Coolidge
Milburn Morante, Gale Henry, Heinie Conklin, Billy Franey
One Reel. December 23, 1916

A Tale of a Turk
Written by William Beaudine, Karl Coolidge
Milburn Morante, Gale Henry, Heinie Conklin, Billy Franey, Lillian Peacock, Jack Conally
One Reel. December 30, 1916

Love in Suspense
Written by William Beaudine, Karl Coolidge
Milburn Morante, Gale Henry, Heinie Conklin, Billy Franey, John Cook
One Reel. January 6, 1917

When Damon Fell for Pythias
Written by William Beaudine
Gale Henry, Heinie Conklin, Billy Franey, Lydia Yeamans Titus,
One Reel. January 11, 1917

Mines and Matrimony
Written by Paul Coolidge, Irene Blake
Milburn Morante, Gale Henry, Heinie Conklin, Billy Franey, Harry Mann, Yvonne Mitchell
One Reel. January 13, 1917

Barred From the Bar
Written by Karl Coolidge
Milburn Morante, Gale Henry, Heinie Conklin, Billy Franey, Lillian Peacock
One Reel. January 20, 1917

Love Me, Love My Biscuits
Written by Karl Coolidge
Milburn Morante, Gale Henry, Billy Franey, Dolly Ohnet
One Reel. January 27, 1917

His Coming Out Party
Written by Karl Coolidge

Milburn Morante, Gale Henry, Heinie Conklin, Billy Franey, Lillian Peacock
One Reel. February 3, 1917

Out for the Dough
Written by Jack Cunningham
Milburn Morante, Gale Henry, Billy Franey, Lillian Peacock, John Cook
One Reel. February 10, 1917

Mule Mates
Written by Jack Cunningham
Milburn Morante, Gale Henry, Billy Franey, Lillian Peacock, Fred Woodward
One Reel. February 17, 1917

Rosie's Rancho
Written by Jack Cunningham
Milburn Morante, Gale Henry, Billy Franey, Lillian Peacock,
One Reel. February 24, 1917

Passing the Grip
Written by Walter Newman
Milburn Morante, Gale Henry, Billy Franey, Lillian Peacock, Heinie Conklin
One Reel. March 3, 1917

Wanna Make a Dollar?
Written by Jack Cunningham
Milburn Morante, Gale Henry, Billy Franey, Lillian Peacock, John Cook
One Reel. March 10, 1917

Art Aches
Written by Jack Cunningham
Milburn Morante, Gale Henry, Billy Franey, Lillian Peacock, John Cook, Bobby Mack
One Reel. March 17, 1917

Whose Baby?
Written by Jack Cunningham
Milburn Morante, Gale Henry, Billy Franey, Lillian Peacock
One Reel. March 24, 1917

What the ---?
Written by Jack Cunningham

Milburn Morante, Gale Henry, Billy Franey, Lillian Peacock, Kewpie Morgan, Bobbie Mack, Martha Mattox
One Reel. March 31, 1917

A Boob For Luck
Written by Jack Cunningham, William Beaudine
Milburn Morante, Gale Henry, Billy Franey, Lillian Peacock, Bobbie Mack, Billy Human
One Reel. April 7, 1917

The Careless Cop
Written by Jack Cunningham
Milburn Morante, Gale Henry, Billy Franey, Lillian Peacock, RJ Craven
One Reel. April 13, 1917

Take Back Your Wife
Written by Charles J. Wilson
Milburn Morante, Gale Henry, Billy Franey, Lillian Peacock, Heinie Conklin
One Reel. April 21, 1917

The Leak
Written by Jack Cunningham
Milburn Morante, John Cook, Billy Franey, Lillian Peacock, Milton Uhl
One Reel. April 28, 1917

Left in the Soup
Written by Jack Cunningham
Milburn Morante, Gale Henry, Billy Franey, Lillian Peacock
One Reel. May 5, 1917

The Man With a Package
Written by C.O. Hoadley
Milburn Morante, Gale Henry, Billy Franey, Lillian Peacock
One Reel. May 12, 1917

The Last Scent
Written by Billy Franey, C.O. Hoadley
Milburn Morante, Gale Henry, Billy Franey, Lillian Peacock,
One Reel. May 19, 1917

Boss of the Family
Written by C.O. Hoadley
Milburn Morante, Gale Henry, Billy Franey, Lillian Peacock
One Reel. May 26, 1917

Uneasy Money
Written by Jack Cunningham
Milburn Morante, Gale Henry, Billy Franey, Lillian Peacock
One Reel. June 2, 1917

One Damp Day
Written by Jack Cunningham
Milburn Morante, Gale Henry, Billy Franey, Lillian Peacock, Bobbie Mack
One Reel June 16, 1917

A Desert Dilemma
Written by C.O. Hoadley
Milburn Morante, ZaSu Pitts
One Reel June 23, 1917

His Fatal Beauty
Written by Jack Cunningham
Milburn Morante, ZaSu Pitts, Billy Franey, Lillian Peacock
One Reel June 25, 1917

He Had 'Em Buffaloed
Written by C.O. Hoadley
Milburn Morante, ZaSu Pitts, Billy Franey, Lillian Peacock, Bobbie Mack
One Reel. July 21, 1917

Canning the Cannibal King
Written by C.O. Hoadley
Milburn Morante, ZaSu Pitts, Billy Franey, Lillian Peacock, Bobbie Mack
One Reel. July 28, 1917

The Battling Bellboy
Written by Jack Cunningham
Milburn Morante, ZaSu Pitts, Billy Franey, Lillian Peacock, Bobbie Mack, John Cook
One Reel. August 2, 1917

O-My The Tent Mover
Written by Tom Gibson, E.M McCall
Milburn Morante, ZaSu Pitts, Billy Franey, Lillian Peacock, Eddie Baker
One Reel. August 11, 1917

Out Again, In Again
Written by Tom Gibson
Billy Franey, Harry Mann, Eileen Roberts, Milburn Morante
One Reel. August 18, 1917

Behind the Map
Written by William Beaudine, Tom Gibson
Milburn Morante, ZaSu Pitts, Billy Franey, Lillian Peacock, Eddie Baker
One Reel. August 25, 1917

Why They Left Home
Written by C.O. Hoadley
Milburn Morante, ZaSu Pitts, Billy Franey, Lillian Peacock, Bobbie Mack, Burton Law
One Reel. August 27, 1917

Officer, Call a Cop!
Written by Arthur F. Statter
Billy Franey, Janet Eastman, Milburn Morante, Scott Pembroke
One Reel. September 3, 1917

Hawaiian Nuts
Written by William Beaudine, Robert A. Dillon
Milburn Morante, Gail Henry, Billy Franey, Milton Sims, Eddie Baker
One Reel. September 17, 1917

The Fountain of Trouble
Written by Arthur F. Statter
Milburn Morante, Billy Franey, Ida Tenbrook, Nellie Allen
One Reel. September 24, 1917

Who Done It
Written by Robert A. Dillon
Milburn Morante, Gail Henry Billy Franey, Milton Sims, Eddie Baker
One Reel. October 15, 1917

The Cross Eyed Submarine
Written by Jack Cunningham
Milburn Morante, ZaSu Pitts, Billy Franey, Lillian Peacock
One Reel. October 18, 1917

NESTOR FILM COMPANY

What Will We Do With Uncle?
Written by King Vidor

Henry Murdock, Mildred Davis, Milton Uhl, Eddie Baker
One Reel. October 22, 1917

A Bad Little Good Man
Written by King Vidor
Mathilde Comont, Henry Murdock, Eddie Baker
One Reel. October 29, 1917

KEYSTONE-TRIANGLE

Won By a Fowl
Written by William Beaudine
Claire Anderson, Joseph Belmont, Paddy McGuire, Peggy Pearce, Fritz Schade
Three Reels. November 25, 1917

A Sanitarium Scandal
Written by William Beaudine
Joseph Belmont, Paddy McGuire, Blanche Payson, Peggy Pearce, Earle Rodney, Fritz Schade
One Reel. December 17, 1917

Mud
Written by William Beaudine
Raymond Griffith, Max Asher, Peggy Pearce, Henry Depp
Two Reels. March 17, 1918

Mr. Briggs Closes The House
Written by William Beaudine
Myrtle Rishell, Ed Brady, Anna Dodge, Fred Mack, Frank Caffray
One Reel. April 14, 1918

Mr Smith's Economy
Written by William Beaudine
Ed Brady, Charles Dorian
One Reel. April 28, 1918

The Poor Fish
Written by William Beaudine
Ed Brady, Clarie Anderson, Fritzi Ridgeway, Thornton Edwards, Josie Sedgwick, Gino Corrado, Percy Challenger.
One Reel. June 2, 1918

Flapjacks
Written by William Beaudine

George Hernandez, Josie Sedgwick, Frank MacQuarrie
One Reel. June 9, 1918

MISC

The Pie Eyed Piper
Written by C.B. Hoadley
ZaSu Pitts, Billy Franey, Milburn Morante, Lillian Peacock, Bobbie Mack
One Reel. August 19, 1918. Nestor

A High Diver's Last Kiss
Written by William Beaudine
Slim Summerville, Elizabeth R. Carpenter, Bobby Dunn, Frank J. Coleman
One Reel. August 25, 1918. Fox Film Corporation

Dan Cupid M.D.
Written by Karl Coolidge
Harry Depp, Elinor Field
One Reel. December 4, 1918. Southern California Production Co.

Easy Payments
Written by Karl Coolidge
Harry Depp, Elinor Field, George Pierce
One Reel. January 26, 1919. Southern California Production Co

Mixed Wives
Written by Arthur Stratter
Billy Franey, Elsie Cort, Milburn Morante, Beulah Lewis
One Reel. February 16, 1919. Nestor

CHRISTIE COMEDIES

Brides For Two
Written by Al Christie, John Newton
Dorothy Devore, Roscoe Karns, Ethel Lynne, Earle Rodney
One Reel. March 1, 1919

Sea Sirens
Written by Royce Alton
Bobby Vernon, Patricia Palmer, George B. French
One Reel. April 28, 1919

A Rustic Romeo
Written by Al Christie
Vera Steadman, Bobby Vernon
One Reel. May 12, 1919

He Who Hesitates
Written Al Christie
Ethel Lynne, Bobby Vernon
One Reel. June 1, 1919

Save Me Sadie
Written by Scott Darling
Eddie Barry, Helen Darling, Earle Rodney, Fay Lemport, Edith Clark
One Reel. February 7, 1920

Eat-a-Bite-a-Pie
Written by William Beaudine
Bobby Vernon, Vera Steadman, Victor Rodman
One Reel. March 11, 1920

Watch Your Step, Mother
Written by Al Christie
Bobby Vernon, Vera Steadman
One Reel. April 1, 1920

Hearts and Diamonds
Written by Scott Darling
Katherine Lewis, James Liddy
One Reel. April 5, 1920. Supreme Feature Films Company

The Captivating Captive
Written by Scott Darling
Earle Rodney, Charlotte Merriam
One Reel. May 8, 1920. Universal Film Manufacturing Company

Petticoats and Pants
Written by Frank Conklin, Scott Darling
Bobby Vernon, Helen Darling, Elinor Field
One Reel. May 20, 1920

Why Be Jealous
Written by Harry Depp
Harry Depp, Teddy Sampson,
One Reel. May 26, 1920

A Husband in Haste
Written by Frank Conklin, Jack Jevne
Earle Rodney, Helen Darling, Eddie Barry
One Reel. June 16, 1920

A Seaside Siren
Written by Scott Darling, M.B. Hageman
Earle Rodney, Fay Tincher, Charlotte Merriam, James Harrison, Eddie Baker, Helen Darling, Virginia Ware
One Reel. July 25, 1920

Fit to Fight
Written by Scott Darling
Bobby Vernon, Vera Steadman, George B. French
One Reel. August 1, 1920

Seven Bald Pates
Written by Frank Conklin, Scott Darling
Bobby Vernon, Dorothy Devore, Victor Rodman, Francis Feeney
One Reel. August 22, 1920

A Home Spun Hero
Written by Frank Conklin, Scott Darling
Bobby Vernon, Vera Steadman, Helen Darling, George Ford
Two Reels. October 2, 1920

Shuffle The Queens
Written by Al Christie, Scott Darling
Earle Rodney, Charlotte Merriam, Vera Steadman, Neal Burns, Eddie Barry, Lydia Yeamans Titus.
One Reel. October 17, 1920

Tea For Two
Written by Frank Conklin, Jack Jevne
Eddie Barry, Charlotte Merriam, Gino Corrado
One Reel. December 5, 1920

Back From the Front
Written by Frank Conklin, Scott Darling
Bobby Vernon, Vera Steadman, Laura La Plante, Neal Burns, William Sloan, Francis Feeney
Two Reels. December 12, 1920

Why Men Go Wild
Written by Scott Darling
Bobby Vernon, Vera Steadman, James Harrison
Two Reels. December 28, 1920

Movie Mad
Written by Frank Conklin, Scott Darling

Dorothy Devore, Neal Burns, Gino Corrado, George B. French
One Reel. January 2, 1921

Ouija Did It
Written by Clyde Campbell, Jack Jevne
Bobby Vernon, Vera Steadman, Neal Burns, Henry Murdock
One Reel. January 30, 1921

Dead Easy
Written by Walter Graham
Earle Rodney, Irene Dalton
One Reel. March 27, 1921

Twin Husbands
Written by William Beaudine
Dorothea Wolbert, Helen Darling
One Reel. March 28, 1921. Universal Film Manufacturing Company

Who Kissed Me?
Written by William Beaudine
Dorothea Wolbert
One Reel. April 4, 1921 Universal Film Manufacturing Company
CHRISTIE continued

Short and Snappy
Written by Jack Jevne
Bobby Vernon, Vera Steadman, Billy Bletcher, Gus Alexander, Eddie Barry
One Reel. April 10, 1921

Hubby Behave
Written by Walter Graham
Earle Rodney, Irene Dalton, Harry Edwards, Henry Murdock
One Reel. April 12, 1921

Short and Sweet
Written by William Beaudine
Dorothea Wolbert
One Reel. April 18, 1921 Universal Film Manufacturing Company

Zulu Love
Written by William Beaudine
Eddie Barry
One Reel. May 9, 1921 Universal Film Manufacturing Company

Hero Pro Tem
Written by Jack Jevne
Henry Murdock, Teddy Sampson, George George
One Reel. June 26, 1921

Ninety Days or Life
Written by Jack Jevne
Donald Keith, Irene Dalton, Thornton Edwards, Gus Leonard
One Reel. July 3, 1921

Oh Buddy!
Written by Frank Conklin
Neal Burns, Vera Steadman, Ogden Crane, Victor Rodman
One Reel. August 21, 1921

Falling For Fanny
Written by Frank Conklin
Eddie Barry, Helen Darling, Victor Rodman
One Reel. September 19, 1921

Pure and Simple
Written Frank Conklin
Bobby Vernon, Josephine Hill, Ward Caufield, Victor Rodman, Virginia Ware
One Reel. October 30, 1921

Fresh From The Farm
Written by Frank Conklin
Bobby Vernon, Josephine, Hill, George C. Pearce, Victor Rodman
One Reel. November 27, 1921

Watch Your Step
Written by Julien Josephson
Cullen Landis, Patsy Ruth Miller, Bert Woodruff, George C. Pearce, Raymond Cannon, Gus Leonard, Harry Rattenberry, Joel Day, LJ O'Connor, John Cossar, Lillian Sylvester, Louis King, Cordelia Callahan, Alberta Lee.
Five Reels. February 8, 1922. Goldwyn Pictures Corporation

Step Forward
Writer unknown
Ben Turpin, Phyllis Haver, Heinie Conklin, Kewpie Morgan, Jack Richardson, Kalla Pasha, Fanny Kelly, Andy Clyde, George Nichols, Patrick Kelly, Dave Anderson, Gordon Lewis, Joe Bordeaux, Marvin Loback, James Donnelly, Teddy the Dog.

Two Reels. April 13, 1922. Mack Sennett Comedies
(Beaudine shot retakes on this film according to Brent Walker's book
  Mack Sennett's Fun Factory)

Punch The Clock
Writer unknown
Snub Pollard, Marie Mosquini, Eddie Baker, Wililiam Gillespie, Mark
  Jones, George Rowe, Wallace Howe.
One Reel. June 4, 1922. Hal Roach productions

Strictly Modern
Writer Unknown
Snub Pollard, Marie Mosquini, Leo Willis
One Reel. June 11, 1922. Hal Roach production

Pardon My Glove
Written by Scott Darling
Bobby Vernon, Vera Steadman, Ward Caufield, George C. Pearce,
  Tom O'Brien, Zack Williams.
One Reel. September 17, 1922. Christie Film Company

The Chased Bride
Written by Scott Darling
Neal Burns, Vera Steadman, George C. Pearce, Victor Rodman
One Reel. December 3, 1922. Christie Film Company

Catch My Smoke
Written by Jack Sturmwasser, Joseph Bushnell Ames
Tom Mix, Lillian Rich, Claude Payton, Gordon Griffith, Harry Griffith,
  Robert Milasch, Pat Chrisman, C.E. Anderson, Ruby Lafayette.
Five reels. December 11, 1922. Fox Film Corporation

Heroes of the Street
Written by Mildred Considine, Edmund Goulding, Isabel Johnston,
  Lee Parker
Wesley Barry, Marie Prevost, Jack Mulhall, Philo McCullough, Will Walling,
  Agnes Herring, Wilfred Lucas, Wedgwood Nowell, Phil Ford, Peaches
  Jackson, Joe Butterworth, William Beaudine jr, Cameo the Dog
60 minutes. December 24, 1922. Warner Brothers

Her Fatal Millions
Written by Arthur F. Statter, William Dudley Pelley
Viola Dana, Huntley Gordon, Allan Forrest, Peggy Browne, Kate Price,
  Joy Winthrop,
62 minutes. April 9, 1923. Metro Pictures

Penrod and Sam
Written by Hope Loring and Louis Lighton, based on the story by Booth Tarkington
Ben Alexander, Joe Butterworth, Buddy Messinger Newton Hall, Gertrude Messinger, Joe McGray, Eugene Jackson, Rockliffe Fellowes, Gladys Brockwell, Mary Philbin, William Mong, Victor Potel, Martha Mattox.
70 minutes. June 23, 1923. Associated First National Pictures

The Printer's Devil
Written by Julien Josephson
Wesley Barry, Harry Myers, Kathryn McGuire, Louis King, Goerge Pearce, Raymond Cannon, Mary Halter, Harry Rattenberry
61 minutes. August 21, 1923. Warner Brothers.

The Country Kid
Written by Julien Josephson
Wesley Barry, Spec O'Donnell, Bruce Guerin, Kate Toncray, Helen Jerome Eddy, George Nichols, Edmund Burns, George Pearce, Buddy the Dog.
60 minutes. November 4, 1923. Warner Brothers.

Boy of Mine
Written by Louis Lighton
Ben Alexander, Rockliffe Fellowes, Henry B. Waithall, Irene Rich, Dot Farley, Lawrence Licalzi.
70 minutes. December 30, 1923. Associated First National Pictures.

Daring Youth
Written by Alexander Neal, Dorothy Farnum
Bebe Daniels, Norman Kerry, Lee Moran, Arthur Hoyt, Lillian Langeon, George Pearce
60 minutes. February 1, 1924. Principal Distributing

Wandering Husbands
Written by C.Gardner Sullivan
James Kirkwood, Lila Lee, Margaret Livingston, Eugene Pallette, Muriel Fracnes Dana, Turner Savage, Georce C. Pearce, George B. French
70 minutes. April 20, 1924. Regal Pictures

Daughters of Pleasure
Written by Harvey Thew, based on the novel by Caleb Proctor
Marie Prevost, Monte Blue, Clara Bow, Edythe Chapman, Wilfred Lucas
57 minutes. June 15, 1924

A Self Made Failure
Written by Violet Clark, John Grey, Lex Neal, Tamar Lane, J.K. McDonald
Lloyd Hamilton, Ben Alexander, Matt Moore, Patsy Ruth Miller, Mary Carr, Sam De Grasse, Charles Reisner, Victor Potel, Dan Mason, Harry Todd, Alta Allen, Doris Duane, Priscilla Moran, Joe McGray, Cameo the Dog.
80 minutes. June 29, 1924. Associated First National Pictures

Cornered
Written by Louis Lighton, Hope Loring, based on the play by Dodson Mitchell and Zelda Sears
Marie Prevost, Rockliffe Fellowes, Raymond Hatton, John Roche, Cissy Fitzgerald, Vera Lewis, George Pearce, Bartine Burkett, Billy Bletcher, Ruth Dwyer, Bertram Johns, Wilfred Lucas, Virginia Marshall.
70 mionutes. August 1, 1924. Warner Brothers.

The Narrow Street
Written by Julien Josephson based on the novel by Edwin Bateman Morris.
Matt Moore, Dorothy Devore, David Butler, George Pearce, Russell Simpson, Gertrude Short, Joe Butterworth, Kate Toncray, Tempe Pigott, Madame Sul-Te-Wan.
71 minutes. January 11, 1925 Warner Brothers

A Broadway Butterfly
Written by Gregory Rogers (Darryl Zanuck) from a story by Pearl Keating
Dorothy Devore, Louise Fazenda, Willard Louis, John Roche, Cullen Landis, Lilyan Tashman, Wilfred Lucas, Eugenie Gilbert, Margaret Seddon
67 minutes. March 29, 1925. Warner Brothers.

How Baxter Butted In
Written by Owen Davis, Julien Josephson
Dorothy Devore, Matt Moore, Ward Crane, Wilfred Lucas, Adda Gleason, Turner Savage, Virginia Marshall, Otis Harlan, Cameo the Dog.
72 minutes. July 25, 1925. Warner Brothers.

Little Annie Rooney
Written by Catherine Hennessey (Mary Pickford), Hope Loring, Louis Lighton, Tom McNamara.
Mary Pickford, William Haines, Walter James, Gordon Griffith, Carlo Schipa, Spec O'Donnell, Hugh Fay, Vola Vale, Joe Butterworth, Oscar Rudolph.
94 minutes. October 18, 1925. United Artists

My Sweedie
Written by Sig Herzig
Neil Burns, Vera Steadman, Anita Garvin, William Irving
Two Reels. December 13, 1925. Christie Film Company

That's My Baby
Written by Wade Boteler, Goerge Crone
Douglas MacLean, Margaret Morris, Claude Gillingwater, Eugenie Forde, Wade Boteler, Richard Tucker, Fred Kelsey, Harry Earles, William Orlamond.
72 minutes. April 19, 1926. Famous Players-Lasky/Paramount Pictures

The Social Highwayman
Written by Phillip Klein, Edward T. Lowe jr, Darryl Zanuck
John Patrick, Dorothy Devore, Montagu Love, Russell Simpson, George Pearce, Lynn Cowan, James Gordon, Frank Brownlee, Fred Kelsey, Charlies Hill Mailes
70 minutes. May 9, 1926. Warner Brothers

Hold That Lion!
Written by Joseph Franklin Poland, Rosalie Mulhall
Douglas MacLean, Walter Hiers, Constance Howard, Cyril Chadwick, Wade Boteler, George Pearce
63 minutes. September 4, 1926. Douglas MacLean Productions/Paramount

Sparrows
Written by George Marion and Winifred Dunne
Mary Pickford, Roy Stewart, Mary Louise Miller, Gustav von Seyffertitz, Charlotte Mineau, Spec O'Donnell, Lloyd Whitlock, Billy Butts, Monty O'Grady, Jack Lavine, Billy Jones, Muriel MacCormac, Florence Rogan, Mary McLean, Sylvia Bernard, Seeseell Johnson, Cammilla Johnson, A.L. Schaefer, Mark Hamilton.
110 minutes. September 19, 1926. Pickford Corporation/United Artists

The Canadian
Written by Arthur Stringer, Julian Johnston, J Clarkston Miller, Howard Emmett Rogers, from a play by W. Somerset Maugham.
Thomas Meighan, Mona Palma, Wyndham Standing, Dale Fuller, Charles Winninger, Billy Butts.
81 minutes. November 27, 1926. Famous Players-Lasky/Paramount

Frisco Sally Levy
Written by Alfred A. Cohn
Tenen Holtz, Kate Price, Sally O'Neill, Leon Holmes, Turner Savage, Helen Levine, Roy D'Arcy, Charles Delaney, Cameo the Dog.
68 minutes. April 2, 1927. Metro-Goldwyn-Mayer

Wild Wallops
Written by Hal Conklin
Billy Dooley, Olive Hasbrouck, Kalla Pasha, William Irving, Cliff Lancaster, William Blaisdell.
Two Reels. June 26, 1927. Christie Film Company

The Life of Riley
Written by Curtis Benton, Howard J. Green, Sidney Lazarus, Mann Page, Gene Towne
Charlie Murray, George Sidney, Stephen Carr, June Marlowe, Myrtle Stedman, Sam Hardy, Bert Woodruff, Edwards Davis.
69 minutes. September 3, 1927. First National Pictures/Warner Brothers

The Irresistible Lover
Witten by Albert DeMond, Evelyn Campbell, Edward I. Luddy, James Tynan, Beatrice Van.
Norman Kerry, Lois Moran, Gertrude Astor, Lee Moran, Myrtle Stedman, Phillips Smalley, Arthur Lake, Walter James, George Pearce.
72 minutes. October 21, 1927. Universal Pictures

The Cohens and Kellys in Paris
Written by Alfred Cohn
George Sidney, J. Farrell MacDonald, Vera Gordon, Kate Price, Charles Delaney, Sue Carol, Gertrude Astor, Gino Corrado, Charlie Murray
78 minutes. January 15, 1928. Universal Studios

Heart to Heart
Written by Dainelle Benthall, Adelaide Heilbron, Rufus McCosh, from a story by Juliet Wilbur Tompkins.
Mary Astor, Lloyd Hughes, Louise Fazenda, Lucien Littlefield, Thelma Todd, Raymond McKee, Virginia Grey, Aileen Manning.
69 minutes. July 22, 1928. First National Pictures/Warner Brothers

Home, James
Written by Mort Blumenstock, Albert DeMond, Gladys Johnson.
Laura La Plante, Charley Delaney, Aileen Manning, Joan Standing, George Pearce, Arthur Hoyt, Sidney Bracey
72 minutes. September 2, 1928. Universal Studios

Do Your Duty
Written by Vernon Smith Casey Robinson, Gene Towne, Julien Josephson

Charles Murray, Lucien Littlefield, Charles Delaney, Ed Brady Blue Washington, Doris Dawson, Aggie Herring, George Pearce, Marie Mosquini

70 minutes. October 14, 1928. First National Pictures/Warner Brothers

Give and Take
Written by Albert Demond
Jean Hersholt, George Sindey, George Lewis, Sharon Lynn, Sam Hardy, Rhoda Cross, Charles Hill Mailes
67 minutes. December 23, 1928. Universal Studios.

Fugitives
Written by Rowland Brown
Madge Bellamy, Don Terry, Arthur Stone, Earle Foxe, Matthew Betz, Lumsden Hare, Edith Murgatroyd, Jean Laverty, Hap Ward.
57 minutes. January 27, 1929. Fox Film Corporation

Two Weeks Off
Written by Joseph Poland, Thomas Barrows, Kenyon Nicholson
Dorothy Mackaill. Jack Mulhall, Gertrude Astor, James Finlayson, Kate Price, Jed Prouty, Eddie Gribbon, Dixie Gay, Gertrude Messinger, Wayne LaFever, Helen and Margaret Beaudine.
88 minutes. May 12, 1929. First National Pictures/Warner Brothers

Hard To Get
Written by James Gruen, Richard Weil from the story *Classified* by Edna Ferber.
Dorothy Mackaill, Charles Delaney, James Finlayson, Louise Fazenda, Jack Oakie, Edmund Burns, Clarissa Selwynne, Margaret Beaudine.
81 minutes. August 4, 1929. First National Pictures/Warner Brothers

The Girl from Woolworth's
Written by Adele Comandini
Alice White, Gladden James, Bert Moorhouse, Patricia Caron, William Orlamond, Charles Delaney, Wheeler Oakman, Rita Flynn, Ben Hall.
60 minutes. October 27, 1929. First National Pictures/Warner Brothers

Wedding Rings
Written by Ray Harris
H.B. Warner, Lois Wilson, Olive Borden, Hallam Cooley, James Ford, Kathlyn Williams, Aileen Manning.
74 minutes. December 29, 1929. First National Pictures/Warner Brothers

Those Who Dance
Written by Joseph Jackson
Monte Blue, Lila Lee, William "Stage" Boyd, Betty Compson, William Janney, Wilfred Lucas, Cornelius Keefe, DeWitt Jennings, Gino Corrado, Bob Perry, Charles McAvoy, Kernan Cripps, Richard Cramer, Harry Semels, Nick Thompson.
76 minutes. April 19, 1930. Warner Brothers

Road to Paradise
Written by F. Hugh Herbert, from a play by Dodson Mitchell
Loretta Young, Jack Mulhall, Raymond Hatton, George Barraud, Kathlyn Williams, Fred Kelsey, Purnell Pratt, Ben Hendricks, Jr, Dot Farley, Winter Hall, Georgette Rhodes.
74 minutes. July 20, 1930. First National Pictures/Warner Brothers

A Hollywood Theme Song
Written by Jack Jevne, Harry McCoy, Arthur Ripley, Earle Rodney
Harry Gribbon, Yola d'Avril, Patsy O'Leary, Emma Tansey, George Pearce, William McCall, Lew Kelly, Ben Turpin, Heinie Conklin.
Two Reels. December 7, 1930. Mack Sennett Comedies.

One Yard To Go
Written by John A. Waldron, Walter Weems, Jack Jevney, and Earle Rodney
Bobby Vernon, Marjorie Beebe, Dot Farley, Frank Eastman, Cyril Chadwick, Hugh Saxon, John Wilson, Virginia Whiting, John Francis Dillon, Hubert Diltz, Marvin Loback, Ernie Alexander, George Gray, Barney Hellum, Irene Allen, George Spear.
Two Reels. February 1, 1931. Mack Sennett Comedies

The College Vamp
Written by Jack Jevne, Arthur Ripley, Earle Rodney and Harry McCoy
Andy Clyde, Yola d'Avril, Patsy O'Leary, Dick Stewart, Nellie Nichols, Bobby Burns, George Pearce, Mildred Pointer, Doris Morton, George Gray, Charles Meakin, Jules Hanft, Ed Hawkins, Fredrick Ko Vert.
Two Reels. February 15, 1931. Mack Sennett Comedies

Father's Son
Written by Hope Loring from the novel by Booth Tarkington
Leon Janney, Lewis Stone, Irene Rich, John Halliday, Mickey Bennett, Robert Dandridge, George Reed, Gertrude Howard, Bertha Mann, Grover Ligon,
76 minutes. March 7, 1931. Warner Brothers

Misbehaving Ladies
Written by Julien Josephson, from the story *Queen of Main Street* by Juliet Wilbur Tompkins
Lila Lee, Ben Lyon, Louise Fazenda, Lucien Littlefield, Julia Swayne Gordon, Emily Fitzroy, Martha Mattox, Virgina Grey, Oscar Apfel, Cameo the dog.
75 minutes. April 18, 1931. Warner Brothers

The Lady Who Dared
Written by Forrest Halsey from the story *The Devil's Playground* by Kenneth J. Saunders
Billie Dove, Sidney Blackmer, Conway Tearle, Judity Vosselli, Cosmo Kyrle Bellew, Ivan Simpson, Lloyd Ingraham, Mathilde Comont, Phillips Smalley
59 minutes. May 29, 1931. Warner Brothers

The Mad Parade
Written by Doris Malloy, Gertrude Orr, Henry McCarthy, Frank Roland Conklin, from the story *Women Like Men* by Orr and Malloy.
Evelyn Brent, Irene Rich, Louise Fazenda, Lilyan Tashman, Marceline Day, Fritzi Ridgeway, June Clyde, Elizabeth Keating, Helen Keating.
63 minutes. September 18, 1931. Paramount Pictures

Penrod and Sam
Written by Waldemar Young from the story by Booth Tarkington
Leon Janney, Frank Coghlan jr, Margaret Marquis, Billy Lord, Michael Stuart, Jimmy Robinson, Matt Moore, Dorothy Peterson, Helen Beaudine, Johnny Arthur, ZaSu Pitts, Charles Sellon, Cameo the Dog.
71 minutes. October 3, 1931. First National Pictures/Warner Brothers

The Great Junction Hotel
Written by Ralph Ceder and Lew Lipton
Edward Everett Horton, Patsy Ruth Miller, Harry Gribbon, Richard Carle, Leionel Belmore, Frank McHugh, Lucien Littlefield, Tom Dugan, Hank Mann, Bobby Vernon, Luis Alberni, Mack Swain, Harry Stubbs, Maurice Black George Chandler, Glenn Tryon, Richard Carlyle.
Two Reels. October 26, 1931. Masquers Club of Hollywood

Men in Her Life
Robert Riskin, Samuel Hopkins Adams
Lois Moran, Charles Bickford, Victor Varconi, Don Dillaway, Luis Alberni, Adrienne D'Ambicourt, Barbara Weeks, Wilson Benge, Oscar Apfel, Hooper Atchley.
70 minutes. December 10, 1931. Columbia Pictures

Three Wise Girls
Written by by Robert Riskin and Agnes Christine Johnson from the story Blonde Baby by Wilson Collison
Jean Harlow, Mae Clarke, Marie Prevost, Walter Byron, Andy Devine, Natalie Moorhead, Jameson Thomas, Lucy Beaumont, Kathrin Clare Ward, Robert Dudley, Armand Kaliz, Walter Miller, Marcia Harris.
68 minutes February 9, 1932. Columbia Pictures

Make Me a Star
Written by Sam Mintz and Walter DeLeon
Joan Blondell, Stuart Erwin, ZaSu Pitts, Bern Turpin, Charles Sellon, Florence Roberts, Helen Jerome Eddy, Arthur Hoyt, George Templeton, Ruth Donnelly, Sam Hardy, Oscar Apfel.
86 minutes. July 1, 1932. Paramount

The Crime of the Century
Written by Brian Marlow and Florence Ryerson based on the oplay by Walter Maria Espe
Jean Hersholt, Wynne Gibson, Stuart Erwin, Frances Dee, Gordon Wescott, Robert Elliot, David Landau, William Janney, Bodil Rosing, Samuel S. Hinds, Torben Meyer, Marion Byron, Isabel Jewell, Pat McKee, Fred Kelsey, Harry Strang, Harry Depp.
73 minutes. February 19, 1933. Paramount

Dream Stuff
(William Beaudine directed under the pseudonym William X. Crowley)
Writer unknown
Walter Catlett, Joyce Compton, Emerson Treacy, Franklin Pangborn, Al Cooke, Harry Bowen, Bobby Burns.
Two Reels. May 12, 1933. Mack Sennett Comedies

See You Tonight
(William Beaudine directed under the pseudonym William X. Crowley)
Writer unknown
Tom Moore, Nora Lane, Edward J. Nugent, Marjorie Beebe, Grady Sutton, Julia Griffith, Si Jenks, Tom Dempsey, Joe Bordeaux, Roger Moore, Harry Ray, Louise Keyes, Callie Eaton.
Two Reels. June 2, 1933. Mack Sennett Comedies

Her Bodyguard
Written by Walter DeLeon and Ralph Spence with Francis Martin and Frank Partos from a story by Corey Ford
Edmund Lowe, Wynne Gibson, Edward Arnold, Alan Dinehart, Marjoie White, Johnny Hines, Fuzzy Knight, Zoila Cana, Louise Beavers, Arthur Housman, Wildred Lucas, Bill Elliot, Don Brodie, Robert

Gleckler, Lona Andre, Mary MacLaren, Harrison Greene, Frank O'Connor, Hector Sarno, Blue Washington, Minvera Urecal, James Burke, Tenen Holtz.
71 minutes. July 21, 1933. Paramount

Trick Golf
(William Beaudine directed under the pseudonym William X. Crowley)
Written by Pete Smith
Narrated by Pete Smith
One Reel. March 4, 1934. Metro Goldwyn Mayer

The Big Idea
(William Beaudine directed under the pseudonym William X. Crowley)
Written by Matty Brooks from a story by Ted Healy
Ted Healy, Muriel Evans, Bonnie Bonnell, Moe Howard, Larry Fine, Jerry (Curly) Howard, Lew Harvey, Billy Engle, Robert Milasch, Heinie Conklin, Buster Brodie, Eddie Bartell, Jimmy Hollywood, Henry Taylor, Tut Mace, MGM Dancing Girls.
Two Reels. May 12, 1934. Metro Goldwyn Mayer

The Old Fashioned Way
Written by Garnett Weston and Jack Cunningham, from a story by Charles Bogle (W.C. Fields).
W.C. Fields, Joe Morrison, Baby LeRoy, Judith Allen, Jan Duggan, Tammany Young, Nora Cecil, Jack Mulhall, Samuel Ethridge, Ruth Marion, Richard Carle, Larry Grenier, William Blatchford, Jeffrey Williams, Donald Brown, Tom Miller, Oscar Apfel, Sam McDaniel, Marvin Loback, Lew Kelly Billy Bletcher, Dorothy Bay, Robert McKenzie, Clarence Wilson, Duke York, Emma Ray, Dell Henderson, Lona Andre.
70 minutes. July 13, 1934. Paramount

So You Won't Talk
Written by Frank Launder and Russell Medcraft from a story by Thomas Geraghty
Monty Banks, Vera Pearce, Bertha Belmore, Enid Stamp-Taylor, Muriel Angelus, Ralph Ince, Claude Dampier, Julian Royce, A. Bromley Davenport, Peter Bernard, Jack Harley.
84 minutes. Released March 11, 1935. Teddington Studios

Dandy Dick
Written by William Beaudine, Will Hay, Clifford Grey, Frank Miller adapted from a play by Arthur Pinero.
Will Hay, Nancy Burne, Esmond Knight, Davy Burnaby, Mignon O'Doherty, Syd Crossley, Robert Nainby John Singer.
70 minutes. March 16, 1935. British International Pictures.

Boys Will Be Boys
Written by Will Hay
Will Hay, Gordon Harker, Jimmy Hanley, Davy Burnaby, Norma Varden, Claude Dampier, Charles Farrell, Percy Walsh
80 minutes. July 11, 1935. Gainsborough Pictures

Get Off My Foot
Written by Robert Edmunds, Frank Launder
Max Miller, Jane Carr, Chili Bouchier, Norma Varden, Morland Graham, Anthony Hankey, Reginald Purdell, Vera Bogetti, Wally Patch, Charles Hawtrey
82 minutes. November 5, 1935. Teddington Studios.

Mr. Cohen Takes a Walk
Written by Brock Williams, Mary Roberts Rinehart
Paul Graetz, Violet Facebrother, Chili Bouchier, Mickey Brantford, Ralph Truman, Barry Livesey, Sam Springson, Kenneth Villiers, Muriel Forbes, George Merritt.
80 minutes. February 12, 1936. Teddington studios.

Two Hearts in Harmony
Written by Robert Edmunds based on a story by Samuel Gibson Brown.
Bernice Claire, George Curzon, Enid Stamp-Taylor, Nora Williams, Gordon Little, Guy Middleton, Paul Hartley, Eliot Makeham, Julian Royce, Charles Farrell, Chick Endor, Sheila Barrett, Jack Harris and his Band.
75 minutes. Released date unkown. Time Pictures

Where There's a Will
Written by Will Hay, William Beaudine, Robert Edmunds from a story by Leslie Arliss, Sidney Gilliat
Will Hay, Graham Moffat, H.F. Maltby, Norma Varden, Peggy SImpson, Gibb McLaughlin, Gina Mao, Harley Power, Eddie Houghton, Hal Walters, John Turnbull, Sybil Brooke, Davina Cooke.
80 minutes. August 10, 1936. Gaumont

It's in the Bag
Written by Brock Williams from a story by Russell Medcraft
Jimmy Nervo, Teddy Knox, Jack Barty, George Carney, Rene Hunter, Ursula Hirst, Aubrey Dexter, Hal Gordon, Ernest Sefton, C. Denier Warren, Geln Alyn, Gaston and Andree, The Trocadero Girls.
80 minutes. September 9, 1936. Teddington Studios.

Educated Evans
Written by Robert Edmunds, Frank Launder from a novel by Edgar Wallace
Max Miller, Nancy O'Neil, Clarice Mayne, Albert Whelan, Hal Walters, George Merritt, Julien Mitchell, Frederick Burtwell, Anthony Shaw, Percy Walsh, Robert English, Prince Monolulu.
86 minutes. September 24, 1936. Teddington Studios

Windbag the Sailor
Written by Will Hay, Marriott Edgar, Stafford Dickens from a story by Robert Stevenson and Leslie Arliss
Will Hay, Moore Marriott, Graham Mofffatt, Norma Varden Kenneth Warrington, Dennis Wyndham, Amy Vaness, George Merritt
87 minutes. December 4, 1936. Gaumont

Feather Your Nest
Written by Austin Melford, Val Valentine, from a story by Ivar and Sheila Campbell
George Formby, Polly Ward, Enid Stamp-Taylor, Gilbert Russell, Davy Burnaby, Jack Barty, Clifford Heatherley, Fredick Burtwell, Ethel Coleridge, Jimmy Godden, Moore Marriott, Syd Crossley, Frank Perfitt.
86 minutes. Released July 19, 1937. Ealing

Take it From Me
Written by John Meehan Jr, J.O.C. Orton, from a story by Reginald Purdell
Max Miller, Betty Lynne, Buddy Baer, Clem Lawrence, Zillah Bateman, James Stephenson, Charlotte Parry, Joan Miller Valaida Snow, Victor Rietti.
78 minutes. October 22, 1937. Teddington.

Said O'Reilly to McNab
Written by Leslie Arliss
Will Mahoney, Will Fyffe, Ellis Drake, Jean Winstanley, James Carney, Sandy McDougal, Marianne Davis, Lillian Uruhart, Percy Parsons, Bob Gall
80 minutes. February 18, 1938. Gainsborough Pictures

Torchy Gets Her Man
Written by Albert DeMond based on charcaters created by Frederick Nebel
Glenda Farrell, Barton MacLane, Tom Kennedy, Willard Robertson, Thomas E. Jackson, George Guhl, Frank Reicher, John Ridgely, Joe Cunningham, Herbert Rawlinson.
63 minutes. November 12, 1938. Warner Brothers

Torchy Blane in Chinatown
Written by George Bricker, based on the story "The Purple Hieroglyph by Will Jenkins, based on characters created by Frederick Nebel
Glenda Farrell, Barton MacLane, Tom Kennedy, Henry O'Neill, Patric Knowles, James DStephenson, Janet Shaw, Frank Shannon, George Guhl, Anderson Lawler, Richard Bond, Eddy Chandler.
58 minutes. February 4, 1939 Warner Brothers

Four Shall Die
No writer credited
Niel Webster, Mantan Moreland, Laurence Criner, Dorothy Dandridge, Vernon McCalla, Monte Hawley, Reginald Fenderson, Jack Carr, Jess Lee Brooks, Edward Thompson, Earle Hall, Harry Levette.
62 minutes. October 15, 1940. Million Dollar Productions

Misbehaving Husbands
Written by Vernon Smith from a story by Cea Sabin
Harry Langdon, Betty Blythe, Esther Muir, Ralph Byrd, Gayne Whitman, Florence Wright, Luana Walters, Frank Jaquet, Charlotte Treadway, Byron Barr (Gig Young) Fred Kelsey, Mary MacLaren.
65 minutes. Released December 20, 1940. Producers Releasing Coropration

Emergency Landing
Written by Martin Mooney
Forrest Tucker, Carol Hughes, Evelyn Brent, Emmett Vogan, William Halligan, George Sherwood, Thornton Edwards, I. Stanford Jolley, Stanley Price, Jack Lescoulie, Paul Scott, Billy Curtis.
64 minutes. Released March 7, 1941. Producers Releasing Corporation

Federal Fugitives
Written by Martin Mooney
Neil Hamilton, Doris Day, Victor Varconi, Charles C. Wilson, George M. Carleton, Frank Shannon, Lyle Latell, Betty Blythe, Gerald Oliver Smith, Frank Moran
66 minutes. March 29, 1941. Producers Releasing Corporation

Mr. Washington Goes to Town
Written by Walter Weems
F.E. Miller, Mantan Moreland, Marguerite Whiten, Henry Hastings, Charlie Hawkins, Monte Hawley, DeForest Cowan, Slick Garrison, John Lester Johnson.
64 minutes. May 9, 1941. Dixie National Pictures

Desperate Cargo
Written by Morgan Cox from the story "Loot Below" by Eustace Adams
Ralph Byrd, Charlo Hughes, Jack Mulhall, Julie Duncan, I. Stanford Jolley, Kenneth Harlan, Richard Clarke, Johnstone White, Paul Bryar, Thornton Edwards, Rick Vallin.
67 minutes. July 4, 1941. Producers Releasing Corporation

Mr. Celebrity
Written by Martin Mooney
Robert "Buzz" Henry, James Seay, Doris Day, William Halligan, Laura Treadwell, Gavin Gordon, Frank Hagney, John Berkes, John Ince, Francis X. Bushman, Clara Kimball Young, James J. Jeffries, Larry Grey, Jack Baxley, Billy Mitchell.
67 minutes. Released October 10, 1941. Producers Releasing Corporation

The Miracle Kid
Written by Gerald D. Adams and John T. Coyle
Tom Neal, Carol Hughes, Vickie Lester, Betty Blythe, Ben Taggart, Alex Callam, Thornton Edwards, Joe Gray, Paul Bryar, Pat Gleason, Billy McGowan, John Ince, Gene O'Donnell, Warren Jackson, Larry McGrath.
69 minutes. November 14, 1941 Producers Releasing Corporation

Blonde Comet
Written by Martin Mooney
Virginia Vale, Robert Kent, Barney Oldfield, Vince Barnett, William Halligan, Joey Ray, Red Knight, Diana Hughes.
67 minutes. December 26, 1941. Producers Releasing Corporation

Up Jumped the Devil
Writer unknown
Mantan Moreland, Maceo Bruce Sheffield, Shelton Brooks, Laurence Criner, Myrtle Fortune, Patsy Hunter, Millie Monroe, Suzette Harbin, Avanelle Harris, Earle MOrris, Doris Ake, Florence O'Brien, Clarence Brooks.
61 minutes. Released December 31, 1941. Dixie National Pictures
Beaudine was credited as William X. Crowley.

Broadway Big Shot
Written by Martin Mooney
Ralph Byrd, Virginia Vale, William Halligan, Dick Rich, Herbert Rawlinson, Cecil Weton, Tom Herbert, Harold Kruger, Frank Hagney, Jack Buckley, Harry Depp, Jack Roper, Al Goldsmith, John Ince, Joe Oakie.
59 minutes. Released February 6, 1942. Producers Releasing Corporation

Lady Luck
Written by Vernon Smith and Lex Neal
Mantan Moreland, F.E. Miller, Maceo Bruce Sheffield, Arthur Ray, Florence O'Brien, Harold Garrison, Jessie Cryer, Nappie Whiting, Jess Lee Brooks, Ida Coffin, Nathan Curry, Millie Monroe, Louise Franklin, Lucille Battle Avanelle Harris
61 minutes. Released February 10, 1942. Dixie National Pictures
Beaudine was credited as William X. Crowley.

Professor Creeps
Written by William Beaudine, Jed Buell, Roy Clements, Robert Edmunds
Mantan Moreland, F.E. Miller, Arthur Ray, Florence O'Brien, Maceo Brice Sheffield, Marguerite Whitten, Shelton Brooks, Jessie Cryer, Billy Mitchell, Zack Williams, Charles Hawkins, Clarence Hargrave, John Lester Johnson, Nappy Whiting
63 minutes. Released February 28, 1942. Dixie National Pictures

The Panther's Claw
Written by Martin Mooney from the story "The Perfect Crime of Mr. Digberry" by Anthony Abbot/Fulton Oursler
Sidney Blackmer, Rick Vallin, Byron Foulger, Herbert Rawlinson, Lynn Starr, Barry Bernard, Gerta Rozan, Thornton Edwards, John INce, Martin Ashe, Walter James, Frank Darien, William Castello, Joseph DeVillard.
70 minutes. Released May 15, 1942. Motion Picture Associates.

Men of San Quentin
Written by Ernest Booth from a story by Martin Mooney.
J. Anthony Hughes, Eleanor Stewart, Dick Curtis, Charles Middleton, Jeffrey Sayre, George P. Breakston, Art Mills, Michael Mark, John Ince, Joe Whitehead, John "Skins" Miller, John Shay, Jack Cheatham, Drew Demarest, Nancy Evans.
80 minutes. Released May 15, 1942. Producers Releasing Corporation

Gallant Lady
Written by Arthur St Claire from a story by Octavus Roy Cohen
Rose Hobart, Sidney Blackmer, Claire Rochelle, Lynn Starr, Jane Novak, Vince Barnett, Jack Baxley, Crane Whitley, John Ince, Frank Brownlee, Richard Clarke, Spec O'Donnell, Inez Cole, Pat McKee, Ruby Dandridge.
68 minutes. Released May 29, 1942. Motion Picture Associates.

One Thrilling Night
Written by Joseph Hoffman

John Beal, Wanda McKay, Warren Hymer, J. Farrell MacDonald, Barbara Pepper, Tom Neal, Ernie Adams, Lynton Brent, Pierce Lyden, Gene O'Donnell, Jimmy O'Gatty, Tom Herbert
69 minutes. Released June 5, 1942. Monogram Pictures

Phantom Killer
Written by Karl Brown
Dick Purcell, Joan Woodbury, John Hamilton, Warren Hymer, Mantan Moreland, J. Farrell MacDonald, Gayne Whitman, Kenneth Harlan, George J. Lewis, Karl Hackett, Harry Depp, Isabel La Mal, Robert Carson, Frank Ellis.
61 minutes. October 2, 1942. Monogram Pictures

Foreign Affair
Written by John Krafft from a story by Martin Mooney.
John Shelton, Gale Storm, Ivan Lebedeff, George Travell, Patsy Moran, Lyle Latell, Hans Schumm, William Halligan, Kenneth Harlan, Herbert Rawlinson, Boyd Irwin, David Clarke, Fay Wall, Edward Peil, Paul Bryar.
64 minutes. Released October 9, 1942. Monogram Pictures

The Living Ghost
Written by Joseph Hoffman from a story by Howard Dimsdale
James Dunn, Joan Woodbury, Paul McVey, Vera Gordon, Norman Willis, J. Farrell MacDonald, Minerva Urecal, Goerge Eldredge, Jan Wiley, Edna Johnson, Danny Beck, Gus Glassmire, Lawrence Grant, Howard Banks, J. Arthur Young.
61 minutes. Released November 27, 1942. Monogram Pictures

The Ape Man
Written by Barney Sarecky from the story "The Creep in the Dark" by Karl Brown
Bela Lugosi, Louise Currie, Wallace Ford, Henry Hall, Minerva Urecal, Emil Van Horn, J. Farrell MacDonald, Wheeler Oakman, Ralph Littlefield, Juack Mulhall, Charles Jordan.
68 minutes Released March 5, 1943. Monogram Pictures

Clancy Street Boys
Written by Harvey Gates
Leo Gorcey, Huntz Hall, Bobby Jordan, Noah Beery, Amelita Ward, Benny Bartlett, Rick Vallin, Billy Benedict, J. Farrell MacDonald, Jan Rubini, Martha Wentworth, Ernest "Sunshine Sammy" Morrison, Dick Chandlee, Eddie Mills, George DeNormand.
66 minutes. Released April 23, 1943. Monogram Pictures.

Ghosts on the Loose
Written by Kenneth Higgins
Leo Gorcey, Huntz Hall, Bobby Jordan, Bela Lugosi, Ava Gardner, Rick Vallin, Ernest "Sunshine Sammy" Morrison, Billy Benedict, Stanley Clements, Bobby Stone, Minerva Urecal, Wheeler Oakman, Peter Seal, Frank Moran, Jack Mulhall.
65 minutes. Released June 30, 1943. Monogram Pictures.

Here Comes Kelly
Written by Charles R. Marion from a story by Dore Schary
Eddie Quillan, Joan Woodbury, Maxie Rosenbloom, Armida, Sidney Miller, Mary Gordon, Ian Keith, Luis Alberni, Charles Jordan, Emmett Vogan, John Dilson.
64 minutes. September 9, 1943. Monogram Pictures.

Spotlight Scandals
Written by Beryl Sachs and William Beaudine (billed as William X Crowley)
Billy Gilbert, Frank Fay, Bonnie Baker, Billy "Butch" Lenhart and Kenneth "Buddy" Brown, Harry Langdon, Iris Adrian, James Bush, Claudia Dell, Eddie Parks, Betty Blythe, Wheeler Oakman, Lottie Harrison, Jim Hope, Jack Boyle, Henry King's Orchestra, Herb Miller and his Orchestra, The Radio Rogues.
79 minutes. September 24, 1943. Monogram Pictures

Mr. Muggs Steps Out
Written by Beryl Sachs and William Beaudine (billed as William X Crowley)
Leo Gorcey, Huntz Hall, Gabriel Dell, Billy Benedict, Joan Marsh, Bobby Stone, Buddy Gorman, David Durand, Jimmy Strand, Patsy Moran, Eddie Gribbon, Halliwell Hobbes, Stanley Brown, Betty Blythe, Emmett Vogan.
63 minutes. October 29, 1943. Monogram Pictures.

The Mystery of the 13th Guest
Written by Tim Ryan and Charles R. Marion
Dick Purcell, Helen Parrish, Tim Ryan, Frank Faylen, Johnny Duncan, John Dawson, Addison Richards, Jacqueline Dalya, Cyril Ring, Paul McVey, Lloyd Ingraham
60 minutes. November 5, 1953. Monogram Pictures.

What a Man!
Written by Beryl Sachs and William Beaudine (billed as William X Crowley)

Johnny Downs, Wanda McKay, Robert Kent, Etta McDaniel, Harry Holman, I. Stanford Jolley, Wheeler Oakman, Lillian Bronson, Jack Baxley, Jack Baxley, John Ince, Betty Sinclair, Dick Rush, Jim Farley, Henry Hall, Ralph Cathey
67 minutes. January 31, 1944. Monogram Pictures

Voodoo Man
Written by Robert Charles
Bela Lugosi, John Carradine, George Zucco, Wanda McKay, Louise Currie, Tod Andrews, Ellen Hall, Terry Lwalker, Mary Currier, Claire James, Henry Hall, Dan White, Pat McKee, Mici Goty.
62 minutes February 21, 1944 Monogram Pictures

Hot Rhythm
Written by Tim Ryan and Charles R. Marion
Robert Lowery, Dona Drake, Tim Ryan, Irene Ryan, Sidney Miller, Jerry Cooper, Harry Langdon, Robert Kent, Lloyd Ingraham, Cyril Ring, Joan Curtis, Paul Porcasi
79 minutes. April 22, 1944. Monogram Pictures

Detective Kitty O'Day
Written by Tim Ryan and Victor Hammond from a story by Hammond
Jean Parker, Peter Cookson, Tim Ryan, Veda Ann Borg, Edward Gargan, Douglas Fowley, Pat Gleason, Olaf Hytten, Edward Earle, Herbert Heyes.
61 minutes. May 13, 1944. Monogram Pictures

Follow the Leader
Written by Beryl Sachs and William Beaudine (billed as William X Crowley) from the story "East of the Bowery" by Ande Lamb.
Leo Gorcey, Huntz Hall, Gabriel Dell, Billy Benedict, Jack La Rue, David Durand, Bobby Stone, Jimmy Strand, Buddy Gorman, Bryant Washburn, J. Farrell MacDonald, Joan Marsh, Gene Austin, Doris and Grace Sherrill, Bernard Gorcey, Mary Gordon, Marie Windsor, Ernie "Sunshine Sammy" Morrison.
65 minutes. June 3, 1944. Monogram Pictures

Leave it to the Irish
Written by Eddie Davis and Tim Ryan
James Dunn, Wanda McKay, Jack La Rue, Dick Purcell, Arthur Loft, Babara Wooddell, Vince Barnett, Joseph DeVillard, Olaf Hytten, Eddie Allen, Dick Scott, Ted Stanhope
71 minutes. August 26, 1944. Monogram Picture

Oh, What a Night!
Written by Paul Gerard Smith from a story by Marion Orth
Edmund Lowe, Jean Parker, Marjorie Rambeau, Alan Dinehart, Pierre Watkin, Ivan Lebedeff, Claire Du Brey, Charles MIller, Olaf Hytten, Karin Lang, George J. Lewis, Crane Whitney, Charles Jordan, Dick Rush
72 minutes. September 2, 1944. Monogram Pictures

Shadow of Suspicion
Written by Albert Demond, Earle Snell, Tim Ryan, from a story by Harold Goldman
Marjorie Weaver, Peter Cookson, Tim Ryan, Pierre Watking Clara Blandick, J. Farrell MacDonald, John Hamilton, Tom Herbert, Anthony Warde, George J. Lewis, Frank Scannell, Ralph Lewis, Cyril Delevanti, Ralph Littlefield, Wilburn Mack, Charlotte Treadway, Jimmy Aubrey, Dudley Dickerson.
68 minutes. September 23, 1944. Monogram Pictures.

Bowery Champs
Screenplay by Earle Snell, Morey Amsterdam
Leo Gorcey, Huntz Hall, Billy Benedict, Bobby Jordan, Gabriel Dell, Thelma White, Evelyn Brent, Ian Keith, Frank Jaquet, Fred Kelsey, Anne Sterling, William Ruhl, Wheeler Oakman, Buddy Gorman, Jimmy Strand.
62 minutes. November 25, 1944. Monogram Pictures

Crazy Knights
Screenplay by Tim Ryan
Billy Gilbert, Shemp Howard, Maxie Rosenbloom, Tim Ryan, Jayne Hazard, Tay Dunn, Minerva Urecal, John Hamilton, Bernard Sell, Betty Sinclair, Buster Brodie, Art Miles, Dan White.
63 minutes. December 8, 1943. Monogram Pictures.
alternate title: *Ghost Crazy*

Mom and Dad
Written by Mildred Horn and Kroger Babb, from a story by Horn
June Carlson, Losi Austin, George Eldredge, Jimmy Clark, Hardie Albright, Bob Lowell, Willa Pearl Curtis, Jimmy Zahner, Jane Isbell, Robert Filmer, Forrest Taylor, John Hamilton, Virginia Vane, Kaye Renard, Elliot Forbest, Wheeler Oakman, Francis Ford, Jack Roper, Lucille Vance, Betty Sinclair.
97 minutes. January 3, 1945 (premiere). Hallmark Productions

Adventures of Kitty O'Day
Written by George Callahan, Tim Ryan, and Victor Hammond from the story "Kitty O'Day Comes Through by Hammond.
Jean Parker, Peter Cookson, Tim Ryan, Lorna Gray, Jan Wiley, Ralph Sanford, William Forrest, Byron Foulger, Hugh Prosser, Dick Elliot, William Ruhl, Shelton Brooks.
63 minutes. January 19, 1945. Monogram Pictures

Fashion Model
Written by Tim Ryan and Victor Hammond from a story by Hammond
Robert Lowery, Marjorie Weaver, Tim Ryan, Lorna Gray, Dorothy Christy, Dewey Robinson, Sally Yarnell, Jack Norton, Harry Depp, Nell Craig, Edward Keane, John Valentine.
61 minutes. March 2, 1945. Monogram Pictures.

Blonde Ransom
Written by M. Coates Webster from a story by Robert T. Shannon
Donald Cook, Virginia Grey, Pinky Lee, Collete Lyons, George Barbier, Jerome Cowan, George Meeker, Ian Wolfe, Joe Kirk, Charles Delaney, Frank Reicher, William B. Davidson, Chester Clute, Janina Frostova.
68 minutes. May 7, 1945. Universal Studios.

Swingin' on a Rainbow
Written by Olive Cooper and John Grey
Jane Frazee, Stanley Brown, Harry Langdon, Minna Gombell, Amelita WEard, Tim Ryan, Paul Harvey Wendell Niles, Richard Davies, Helen Talbott.
72 minutes. September 1, 1945. Republic Pictures

Come Out Fighting
Written by Earle Snell
Leo Gorcey, Huntz Hall, Billy Benedict, Gabriel Dell, June Carlson, Amelita Ward, Addison Richards, George Meeker, Johnny Fucnan, Buddy Gorman, Fred Kelsey, Douglas Wood, Milton Kibbee, Pat Gleason, Robert Homans.
62 minutes. September 29, 1945. Monogram Pictures.

Black Market Babies
Written by George Wallace Sayre, based on a story by George Maurice which was based on an article by Virginia Reid.
Ralph Morgan, Kane Richmond, Jayne Hazard, Teala Loring, Marjoie Hoshelle, George Meeker, Maris Wrixton, Nana Bryant, Addison Richards, Anthony Warde, Selmer Jackson, Dewey Robinson, Alan Foster, Parker Gee, John Gallaudette, Dorothy Christy.
71 minutes. December 15, 1945. Monogram Pictures.

Girl on the Spot
Written by Dorcas Cochran and Jerry Warner from a story by George Blake and Jack Hartfield with additional dialog by Stanley Davis.
Lois Collier, Jess Barker, George Dolenz, Fuzzy Knight, Ludwig Stössel, Richard Lane, Donald Mac Bride, Edward Brophy, Sarah Edwards, John Hamilton, Robert Homans, George Lynn, Carol Hughes, Cyril Ring, Ralph Sanford, Ray Walker, Forrest Taylor, Gene Roth. 75 minutes. January 11, 1946. Universal Pictures

The Face of Marble
Written by Michael Jacoby based on a story by Edmund L. Hartmann
John Carradine, Claudia Drake, Robert Shayne, Maris Wrixon, Willie Best, Thomas E. Jackson, Rosa Rey, Neil Burns, Donald Kerr, Allan Ray.
72 minutes. January 19, 1946. Monogram Pictures

One Exciting Week
Written by Jack Townley from a story by Dennis Murray
Al Pearce, Pinky Lee, Jerome Cowan, Shemp Howard, Arlene Harris, Mary Treen, Lorraine Krueger, Maury Dexter, Will Wright, Arthur Loft, Chester Clute, The Teen-Agers.
69 minutes. June 8, 1946, Republic Pictures

Don't Gamble With Strangers
Written by Caryl Coleman and Harvey Gates
Kane Richmond, Bernadene Hayes, Peter Cookson, Gloria Warren, Charles Trowbridge, Freank Dae, Anthony Caruso, Phil Van Zandt, Harold Goodwin, Leonard Mudie, Bill Kennedy, Addison Richards, Ferris Taylor, Edith Evanson.
68 minutes. June 22, 1946. Monogram Pictures.

Below The Deadline
Written by Forrest Judd and Harvey Gates
Warren Douglas, Ramsay Ames, Jan Wiley, Paul Maxey, Phil Van Zandt, John Harmon, Bruce Edwards, George Meeker, Clancy Cooper, Cay Forester, Al Bridge, George Eldredge, William Ruhl, Vera Pavlovska, Charles Sullivan.
65 minutes. August 3, 1946. Monogram Pictures.

Spook Busters
Written by Edmond Seward and Tim Ryan
Leo Gorcey, Huntz Hall, Bobby Jordan, Gabe Dell, Billy Benedict, David Gorcey, Tanis Chandler, Douglas Dumbrille, Bernard Gorcey, Vera Lewis, Charles Middleton, Richard Alexander, Charles Millsfield.
68 minutes. August 24, 1946. Monogram Pictures

Mr. Hex
Written by Cy Endfield from a story by Jan Grippo
Leo Gorcey, Huntz Hall, Bobby Jordan, Gabe Dell, Billy Benedict, Bernard Gorcey, David Gorcey, Gale Robbins, Ben Welden, Ian Keith, Sammy Cohen, William Ruhl, Danny Beck, Rita Lynn, Joe Gray
63 minutes. December 7, 1946. Monogram Pictures.

Phil Vance Returns
Written by Robert E. Kent based on the character created by S.S. Van Dine
William Wright, Vivian Austin, Leon Belasco, Clara Blandick, Ramsay Ames, Famian O'Flynn, Frank Wilcox, Iris Adrian, Ann Staunton, Tim Murdock, Mary Scttt.
64 minutes. April 14, 1947. Producers Releasing Corporation

Hard Boiled Mahoney
Written by Cyr Endfield and Edmond Seard
Leo Gorcey, Huntz Hall, Bobby Jordan, Gabe Dell, Betty Compson, Billy Benedict, David Corcey Teala Loring, Dan Seymour, Byron Foulger, Patti Brill.
63 mi9nutes. May 10, 1947. Monogram Pictures

Too Many Winners
John Sutherland, Fred Myton, Scott Darling, from a story by Brett Halliday based on his characters.
Hugh Beaumont, Trudy Marshall, Ralph Dunn, Claire Carleton, Charles Mitchell, John Hamilton, Ben Welden, Byron Foulger, Grandon Rhodes, George Meader
61 minutes. May 24, 1947. Producers Releasing Corporation.

Killer at Large
Written by Fenton Earnshaw and Thomas W Blackburn
Robert Lowery, Anabel Shaw, Charles Evans, Frank Ferguson, George Lynn, Dick Rich, Ann Stanton, Leonard Penn, Eddie Parks, Stanley Blystone
61 minutes. May 31, 1947. Producers Releasing Corporation
(a 26 minute edit was released to television)

Gas House Kids Go West
Written by Robert Kent, Robert McGowan, Eugene Conrad from a story by Sam Baerwitz
Emory Parnell, Chili Williams, Vince Barnett, William Wright, Carl "Alfalfa' Switzer, Benny Bartlett, Rudy Wissler, Tommy Bond, Lela Bliss
62 minutes. June 12, 1947. Producers Releasing Corporation.

News Hounds
Written by Edmond Seard and Tim Ryan
Leo Gorcey, Huntz Hall, Bobby Jordan, Gabe Dell, Billy Benedict, David Gorcey, Christine McIntyre, Tim Ryan, Anthony Caruso. Bill Kennedy, Ralph Dunn, Nita Bieber, John Hamilton, Terry Goodman, Robert Emmett Keane.
68 minutes. September 13, 1947. Monogram Pictures

Bowery Buckaroos
Written by Edmond Seward and Tim Ryan
Leo Gorcey, Huntz Hall, Bobby Jordan, Bernard Gorcey, Gabe Dell, Billy Benedict, David Gorcey, Julie Gibson, Russell Simpson, Minerva Urecal, Iron Eyes, Cody, Rosa Turich, Cheif Yowlachie, Sherman Sanders.
66 minutes. November 22, 1947. Monogram Pictures

The Chinese Ring
Written by Scott Darling based on the character created by Earl Derr Biggers
Roland Winters, Warren Douglas, Mantan Moreland, Victor Sen Yung, Phillip Ahn, Byron Foulger, Thayer Roberts, Jean Wong, Dimples Cooper, George Spaulding.
68 minutes. December 6, 1947. Monogram Pictures.

Angels Alley
Written by Edmond Seward, Tim Ryan, and Geral Schnitzer
Leo Gorcey, Huntz Hall, Gabriel Dell, Billy Benedict, David Gorcey, Frankie Darro, Nestor Paiva. Rosemary La Planche, Geneva Gray Benny Bartlett, John Eldredge, Nelson Leigh. Thomas Menzies, Mary Gordon, Dick Paxoton.
67 minutes. March 7, 1948, Monogram Pictures.

Jinx Money
Written by Edmond Seward, Tim Ryan, Gerald Schnitzer, from a story by Jerome T. Gollard.
Leo Gorcey, Huntz Hall, Gabriel Dell, Billy Benedict, Bernard Gorcey, Benny Bartlett, David Gorcey, Sheldon Leonard, Conald MacBride, Betty Caldwell, John Eldredge, Ben Welden, Lucien Littlefield, Benny Baker, Ralph Dunn
68 minutes. Released June 27, 1948. Monogram Pictures.

Shanghai Chest
Written by Samuel Newman and Scott Darling from a story by Newman, based characters by Earl Derr Biggers.

Roland Winters, Mantan Moreland, Tim Ryan, Victor Sen Yung, Deannie Best, Tristam Coffin, John Alvin, Russell Hicks, Pierre Watkin, Phillip Van Zandt, Milton Parsons, Olaf Hytten, Erville Alderson, George Eldredge, Lois Austin, Willie Best, Chabing, Eddie Coke.
65 minutes. Released July 11, 1948. Monogram Pictures

The Golden Eye
Written by Scott Darling based characters by Earl Derr Biggers.
Roland Winters, Wanda McKay, Mantan Moreland, Victor Sen Yung, Bruce Hellogg, Tim Ryan, Evelyn Brendt, Ralph Dunn, Lois Austin, Forrest Taylor, Lee Lasses White
69 minutes. Released August 29, 1948. Monogram Pictures

Smuggler's Cove
Written by Edward Seward and Tim Ryan
Leo Gorcey, Huntz Hall, Gabe Dell, Billy Benedict, Benny Bartlett, David Gorcey, Martin Kosleck, Paul Harvey, Amelita Ward, Jacqueline Dalya, Eddie Gribbon, Hans Schumm, Gene Roth, Emmett Vogan, Buddy Gorman.
66 minutes. October 10, 1948. Monogram Pictures

Incident
Written by Fred Niblo Jr from a story by Harry Lewis.
Warren Douglas, Jane Frazee, Robert Osterloh, Joyce Compton, Harry Lauther, Anthony Caruso, Eddie Dunn, Meyer Grace, Pierre Watkin, Ralph Dunn, John Shay, Lynn Millan, Harry Cheshire, Robert Emmett Keane.
66 minutes. October 30, 1948. Monogram Pictures

Kidnapped
Written by Scott Darling based on the novel by Robert Louis Stevenson
Roddy McDowall, Sue England, Dan O'Herlihy, Roland Winters, Jeff Corey, Houseley Stevenson, Erskine Sanford, Alex Frazer, Winifriede McDowall, Robert J. Anderson, Janet Murdoch, Olaf Hytten, Erville Alderson
81 minutes. November 28, 1948. Monogram Pictures.

Jiggs and Maggie in Court
Written by Barney Gerard based on the characters by George McManus
Joe Yule, Renie Riano, George McManus, June Harrison, Riley Hill, Tim Ryan, Robert Lowell, Pat Goldin, Dick Ryan, Cliff Clark, Jimmy Aubrey, Jean Fenwich, Frank Austin, Russell Hicks, Chester Clute.
62 minutes. December 12, 1948. Monogram Pictures.

The Feathered Serpent
Written by Oliver Drake from his story "Riders of the Whistling Skull," based on characters created by Earl Derr Biggers.
Roland Winters, Keye Luke, Mantan Moreland, Victor Sen Yung, Carol Forman, Robert Livingston, Nils Asther, Beverly Jons, Martin Garralaga, George J. Lewis, Leslie Denison.
61 minutes. December 19, 1948. Monogram Pictures

The Lawton Story
Written by Scott Darling from a story by Mildred Horn and Mark QWallock.
Ginger Prince, Forrest Taylor, Millard Coody, Ferris Taylor, Gwyn Shipman, Darlene Bridges, Maude Eburne, Willa Pearl Curtis. Raymond Largay, A.S. Fischer, Hazel Lee Becker, William Ruhl, Russ Whiteman, Knox Manning, Lydia McKim.
120 minutes. April 1, 1950. Hallmark Productions
Also known as The Prince of Peace

Tuna Clipper
Written by Scott Darling
Roddy McDowall, Elena Verdugo, Roland Winters, Peter Mamkos, Rick Vallin, Michael Vallon, Russell Simpson, Doris Kemper, Dickie Moore, Richard Avonde Victor Sen Yung.
77 minutes. April 10, 1949. Monogram Pictures

Forgotten Women
Written by Scott Darling based on a story by Jerry Bernerd
Elyse Knox, Edward Norris, Robert Shayne, Theodora Lynch, Veda Ann Borg, Noel Neill, Tim Ryan, Bill Kennedy, Warren Douglas, Selmer Jackson, Paul Frison.
65 minutes. July 17, 1949. Monogram Pictures

Trail of the Yukon
Written by Oliver Drake, from the story "The Gold Hunters" by James Oliver Curwood
Kirby Grant, Suzanne Dalbert, Bill Edwards, Iris Adrian, Dan Seymour, Anthony Warde, Maynard Holmes, Peter Mamakos, Guy Beach, Stanley Andrews, Dick Elliott, Jay SIlverheels, Bill Kennedy, Harrison Hearne.
67 minutes. July 31, 1949. Monogram Pictures.

Jiggs and Maggie in Jackpot Jitters
Written by Barney Gerard based on characters created by George McManus.

Joe Yule, Renie Riano, George McManus, Tim Ryan, Pat Goldin, June Harrison, Sam Hayes, Joe Hernandez.
67 minutes. August 28, 1949. Monogram Pictures

Tough Assignment
Written by Milton Luban from a story by Carl Hittleman
Don "Red" Barry, Marjorie Steele, Steve Brodie, Marc Lawrence, Ben Welden, Sid Melton, John Cason, Frank Richards, Fred Kohler jr, Michael Whalen, Edith Apgold, Leander DeCordova, Stanley Andrews, Stanley Price, Iris Adrian
64 minutes. November 15, 1949. Lippert Pictures.

Blue Grass of Kentucky
Written by Scott Darling
Bill Williams, Jane Nigh, Ralph Morgan, Russell Hicks, Buzz Henry, Ted Hecht, Dick Foote, Jack Howard, Bill Terrell, Stephen Harrison, Pierre Watkin, Harry Lauter.
72 minutes. January 22, 1950. Monogram Pictures

Blonde Dynamite
Written by Charles R. Marion
Leo Gorcey, Huntz Hall, Gabriel Dell, Billy Benedict, Buddy Gorman, David Gorcey, Bernard Gorcey, Adele Jergens, Harry Lewis, Murray Alper, Jody Gilbert, John Harmon, Michael Ross, Lynn Davies, Beverlee Crane.
66 minutes. February 12, 1950. Monogram Pictures

Jiggs and Maggie Out West
Written by Barney Gerard based on characters created by George McManus
Joe Yule, Renie Riano, George McManus, Tim Ryan, Jim Bannon, Riley Hill, Pat Goldin, June Harrison, Henry Kulky, Terry McGinnis, Billy Griffith
66 minutes. April 23, 1950. Monogram Pictures.

Lucky Losers
Written by Charles R. Marion with additional dialog by Bert Lawrence
Leo Gorcey, Huntz Hall, Gabriel Dell, Billy Benedict, David Gorcey, Buddy Gorman, Bernard Gorcey, Hillary Brooke, Lyle Talbot, Joe Turkel, Harry Tyler, Harry Cheshire, Frank Jenks, Douglas Evans, Wendy Waldron.
70 minutes. May 14, 1950. Monogram Pictures

County Fair
Written by Scott Darling
Rory Calhoun, Jane Nigh, Florence Bates, Warren Douglas, Raymond Hatton, Emory Parnell, Rory Mallinson, Harry Cheshire, Milton Kibbee, Roy E. Shudt
76 minutes. July 20, 1950. Monogram Pictures

A Wonderful Life
Written by Alan Shilin
James Dunn, Allene Roberts, Isabel Withers, Arthur Shields, Robert Board, Madge Crane, Andrew Tombes, Donna Jo Boyce, Jack Larson, David Kasday, Sam Flint, Dorothy Vaughan, Isabel Randolph, Ray Walker, Bob Lowell
43 minutes. August 14, 1950. Protestant Film Commission

Second Chance
Written by Robert Presnell Sr. based on a story by Faith Baldwin
Ruth Warrick, John Hubbard, Hugh Beaumont, David Holt, Pat Combs, Ellye Marshall, John Holland, Joan Carroll, John Marston, Jamesson Shade, Fay Kern.
72 minutes. September 6 1950. Protestant Film Commission

Blues Busters
Written by Charles Marion
Leo Gorcey, Huntz Hall, Gabriel Dell, Billy Benedict, David Gorcey, Buddy Gorman, Bernard Gorcey, Adele Jergens, Craig Stevens, Phyllis Coates, Paul Bryar, Matty King, Sailor Vincent.
67 minutes. October 29, 1950. Monogram Pictures

Again...Pioneers
Written by Oviatt McConnell with additional dialog by Alan Shilin
Colleen Townsend, Tom Powers, Sarah Padden, Regis Toomey, Jimmy Hunt, Evelyn Brent, Larry Olsen, Larry Carr, Erville Alderson, Peggy Wynne, Melinda Casey, Gene Roth, Judith Allen, Harry Cheshire, Hart Wayne.
72 minutes. November 2, 1950. Protestant Film Commission

Bowery Battalion
Written by Charles Marion with additional dialog by Bert Lawrence
Leo Gorcey, Huntz Hall, Billy Benedict, Buddy Gorman, David Gorcey, Bernard Gorcey, Donald MacBride, Virginia Hewitt, Russell Hicks, John Bleifer, Al Eben, Frank Jenks, Selmer Jackson.
69 minutes. January 24, 1951. Monogram Pictures

Cuban Fireball
Written by Charles Roberts
Estelita Rodriguez, Warren Douglas, Mimi Auglia, Leon Belasco, Donald MacBride, Rosa Turich, John Litel, Tim Ryan, Russ Vincent, Edward Gargan, Victoria Horne, Jack Kruschen, Pedro de Cordoba, Olan Soule, Tony Barr.
78 minutes. March 5, 1951. Republic Pictures

Ghost Chasers
Written by Charles Marion with additional dialog by Bert Lawrence
Leo Gorcey, Huntz Hall, Billy Benedict, Buddy Gorman, David Gorcey, Bernard Gorcey, Lloyd Corrigan, Lela Bliss, Phil Van Zandt, Jan Kayne, Argentina Brunetti, Marshall Bradford, Robert Coogan, Michael Ross.
69 minutes. April 29, 1951. Monogram Pictures

Let's Go Navy
Written by Leonard Stern with additional dialog by Bert Lawrence
Leo Gorcey, Huntz Hall, Bill Benedict, Buddy Gorman, David Gorcey, Bernard Gorcey, Allen Jenkins, Tom Neal, Charlita, Richard Benedict, Paul Harvey, Jonathan Hale, Emory Parnell, Douglas Evans, Frank Jenks
68 minutes. July 29, 1951. Monogram Pictures

Havanna Rose
Written by Charles Roberts and Jack Townley
Estelita Rodriguez, Bill WIlliams, Hugh Herbert, Florence Bates, Fortunio Bonanova, Leon Belasco, Nacho Galindo, Martin Garralaga, Rosa Turich, Tom Kennedy, Manuel Paris, Bob Easton, Evelynne Smith, Felix and his Martiniques, Geri Galian and his Rhumba Band.
77 minutes. September 15, 1951. Republic Pictures

Crazy Over Horses
Written by Tim Ryan
Leo Gorcey, Huntz Hall, Billy Benedict, David Gorcey, Benny Bartlett, Bernard Gorcey, Ted de Corsia, Allen Jenkins, Gloria Saunders, Tim Ryan, Micahel Ross, Russell Hicks, Peggy Wynne, Sam Balter, Leo "Ukie" Sherin.
65 minutes. November 18, 1951. Monogram Pictures.

Rodeo
Written by Charles Marion
Jane Nigh, John Archer, Wallace Ford, Gary Gray, Frances Rafferty, Sara Haden, Frank Ferguson, Myron Healey, Fuzzy Knight, Robert Karnes, Jim Bannon, I. Stanford Jolley.
70 minutes. March 9, 1952. Monogram Pictures

Hold That Line
Written by Tim Ryan and Charles Marion
Leo Gorcey, Huntz Hall, David Gorcey, Benny Bartlett, Bernard Gorcey, Gil Stratton, John Bromfield, Veda Ann Borg, Mona Knox, Gloria Winters, Taylor Holmes, Francis Perlot, Pierre Watkin, Bob Nichols, Paul Bryar.
67 minutes. March 23, 1952. Monogram Pictures

Jet Job
Written by Charles Marion
Stanley Clements, Elena Verdugo, John Litel, Robert Nichols, Tom Powers, Dorothy Adams, Todd Karns, Paul Stanton, Dave Willock, John Kellogg, Russ Conway, Stephen Roberts, Arthur Space, William Forrest, William Tannen.
63 minutes. April 6, 1952. Monogram Pictures

Here Come The Marines
Written by Tim Ryan and Charles Marion
Leo Gorcey, Huntz Hall, David Gorcey, Benny Bartlett, Gil Stratton, Bernard Gorcey, Hanley Stafford, Myrna Dell, Murray Alper, Arthur Space, Tim Ryan, Paul Maxey, William Newell, Lisa Wilson, Riley Hill.
66 minutes. June 29, 1952. Monogram Pictures.

The Rose Bowl Story
Written by Charles R. Marion
Marshall Thompson, Vera Miles, Richard Rober, Natalie Wood, Keith Larsen, Tom Harmon, Ann Doan, James Dobson, Jim Backus, Clarence Kolb, Barbara Woodell, Bill Welsh.
73 minutes. August 24, 1952. Monogram Pictures

Bela Lugosi Meets a Brooklyn Gorilla
Written by Tim Ryan
Bela Lugosi, Duke Mitchell, Sammy Petrillo, Charlita, Muriel Landers, Al Kikume, Mickey Simpson, Milton Newberger, Martin Garralaga
74 minutes. October 8, 1952. Realart Pictures

Feudin' Fools
Written by Bert Lawrence and Tim Ryan
Leo Gorcey, Huntz Hall, David Gorcey, Benny Bartlett, Bernard Gorcey, Dorothy Ford, Lyle Talbot, Benny Baker, Anne Kimbell, Oliver Blake, Fuzzy Knight Robert Easton, O.Z. Whitehead, Paul Wexler, Russell Simpson
63 minutes. September 21, 1952. Monogram Pictures

No Holds Barred
Written by Jack Crutcher, Bert Lawrence, Tim Ryan
Leo Gorcey, Huntz Hall, David Gorcey Benny Bartlett, Bernard Gorcey, Marjorie Reynolds, Leonard Penn, Henry Kulky, Hombre Montana, Sandra Gould, Tim Ryan, Lisa Wilson, Murray Alper, Barbara Gray, Ukie Sherin.
65 minutes. November 23, 1952. Monogram Pictures.

Jalopy
Written by Jack Crutcher and Tim Ryan with additional dialog by Bert Lawrence
Leo Gorcey, Huntz Hall, David Gorcey, Benny Bartlett, Bernard Gorcey, Robert Lowery, Leon Belasco, Richard Benedict, Jane Easton, Murray Alper, Tom Hanlon, Mona Knox
62 minutes. February 15, 1953. Monogram Pictures

Born to the Saddle
Written by Adele Buffington from the novel by Gordon Ray Young
Leif Erickson, Donald Woods, Rand Brooks, Chuck Courtney, Karen Morley, Glenn Strange, Robert J. Anderson, Milton Kibbee, Boyd Davis, Lucille Thompson, Dolores Prest, Fred Kohler Jr, Dan White
77 minutes. March 15, 1953. Astor Pictures

Roar of the Crowd
Written by Charles Marion
Howard Duff, Helene Stanley, Dave Willock, Louise Arthur, Minor Watson, Harry Shannon, Don Haggerty, Edna Holland, Ray Walker, Paul Bryar, Johnnie Parsons, Henry Banks, Manuel Ayulo, Duke Nalon, Bill Vukovich
71 minutes. May 31, 1953. Monogram Pictures

Murder Without Tears
Written by Jo Pagano and William Raynor
Craig Stevens, Joyce Holden, Richard Benedict, Edward Norris, Clair Regis, Tom Hubbard, Murray Alper, Robert Carson, Murray Pollack, Edith Angold, Leonard Penn, Hal Gerard, Burt Wenland, Fred Kelsey, Gregg Sanders
65 minutes. June 14, 1953. Allied Artists

For Every Child
William Ching, June Whitney Taylor, Regis Toomey, Susan Odin, B.G. Norman, Helen Burnett, David Saber, Phil Bonnell, Robert Livingston.
28 minutes. Protestant Film Commission

High Society
Written by Jerome Gottler from a story by Edward Bernds and Ellwood Ullman
Leo Gorcey, Huntz, Hall, Bernard Gorcey, Amanda Blake, David Gorcey, Benny Bartlett, Addison Richards, Paul Harvey, Dayton Lummis, Ronald Keith, Gavin Gordon, Dave Barry, Kem Dibbs.
61 minutes. April 17, 1955. Allied Artists

Jail Busters
Written by Edward Bernds and Ellwood Ullman
Leo Gorcey, Huntz Hall, Bernard Gorcey, Barton MacLane, Anthony Caruso, Percy Helton, David Gorcey, Benny Bartlett, Lyle Talbot, Michael Ross, John Harmon, Murray Alper.
61 minutes. September 18, 1955. Allied Aritsts

The Beginning
Written by Morton Wishengrad
43 minutes. Protestant Film Commission

Each According to His Faith
45 minutes. Protestant Film Commission

Design for Dreaming
Tad Tadlock, Marc Breaux, Thurl Ravenscroft
10 minutes. Coronet Media

Westward Ho, The Wagons
Written by Tom Blackburn based on the novel by Mary Jane Carr
Fess Parker, Kathleen Crowley, Jeff York, David Stollery, Sebastian Cabot, George Reeves, Doreen Tracey, Barbara Wooddell, John War Eagle, Cubby O'Brien, Tommy Cole, Leslie Bradley, Morgan Woodward, Iron Eyes Cody, Anthony Numkena
90 minutes. December 20, 1956. Walt Disney Productions

Up in Smoke
Written by Jack Townley and Bert Lawrence from a story by Lawrence
Huntz Hall, Stanley Clements, David Gorcey, Eddie LeRoy, Dick Elliott, Judy Bamber, Byron Foulger, Ralph Sanford, Ric Roman, Joe Devlin, Fritz Feld, Benny Rubin, James Flavin, Earle hodgins, John Mitchum.
61 minutes. December 22, 1957. Allied Artists

In The Money
Written by Al Martin and Ellwood Ullman from a story by Martin
Huntz Hall, Stanley Clements, Patricia Donahue, Paul Cavanaugh, David Gorcey Eddie LeRoy, Leonard Penn, John Dodsworth, Jack Mulhall

62 minutes. February 16, 1958. Allied Artists
The Secret of the Gift
Written by Fredric Frank, Paul Heard
28 minutes. Protestant Film Commission

Ten Who Dared
Written by Lawrence Edward Watkin based on the journal by Major John Wesley Powell
Brian Keith, John Beal, James Drury, R.G. Armstrong, Ben Johnson, L.Q. Jones, Dan Sheridan, David Stollery, Stan Jones, David Frankham
92 minutes. November 1, 1960. Walt Disney Productions

Jesse James Meets Frankenstein's Daughter
Written by Carl Hittleman
John Lupton, Narda Onyx, Cal Bolder Estelita Rodriguez, Jim Davis, Steven Geray, Rayford Barnes, William Fawcett, Nestor Paiva, Roger Creed, Rosa Turich, Felipe Turich, Fred Stromsoe, Dan White, Page Slattery
88 minutes. April 10, 1966. Embassy Pictures

Billy the Kid Versus Dracula
Written by Carl Hittleman
John Carradine, Chuck Courtney, Melinda Casey, Virginia Christie, Walter Janovitz, Bing Russell, Olive Carey, Roy Barcroft, Hannie Landman, Richard Reeves, Marjorie Bennett, William Forrest, George Cisar, Harry Carey Jr, Leonard P. Geer
74 minutes. April 10, 1966. Embassy Pictures

TELEVISION

Racket Squad
Reed Hadley
CBS TV
1951-1953

Adventures of Wild Bill Hickock
Guy Madison, Andy Devine
CBS TV
1953

TV's Reader's Digest
Two Episodes
ABC TV
1955

The Mickey Mouse Club
Walt Disney Productions
1955

The Adventures of Spin and Marty
Walt Disney Productions
1955

Treasury Men in Action
ABC (1950)
NBC (1951-1954)
ABC (1955)

Corky and the White Shadow
Walt Disney Productions
1956

Adventures in Dairyland
Walt Disney Productions
1956

Further Adventures of Spin and Marty
Walt Disney Productions
1956

Circus Boy
Micky Dolenz
NBC
1956

Broken Arrow
John Lupton, Michael Ansara
ABC
1956

Naked City
Harry Bellaver, Horace McMahon
ABC
1958

The Adventures of Rin Tin Tin
Lee Aaker, James Brown, Joe Sawyer, Rand Brooks
ABC
1957-1959

Rescue 8
Jim Davis, Lang Jeffries
1958-1959

Lassie
Jon Provost, June Lockhart, Hugh Reilly, Andy Clyde (1957-1964)
Robert Bray (1964-1968)
CBS

Lassie's Great Adventure
Jon Provost
Feature length version of several Lassie TV episodes
1966

The Green Hornet
Van Williams, Bruce Lee
ABC
1966-1967

Flight of the Cougar
Robert Bray
Feature length version of Lassie episodes
1967

Mickey Mouse Anniversary Special
Dean Jones
Walt Disney Productions
NBC
December 22, 1968

The Green Hornet
Feature version of TV episodes
1974
Released posthumously

Fury of the Dragon
Feature version of TV episodes
1976
Released posthumously

NOTE
Several episodes of the Magical World of Disney (aka Walt Disney's Wonderful World of Color) on NBC featured material from William Beaudine's various films for the company including shorts, series, and features broken up and serialized.

BIBLIOGRAPHY

Books

Balducci, Anthony. *Lloyd Hamilton: Poor Boy Comedian of Silent Cinema.* Jefferson, NC. McFarland. 2009

Brownlow, Kevin. *The Parade's Gone By.* NY: Knopf, 1968

Brownlow, Kevin. *The Silent Films of William Beaudine.* American Film Institute. 1972

Bubbeo, Daniel. *The Women of Warner Brothers: The Lives and Careers of 15 Leading Ladies, with Filmographies for Each.* Jefferson, NC: McFarland & Company.

Coghlan, Frank. *They Still Call Me Junior.* Jefferson, NC: McFarland. 1993

Croy, Homer. *Star Maker: The Story of D.W. Griffith* New York. Duell, Sloan and Pierce. 1959

Gallen, Ira H. *D.W. Griffith, Master of Cinema.* Canada. Friesen Press. 2015

Hayes, David and Brent Walker. *The Films of the Bowery Boys.* Secaucus, NJ: Citadel, 1984

Lahue, Karlton and Samuel Gill. *Clown Princes and Court Jesters.* NY: A.S. Barnes, 1970

Maltin, Leonard. *The Disney Films.* NY: Hyperion 1995

Marshall, Wendy L. *William Beaudine: From Silents to Television.* Lanham, MD. Scarecrow Press. 2002

Massa, Steve. *Lame Brains and Lunatics.* Albany, GA: Bear Manor, 2013

Massa, Steve. *Slapstick Divas.* Albany, GA: Bear Manor 2017

Neibaur, James L. *The W.C. Fields Films.* Jefferson, NC: McFarland, 2017

Neibaur, James L. *The Jean Harlow Films.* Jefferson, NC: McFarland, 2019

Pickford, Mary *Sunshine and Shadow* NY: Doubleday, 1955

Spicer, Andrew. *Historical Dictionary of Film Noir.* Scarecrow Press, 2010.

Articles

"American Film Director Must Quit England." *Los Angeles Times.* September 25, 1937

Behind The Movie Sets with Buddy Mason. *The Algona Upper Des Moines.* July 30, 1959

"Boyish Smile, In Spite of Sickness, Gives Hugh Allen a Chance with Mary Pickford". *Lincoln Star* June 14, 1925

Conflict, Dion. "Undiscovered World of William Beaudine, The". *Konflict in the Kino*. Issue 10. December 2003

"Cullen Landis Featured in 'Watch Your Step'" *Motion Picture News* January 24, 1922

"Disney Films New TV Series at Big Bear Lake." *The San Bernardino County Sun*. October 10, 1955

Hedda Hopper's Hollywood. *Los Angeles Times*. October, 10, 1941

"High School to Hollywood" *Oakland Tribune* May 17, 1925

"In Which An Auto Figured" *Film Daily* June 11, 1922

"Just a loveable old so and so" *Film Weekly* December 7, 1934

Jungmeyer, Jack. "Beaudine Friend of Boyhood." *The Reading Times*. June 14, 1924

Lubou, Dorothy. "Grinding Out Grins". *Motion Picture Classic*. May 1929

"The Man on the Cover" *Director* February, 1925

Moak, Bob "Hollywood Draws the Line". *Picture-Play Magazine*. September 1929

Nichols, Harry E. "Are Animals Abused in Films?" *Exhibitors Herald*. November 29, 1924

Scheuer, Phillip. "60 Years in Films." *Action* July-August, 1969

U.W. Cancels Film After Protests. *The Capital Times*. April 3, 1943

"With Fess Parker on the Westward Ho Set" *Lancaster Eagle-Gazette*. February 20, 1956

Wooley, John. "Jesus in the Witchitas" *This Land*, Vol. 5, Issue 7, April 1, 2014.

Reviews:

"Bela Lugosi Meets a Brooklyn Gorilla." *New York Daily News*. September 2, 1952

"Blues Busters." *Variety* October 25, 1950

"Misbehaving Husbands." *The Hollywood Reporter*. December 9, 1940

"The Country Kid" *Bioscope* January 10, 1924

"One Thrilling Night" *Film Daily* July 6, 1942

"Phantom Killer" *Film Daily* August 21, 1942

"Watch Your Step" *Variety* May 19, 1922

"Westward Ho the Wagons" *Variety*. December 19, 1956

INDEX

Abbott and Costello 146
Adventures in Dairy 153-154
Adventures of Kitty O'Day 103
Adventures of Spin and Marty TV 152-154, 160
Adventures of Superman TV 97
Adventures of Wild Bill Hickok TV 148-149
Air Raid Wardens 111
Albright, Hardie 140
Alexander, Ben 24, 26, 2
All Night Long 81
Angels With Dirty Faces 99
Ape Man, The 98
Arthur, Jean 45
Arzner, Dorothy 46
Austin, Lois 140
Autry, Gene 93, 112
Babb, Kroger 140-142, 144
Banks, Monty 59
Barcroft, Roy 160, 161
Barry, Don "Red" 112-113
Barry, Wesley 22, 23, 24, 248
Bartlett, Benny 100, 108, 126
Batman TV 94
Beal, John 94-97, 158
Beatles 132
Beaudine, Helen 47
Beginning, The 143
Benedict, Billy 100, 121
Benny, Jack 146
Berle, Milton 146
Bernds, Edward 125-127, 143
Bevan, Billy 27
Big Idea, The 53
Bitzer, Billy 2
Blonde Comet 86-87
Blondell, Joan 53
Blood and Sand 21
Blues Busters 121-123

Blythe, Betty 83
Bombs and Business 10
Boy of Mine 26-27, 46
Boyd, William 148
Boys of the City 100
Boys Will Be Boys 58-61
Bray, Robert 168
Breakston, George 88
Briggs, O. Henry 86
Bringing Up Father 110
Briskin, Sam 51
Brockwell, Gladys 24
Broder, Jack 132, 133, 135, 136
Brown, Joe E. 123
Brownlow, Kevin 171, 172, 173
Buell, Jed 72-74, 77, 81, 84
Bunker Bean 33
Burr, Cy 8, 10
Burton, Tim 137
Bushman, Francis X 85, 91
Butterworth, Joe 24
Byrd, Ralph 89
Cabot, Sebastian 154
Callahan, Cordeilia 10
Canadian, The 34, 171-174
Cappello, Bill 136
Capra, Frank 49, 125
Carr, Trem 93
Carradine, John 93, 99, 160, 161, 162
Carey, Harry jr. 152, 160
Carey, Olive 160, 161
Case, Carroll 160, 162
Casey, Melinda 161
Chandler, George 167
Chaplin, Charlie 26, 30, 45, 58, 65, 121
Charlita 134, 160
Chaser, The 82
Chatterton, Ruth 46
Children of the Covered Wagon 153-154

Chinese Ring, The 110
Christie, Al 12, 13, 14, 15, 22, 29
Christine, Virginia 160, 161
Circus Boy 149
Cisco Kid TV 146
Clancy Street Boys 100
Clark, Violet 27
Clarke, Mae 50
Clayton, Jan 167
Cleveland, George 167
Cline, Eddie 109-110
Clyde, Andy 53, 167-168, 169
Coghlan, Frank "Junior" 47-48
Cohan, George M. 24
Cohn, Harry 49
Colbert, Claudette 49
Cole, Tommy 153
Colgate Comedy Hour 137, 146
College Vamp 53
Como, Perry 122
Congregation, The 143
Conklin, Heinie 10
Corcoran, Kevin 153, 157, 158
Corky and the White Shadow 152, 153
Corner in Wheat, A 1
Courtney, Chuck 160
Crashing Las Vegas 127
Cross-Eyed Submarine, The 10-11
Crowley Kathleen 154
Country Kid, The 22
Crandall, Irving 43
Crazy Nights 102
Crime School 99
Currie, Louise 98-99
Curtain Pole, The 1
Curtis, Dick 88
Dandy Dick 58-59
Darling, Scott 110
Dash Through The Clouds, A 4-5
Davis, H.O 8, 10, 11
Davis, Jim 161
Davy Crockett 153, 154, 156
Dead End 99
Dell, Gabe 99, 120, 121
Detective Kitty O'Day 103

Disney, Walt 128, 150, 152-160
Donat, Robert 58
Dodd, Jimmie 152
DeForrest, Lee 43
Detour 87
Devine, Andy 148-149
Dolenz, Mickey 149
Dorothy of Haddon Hall 29-30
Drury, James 158
Duncan, Bud. 7, 8, 9, 22, 26
Each According to his Faith 143
East Side Kids 93, 99-103, 108, 113-114, 120-121, 127
Easton, Robert 124-125
Ebsen, Buddy 153
Ed Wood 137
Educated Evans 71
Eldredge, George 140
Emergency Landing 84
Erwin, Stuart 52, 158
Fairbanks, Douglas 30, 32
Farrell, Glenda 66-69, 81
Father's Son 46-48
Fawcett, William 161
Feather Your Nest 61
Feathered Serpent, The 110
Federal Fugitives 84
Fellowes, Rockliffe 24, 26
Feudin' Fools 124-125
Fields, W.C. 27, 53-56, 58, 60
Flying Deuces 103
For Every Child 143
Ford, Eugenie 98
Formby, George 61
Foulger, Byron 127
Franey, Billy 9, 10
Friedrich, James 73
Fugitives 36, 45
Funicello, Annette 153
Gable, Clark 49, 111
Garfield, John 100
Gas House Kids Go West 108-109
Gaskell, Elizabeth 167
George Washington, Jr. 24
Get Off My Foot 71

Ghostbusters 121
Ghosts on the Loose 99
Gilbert, Billy 102-103
Gillespie, Darlene 153, 154
Gladiator, The 124
Goldwyn, Samuel 15, 20, 22, 23, 99
Gone With The Wind 137
Gorcey, Bernard 121, 127
Gorcey, David 121
Gorcey, Leo 100-102, 113, 120-122, 126-127, 143
Grand Illusion 73
Great Dictator, The 121
Green Hornet, The 163, 169, 170
Grey, John 27
Grippo, Jan 113, 114, 120, 124, 125
Griffith, D.W. 1, 2, 7, 20, 25, 30
Guilty Generation, The 49
Gumbel, Bryant 137
Hadley, Reed 148
Half Wits Holiday 123
Hall, Huntz 99-101, 114, 120, 122, 125, 126
Hall, Newton 24
Halop, Billy 99, 103
Ham The Driver 8
Hamilton, John 95-96, 103
Hamilton, Lloyd 7, 8, 9, 26, 27, 28
Hamilton, Neil 94
Hard To Get 36, 45, 47
Harlem on the Prairie 73
Harlow, Jean 22, 49-51, 63, 65
Harrison, Jimmy 13
Hawkins, Jack 58
Hay, Will 58-61, 63, 65
Hays, Will 43
Healy, Ted 53
Heart Trouble 82
Hells Angels 49
Hell's Kitchen 99
Henderson, Dell 5, 20
Henry, Gale 9, 10
Hepburn, Katharine 94, 111
Heroes of the Street 22, 23
Hidden Heart, The 143

Hiers, Walter 36
High School Girl 140
High Society 126-127
His Darker Self 27
His Marriage Wow 82
Hitchcock, Alfred 58
Hoag, H.E. 45
Hold That Line 121, 123
Hold That Lion 35-36
Home James 36
Honeymoon's Over, The 69
Hopalong Cassidy 148
House of Dracula 160
House of Frankenstein 160
Howard, Shemp 102-103, 107
Hughes, Carol 87
Hymer, Warren 94-96
I Love Lucy TV 146
In The Money 127
It Happened One Night 49
It's a Gift 60
Jackson, Eugene 24, 31
Jail Busters 126-127, 143
Jalopy 143
Janney, Leon 46-48
Jazz Singer, The 43-44
Jeffries, Herb 72-73
Jiggs and Maggie in Society 111
Jiggs and Maggie Out West 111-112
Johnson, Ben 158
Johnston, Ray 93
Jonah Jones 28-29
Jordan, Bobby 99, 120
Josephson, Julien 20
Just Tony 21
Karloff, Boris 49
Keaton, Buster 26, 27, 109
Kennedy, Tom 67
Kent, Robert 86
Kenton, Erle C. 142
Kidnapped 112
Kranz, F. W. 43
Landau, Martin 137
Langdon, Harry 81-83, 102
LaPlante, Laura 36

Laurel and Hardy 102, 103, 110
Laurentz, John 122
Lawton Story, The 141-143
Leachman, Cloris 167
Lean David 58
Lee, Bruce 169
Lehrman, Henry 12
Lewis, Jerry 128, 132, 134, 136, 137
Levine, Joseph 160
Life of Riley, The 36
Lights of New York 44
Little Annie Rooney 29-34
Lloyd, Harold 26, 27, 65
Lockhart, June 167
Loose in London 126
Lucky Ghost 75-77
Lugosi, Bela 81, 93, 97-99, 101, 128, 132-137
Luke, Keye 110, 117
Mace, Fred 4-5
MacLean, Douglas 35-36
Mad Parade 46
Madison, Guy 148-149
Make Me a Star 52
Manicure Lady, The 3-4
Martin and Lewis 128, 132-137, 146
Mason, James 58
Master Minds 121
MacLaine, Barton 66-68
Madison, Guy 148
Maltin, Leonard 158
Manners, Sam 162
Martin, Dean 123, 128, 132, 134, 135, 136
Marx Brothers 102
McDonald, Frank 67
McDonald, J.K. 23, 25, 26, 27
McDowall, Roddy 112
McGoldrick, Rita 44
McGray, Joe 24
McGuire, Paddy 11
Kay, Wanda 94-97
Meighan, Thomas
Men in Her Life 49
Men of San Quentin 87-89

Messinger, Buddy 24
Messinger, Gertrude 24
Mickey Mouse Club 152-154
Middleton, Charles 88
Miller, F.E. 74-77
Miller, Max 61
Miller, Patsy Ruth 20, 26
Miller, Rube 8
Mills, John 58
Miracle Kid 87-88
Misbehaving Husbands 81-83
Mitchell, Duke 132-139
Mix, Tom 21, 72
Mom and Dad 140-142, 145
Mong, William 24
Moochie of the Little League 157
Morante, Milburn 10
Moreland, Mantan 74-76, 95-97
Move Along 29
Mr. Celebrity 84-86
Mr. Washington Goes to Town 74-75
Munsters, The TV 162
Murray, Charlie 36
Mystery of the 13th Guest 103
Naked City 149
Neal, Lex 27
Neal, Tom 87
Neilan, Marshall 5, 7, 8, 20, 23
Newman, Samuel 110
Nip and Tuck 27
No Holds Barred 121
Normand, Mabel 27
Ogg, Sammy 153
Okuda, Ted
Oland, Warner 110
Old Fashioned Way, The 53,-56, 58 63, 65, 173
One Thrilling Night 94-97
One Too Many 142
Paiva, Nestor 162
Paris Playboys 126-127
Parker, Fess 154, 155, 156
Parker, Jean 103
Parmalee, Phil 4
Peacock, Lillian 10

Penrod and Sam (1923) 23-27, 31
Penrod and Sam (1931) 47-48, 65
Perry Mason TV 110
Petrillo, Sammy 132-139
Phantom Killer 95-97
Philbin, Mary 24
Pickford, Mary 29-34, 63
Pollard, Snub 14, 15, 52
Porter, Edwin S. 2
Prescott, Vivien 3
Presley, Elvis 132
Prevost, Marie 22, 50
Prince, Ginger 142, 144
Prince of Peace 142
Provost, Jon 167, 168, 169, 170
Punch the Clock 14
Punsly, Bernard 99
Purcell, Dick 95-97
Pygmalion 123
Racket Squad TV 147-148
Rapf, Harry 22
Rattenbury, Henry 20
Reeves, George 154, 155
Reilly, Hugh 167
Riano, Renie 110
Rich, Irene 25-26
Riskin, Robert 49
Roach, Hal 14, 82, 147
Rogers, Roy 94
Rooney, Mickey 111
Rosenbloom, Maxie 102
Rosita 29
Rough Riders 94
Schade, Fritz 11
Schwalb, Ben 125, 126
Searchers, The 161
Shanghai Chest, The 110
Shaw, George Bernard 123
Self-Made Failure, A 26-29, 47
Sen Yung, Victor 110
Sennett, Mack 1, 2, 3, 4, 5, 11, 12, 14, 20, 27, 72, 74, 81, 168
Seven Keys to Baldpate 35
Shepard, David 171
Shepodd, Jon 167

Sidney, George 36
Simpson, Mickey 135
Sky Dragon 110
Smart Blonde 66
So You Won't Talk 59
Sparrows 33-34
Spook Busters 121
St. Clair, Mal 24
Steadman, Vera 13
Step Forward 14
Stevenson, Robert Lewis 112
Stewart, James 148
Stickfaden, Kenneth 163
Swanson, Gloria 12
Switzer, Carl 108
Take it From Me 71
Tarkington, Booth 23, 46-47
Teddy at the Throttle 12
Ten Who Dared 158, 159
Terror of Tiny Town 72
That's My Baby 35
They Made Me a Criminal 100
Three's a Crowd 82
Three Stooges 53, 102, 123
Three Wise Girls 50-51
Those Awful Hats 1
Toddy, Ted 73
Toler, Sidney 109-110
Torchy Blaine in Chinatown 68
Torchy Gets Her Man 67-68
Torchy Runs For Mayor 69
Tough Assignment 113
Trading Places 124
Tranberg, Charles 152
Trail Blazers 94
Turpin, Ben 14, 27, 52
20,000 Leagues Under the Sea 10
Two Weeks Off 36, 47
Up in Smoke 127
Urecal, Minerva 98, 103
Vale, Virginia 86
Valentino, Rudolph 21
Verne, Jules 10
Vernon, Bobby 12-14
Violin Maker of Cremona, A 1

Wallis, Hal 135, 136
Walthall, Henry B. 25, 26, 46
Ward, Chance 8
Warner, Sam 43
Watch your Step 20-23, 26
Wayne, John 93
Weatherwax, Rudd 168
Westword Ho, The Wagons 164-167
What Drink Did 1
Where There's a Will 60
Why Wild Men Go Wild 13
Williams, Roy 152
Williams, Van 169
Winchester 73 148
Windbag the Sailor 60-61
Winters, Roland 110
Won by a Fowl 11
Wood, Ed 137
Woodruff, Bert 20
Wooley, John 141, 142
Wray, Fay 46
Wurtzel, Sol 79
Yates, Herbert J. 93
York, Jeff 154
You're Telling Me 60
Young, Clara Kimball 85
Yule, Joe 111-112
Zanuck, Daryl 79
Zucco, George 99

www.ingramcontent.com/pod-product-compliance
Lightning Source LLC
Chambersburg PA
CBHW050106170426
43198CB00014B/2480